The letter of James the Just, the half-brother of Yesh[...] without its controversy. Often considered to have the most Jewish character of among all the books of the Apostolic Scriptures (New Testament), James' epistle sits between two extremes: those who deny his message, and those who give his message a weight that it was never intended to have. James' letter has a distinctive emphasis on the works of the individual, and so many have viewed what he has to say as actually annulling the grace of God in the process of salvation. Some have denied James' place in the Biblical canon, and others have forgotten who James was as a humble, kind, and patient servant of the Lord.

James' epistle has a universal moral message for all of humanity, and especially the Messianic community today. Written at the emergence of First Century Messianic faith, James was observing some of the controversies and issues creeping in as the gospel message went beyond the Land of Israel, and God's Kingdom was in the process of being restored. Some were causing discord and forgetting the ethics that God requires His people to have in the Torah. When you add to this the early persecutions that the Believers faced, coupled with the fact that corrupt rich people were being shown favor in the assembly, you have a letter that deals with a great deal of practical faith, holy living, and consideration for others. James' admonitions must be heeded, in order for people to find themselves in the will and purpose of the Lord.

In the commentary *James for the Practical Messianic*, Messianic Apologetics editor J.K. McKee addresses what we need to learn as Messianic Believers today from James' epistle. He takes into account the distinct Jewish character of James, considering various passages in the letter with statements made in the Torah and Tanach, the Apocrypha, Philo, Josephus, the Pseudepigrapha, Dead Sea Scrolls, and also the Mishnah and Talmud. He also considers the First Century history behind James' letter, and also parallels that exist between statements in James and remarks made in Greco-Roman classicism. Most importantly, various important theological opinions that have existed over the centuries regarding James are addressed, especially as to whether or not the Epistle of James at all contradicts the theology of the letters of Paul. Some of the current scholastic trends in examination of James are also considered, both enriching and challenging the diligent student who is looking for a distinctive Messianic perspective of this letter.

JAMES

FOR THE PRACTICAL MESSIANIC

JAMES
FOR THE PRACTICAL MESSIANIC

J.K. MCKEE

MESSIANIC APOLOGETICS
messianicapologetics.net

JAMES
FOR THE PRACTICAL MESSIANIC

Cover imagery: J.K. McKee/personal photo

ISBN 978-1484991596 (paperback)
ISBN 979-8740948430 (hardcover)
ASIN B00EN69N0K (eBook)

Published by Messianic Apologetics, a division of Outreach Israel Ministries
P.O. Box 516
McKinney, Texas 75070
(407) 933-2002

outreachisrael.net / outreachisrael.blog
messianicapologetics.net / messianicapologetics.blog

Unless otherwise noted, Scripture quotations are from the *New American Standard, Updated Edition* (NASU), © 1995, The Lockman Foundation.

Unless otherwise noted, quotations from the Apocrypha are from the *Revised Standard Version* (RSV), © 1952, Division of Education of the National Council of the Churches of Christ in the United States of America.

TABLE OF CONTENTS

ABBREVIATION CHART AND SPECIAL TERMS

The following is a chart of abbreviations for reference works and special terms that are used in publications by Outreach Israel Ministries and Messianic Apologetics. Please familiarize yourself with them as the text may reference a Bible version, i.e., RSV for the Revised Standard Version, or a source such as *TWOT* for the *Theological Wordbook of the Old Testament*, solely by its abbreviation. Detailed listings of these sources are provided in the Bibliography.

Special terms that may be used have been provided in this chart:

ABD: *Anchor Bible Dictionary*

AMG: *Complete Word Study Dictionary: Old Testament, New Testament*

ANE: Ancient Near East(ern)

Apostolic Scriptures/Writings: the New Testament

Ara: Aramaic

ASV: American Standard Version (1901)

ATS: ArtScroll Tanach (1996)

b. Babylonian Talmud (*Talmud Bavli*)

B.C.E.: Before Common Era or B.C.

BDAG: *A Greek-English Lexicon of the New Testament and Other Early Christian Literature* (Bauer, Danker, Arndt, Gingrich)

BDB: *Brown-Driver-Briggs Hebrew and English Lexicon*

BECNT: *Baker Exegetical Commentary on the New Testament*

BKCNT: *Bible Knowledge Commentary: New Testament*

C.E.: Common Era or A.D.

CEV: Contemporary English Version (1995)

CGEDNT: *Concise Greek-English Dictionary of New Testament Words* (Barclay M. Newman)

CHALOT: *Concise Hebrew and Aramaic Lexicon of the Old Testament*

CJB: Complete Jewish Bible (1998)

DRA: Douay-Rheims American Edition

DSS: Dead Sea Scrolls

ECB: *Eerdmans Commentary on the Bible*

EDB: *Eerdmans Dictionary of the Bible*

eisegesis: "reading meaning into," or interjecting a preconceived or foreign meaning into a Biblical text

EJ: *Encylopaedia Judaica*

ESV: English Standard Version (2001)

exegesis: "drawing meaning out of," or the process of trying to understand what a Biblical text means on its own

EXP: *Expositor's Bible Commentary*

Ger: German

GNT: Greek New Testament

Grk: Greek

halachah: lit. "the way to walk," how the Torah is lived out in an individual's life or faith community

HALOT: *Hebrew & Aramaic Lexicon of the Old Testament* (Koehler and Baumgartner)

HCSB: Holman Christian Standard Bible (2004)

Heb: Hebrew

HNV: Hebrew Names Version of the World English Bible

ICC: *International Critical Commentary*

IDB: *Interpreter's Dictionary of the Bible*

IDBSup: *Interpreter's Dictionary of the Bible Supplement*

ISBE: *International Standard Bible Encyclopedia*

IVPBBC: *IVP Bible Background Commentary (Old & New Testament)*

Jastrow: *Dictionary of the Targumim, Talmud Bavli, Talmud Yerushalmi, and Midrashic Literature* (Marcus Jastrow)

JBK: New Jerusalem Bible-Koren (2000)

JETS: *Journal of the Evangelical Theological Society*

KJV: King James Version

Lattimore: The New Testament by Richmond Lattimore (1996)

LITV: *Literal Translation of the Holy Bible* by Jay P. Green (1986)

LS: *A Greek-English Lexicon* (Liddell & Scott)

LXE: *Septuagint with Apocrypha* by Sir L.C.L. Brenton (1851)

LXX: Septuagint

m. Mishnah

MT: Masoretic Text

NASB: New American Standard Bible (1977)

NASU: New American Standard Update (1995)

NBCR: *New Bible Commentary: Revised*

NEB: New English Bible (1970)

Nelson: *Nelson's Expository Dictionary of Old Testament Words*

NETS: New English Translation of the Septuagint (2007)

NIB: *New Interpreter's Bible*

NIGTC: *New International Greek Testament Commentary*

NICNT: *New International Commentary on the New Testament*

NIDB: *New International Dictionary of the Bible*

NIV: New International Version (1984)

NJB: New Jerusalem Bible-Catholic (1985)

NJPS: Tanakh, A New Translation of the Holy Scriptures (1999)

NKJV: New King James Version (1982)

NRSV: New Revised Standard Version (1989)

NLT: New Living Translation (1996)

NT: New Testament

orthopraxy: lit. "the right action," how the Bible or one's theology is lived out in the world

OT: Old Testament

PreachC: *The Preacher's Commentary*

REB: Revised English Bible (1989)

RSV: Revised Standard Version (1952)

t. Tosefta

Tanach (Tanakh): the Old Testament

Thayer: *Thayer's Greek-English Lexicon of the New Testament*

TDNT: *Theological Dictionary of the New Testament*

TEV: Today's English Version (1976)

TLV: Tree of Life Messianic Family Bible—New Covenant (2011)

TNIV: Today's New International Version (2005)

TNTC: *Tyndale New Testament Commentaries*

TWOT: *Theological Wordbook of the Old Testament*

UBSHNT: United Bible Societies' 1991 Hebrew New Testament revised edition

v(s). verse(s)

Vine: *Vine's Complete Expository Dictionary of Old and New Testament Words*

Vul: Latin Vulgate

WBC: *Word Biblical Commentary*

Yid: Yiddish

YLT: Young's Literal Translation (1862/1898)

PROLOGUE

It should go without saying that the Epistle of James is a highly valued and appreciated text for many in our broad Messianic faith community. While there are many active discussions and debates pertaining to statements such as, "faith, if it has no works, is dead" (2:17), "a man is justified by works and not by faith alone" (2:24), and the ever-imperative "Pure and undefiled religion in the sight of *our* God and Father is this: to visit orphans and widows in their distress, *and* to keep oneself unstained by the world" (1:27)—on the whole our engagement with the Epistle of James, at least on a surface level, is one that tends to be generally positive. In all of my family's experience in the Messianic community, since 1995, we have never really encountered any Messianic person who does not have some favorable disposition toward reading and applying James' letter to his or her life. We have, however, encountered many of our Christian brothers and sisters, widely ignore or discount the messages of James, or are at least confused in many ways, feeling that James has an irreconcilable message when compared or contrasted to Paul's letters. Likewise, there are Messianic people, who while favorable to James, have probably not let its words penetrate their hearts and minds enough—as this letter certainly presents many challenging statements to the spirituality and behavior of each of us.

When many think of James the Just, they think of a dedicated, godly man, who was committed to a life of complete service to the Body of Messiah. While James the half-brother of Yeshua was likely too young to have been a noticeable part of His teaching ministry, James' contemplative, fair-minded, practical, but also direct approach to the issues of the day, is detectable in the Biblical record we have of him—most notably that of the Acts 15 Jerusalem Council and the letter that bears his name. It is quite easy to peruse through the Epistle of James, and then be compelled to flip to the Sermon on the Mount of Matthew chs. 5-7, noticing a wide variety of parallel words and connections between the concepts elucidated. Many a Messiah follower are greatly moved by the historical record regarding James, as seen in Eusebius' *Ecclesiastical History* (2.1.2, 3; 2.23.4-5), and his fierce dedication to prayer, holiness, and acts of kindness and mercy toward others. When we each reflect upon the example and teachings of James, we all see a figure of faith worthy of emulation, and are significantly reminded of our own mortal limitations.

James for the Practical Messianic was the first real volume issued in the *Practical Messianic* commentary series (when I realized that this would become a series), and the first study conducted for my Wednesday Night Bible Study podcast, which originally started in 2005. James has a timeless moral and ethical message, which we should all cherish deeply, and one which doubtlessly issues many challenges to people in our still-emerging and developing Messianic movement. Over the past year or so (late 2011-2013), as each title released by our ministry has been formatted for paperback and Amazon Kindle eBook, I have had to evaluate the current content status of each, with some revisions and updates required here and there. In the case of the Epistle of James, the letter itself needed to be revisited, not because of any major changes of interpretation or perspective on my part— but more specifically because of the length of time that has passed since this publication's initial release, new challenges present in the Messianic world, and most significantly because of new commentaries and resources issued on James since 2005 (as well as new resources on James acquired for my library).

This commentary on James has gone through a few noticeable updates, which include expansion of previous points, more examination into the Greek source text of the letter, but most especially engagement with some more commentators on the epistle, either released since 2005 or acquired by me (i.e., the volumes by Peter Davids, Luke T. Johnson, Ben Witherington III, Dan G. McCartney, Scot McKnight). More detail has been specifically expelled in investigating various Jamean passages that appear to be in conflict with Pauline passages over the issue of "justification." Is the "justification" in view a remission of sins and a declaration of innocence before the Holy One, or might it pertain more to a demonstration of membership of a man or woman as a part of God's people? Too many are not aware of the wide meanings that justification has for both Hebrew and Greek, which English tends to lack.

Given the almost eight years which have transpired since *James for the Practical Messianic* was first released, while I have given more attention to some new and useful proposals regarding this letter—my primary attention is, as always, to the text, and how James should be considered and applied by individuals within the Messianic movement. There is no question, now in 2013, that the broad Messianic movement really needs to hear what James the Just has to say. Over the past several years, as we have entered into the 2010s, there have been a variety of less-than-useful spiritual and theological perspectives witnessed, which have been deterring us from accomplishing the goals of the Kingdom of God. We need to decisively return to the words and messages of those early Messianic leaders like James, so that we might be useful for the Kingdom. James poignantly says, "you do not know what your life will be like tomorrow. You are *just* a vapor that appears for a little while and then vanishes away" (4:14). Many of us need to be humbled, committing ourselves back to God and His purposes, so that we do not waste any unnecessary time, energy, and resources on those things which do not only take people away from Messiah Yeshua—but do not contribute to the human wholeness that James' letter speaks so prolifically of!

J.K. McKee
Editor, Messianic Apologetics

INTRODUCTION

The Epistle of James[1] has been one of the most debated books of the Bible among theologians, examiners, and many laypeople, for centuries. At the same time, the Epistle of James has also been highly valued by many people seeking instruction on practical matters of faith and obedience, good works, and in making a difference in the world for God. Outside of the Gospels, the letter of James is regarded as probably having the most substantial Jewish character of any of the writings in the Apostolic Scriptures, as it is traditionally the product of James the Just, half-brother of the Lord Yeshua. The letter of James has a very direct message for people who are stagnant in their faith, and are not living up to the essential matters of holiness and piety. It is for these, and many other reasons, why having an appropriate understanding of the Epistle of James—and the role it plays not only for spirituality, but among the other books of the Apostolic canon—is so important for Messiah followers.

That James demonstrated a strong fidelity, to God's Torah and a Jewish way of life (Acts 15:13-21; 21:18-24), is something which bears strongly on this letter, as a great deal of difficulty is present for Christian readers who tend to discount or devalue the importance of God's Law. However, even among those who tend to have a negative disposition, for the Law of Moses in the post-resurrection era, have to admit that James 1:22—"But prove yourselves doers of the word, and not merely hearers who delude themselves"—can surely be regarded as **"the most famous command in the NT"** (Douglas J. Moo),[2] which born again Believers certainly need to obey. Those, who choose to delve into the Epistle of James, see a heavy emphasis upon both faith *and* works, as James intended to address a genuine faith for Believers, manifested in good works of mercy and grace toward others, with a definite concern for the marginalized in society.

A cursory review, of how the Epistle of James has been approached in history, does reveal how this letter has not always been appreciated. James was not immediately accepted as canonical by a wide range of authorities within the emerging Christian Church of the Second and Third Centuries. By the Third Century, Clement of Alexandria recognized James

---

[1] Please note that in spite of the common reference to James as "the Book of James," I am going to purposefully refer to the text as either the Epistle of James or a letter of James, and not use this reference. By failing to forget that this text is a letter written to a specific audience in a specific setting, we can make the common error of thinking that this was a text written *directly to us*. Our goal as responsible interpreters is to try to reconstruct what this letter meant *to its original audience first*, before applying its message in a modern-day setting.

[2] Douglas J. Moo, *Pillar New Testament Commentary: The Letter of James* (Grand Rapids: Eerdmans, 2000), 1.

as being part of "the other general epistles" (Eusebius *Ecclesiastical History* 6.14.1), but it was not universally accepted for instruction among all in early Christianity. Factors, contributing to people tending to ignore James, may have come from the lack of "heavy theology" in James, what appears to be James' emphasis on works contrasted to grace, and perhaps even the fact that the name of Yeshua (Jesus) only appears twice in the letter (1:1; 2:1). While many in ancient Christianity did value James and its message, there was a tendency to focus far more on the Pauline letters, and what was regarded as their "heavy theology," rather than the more "primitive" sayings of James. A negative disposition toward James would appear later in the Reformation, as Martin Luther assigned James to an appendix in his German translation of the Bible, not really knowing what to do with it. Yet, other Reformers and significant Protestant leaders have highly valued James, even if being cautious here or there with it.

Luke T. Johnson indicates how "Luther's view dominated much of the scholarly approach to the letter until very recently. Most readers through the ages...reached a position like that of the patristic interpreters."[3] Throughout much of Christian history, it has been rightly recognized that James and Paul had different vantage points which need to be recognized and appreciated, as they approach the subject of "faith" from different angles, per some of the circumstances of their intended audiences. However, due to the quantity of the Pauline letters, in comparison to the single Epistle of James, even among those who have highly regarded James, there has still not been enough academic engagement on James, perhaps until the past half-century.

Previous negative examination of James, or dismissal or downplaying of James, has been changing in much contemporary Bible scholarship. Some of this has been geared toward various examiners wanting to have a more holistic reading of Scripture, but perhaps more has been geared toward wanting to better understand the Jewish background of the New Testament, and what is likely a very early product of the First Century *ekklēsia*. Given this letter's emphasis on good works, godliness, and the acts of kindness and mercy required by God's Torah—not only have piety and holiness movements in evangelical Christianity appreciated the Epistle of James, but James tends to bear special importance for most of today's Messianic people. With some renewed, and highly important, Christian interest in the Epistle of James detectable over the past few decades, how significant is it that Messianic Believers have a good handle on it?

Today, given the huge bevy of scholastic interest in Second Temple Judaism, emerging Christianity, Biblical history in general—and with it having to navigate conservative, liberal, and other strata—examining the Epistle of James, even with just a passing familiarity with some of the proposals seen, can be a bit daunting. So as we prepare to enter into what James communicates to men and women of faith, this might be the reason why

---

[3] Luke T. Johnson, "The Letter of James," in Leander E. Keck, ed., et. al., *New Interpreter's Bible* (Nashville: Abingdon, 1998), 12:177.

Scot McKnight opens his own commentary on James with the admonition, "read James in light of James!"[4] He further remarks how "James is a one-of-a-kind document...it is the substance of James, combining as it does Torah observance in a new key with both wisdom and eschatology in a Jewish-Christian milieu, that forms its special character."[5] As important as it will be for us to recognize some of the discussions and debates surrounding authorship of this letter, and how various people have under- or over-emphasized it, *ultimately it will be how each of us as readers can appreciate and apply the letter to our lives,* which is what matters the most.

It will be important for each of us to see how various Christian voices, some in past history, but some in more modern history, have approached and applied the Epistle of James. *We will see many perspectives with which we can not only agree, but take direction from.* At the same time, as Messianic Believers in a still-maturing and still-emerging Messianic movement, there are going to be some admonitions that James himself may be said to communicate to us, especially given the high emphasis seen on Torah observance in our faith community. James absolutely believed in the relevance of Moses' Teaching for people of faith, but James also emphasized acts of kindness and mercy toward others. James is highly valued by most of today's Messianic people, but this letter might not always be applied in ways that James originally intended. How easy, or difficult, will it be for Messianic people to possibly make some needed course corrections, reading James' letter in its entirety, and appreciating James for the role it plays among all the books of the Bible?

WHO WAS THE AUTHOR OF JAMES?

When encountering various study Bibles, encyclopedic entries, or commentaries, one will find that there is an evitable amount of discussion about the authorship of the Epistle of James.[6] While there has been longstanding acceptance of the canonicity of James in Christianity, even with some doubts in the Second and Third Centuries (Eusebius *Ecclesiastical History* 3.25.3; 2.23.25), James the Just, half-brother of Yeshua, has widely been regarded as the traditional author, with the material of this letter produced anywhere from the 40s-60s C.E. However, in surveying a history of James' interpretation, not all examiners

---

[4] Scot McKnight, *New International Commentary on the New Testament: The Letter of James* (Grand Rapids: Eerdmans, 2011), 1.

[5] Ibid., pp 2, 3.

[6] Donald Guthrie, *New Testament Introduction* (Downers Grove, IL: InterVarsity, 1990), pp 726-746; D.A. Carson and Douglas J. Moo, *An Introduction to the New Testament,* second edition (Grand Rapids: Zondervan, 2005), pp 621-626; Peter Davids, *New International Greek Testament Commentary: The Epistle of James* (Grand Rapids: Eerdmans, 1982), pp 2-22; Ralph P. Martin, *Word Biblical Commentary: James,* Vol. 48 (Nashville: Thomas Nelson, 1988), pp xxxi-xli; Douglas J. Moo, *Pillar New Testament Commentary: The Letter of James* (Grand Rapids: Eerdmans, 2000), pp 9-20; Ben Witherington III, *Letters and Homilies for Jewish Christians: A Socio-Rhetorical Commentary on Hebrews, James and Jude* (Downers Grove, IL: IVP Academic, 2007), pp 395-401; Dan G. McCartney, *Baker Exegetical Commentary on the New Testament: James* (Grand Rapids: Baker Academic, 2009), pp 8-32; McKnight, pp 13-38.

have been convinced that James, half-brother of Yeshua, was the author or originator of the material in this letter. There are various other candidates for the authorship of the Epistle of James, which have been proposed.

The English name "James" actually renders the Greek *Iakōbos*, which is one of two transliterations for the Hebrew name Jacob or *Ya'akov*. In the Septuagint, the name *Ya'akov*, in reference to the Patriarch Jacob, is rendered as *Iakōb*, and this usage carries over into the Greek New Testament. However, a second form, *Iakōbos*, appears also in the Greek New Testament, perhaps to distinguish *Iakōb* or the Patriarch Jacob from others. Similarly, the English name James is a derivative of the name "Jacob," and it is likely that for this reason it is rendered as such in our English Bibles. In the environs of Jerusalem and Judea, James would have been known as *Ya'akov*, even though when communicating with Greek speakers he would have referred to himself as *Iakōbos*. The difference between *Iakōb* and *Iakōbos* is probably not that substantial, like the difference between Jacob and Jake (or even between James and Jim). In much examination, the adjective Jacobean is often used in reference to the Epistle of James,[7] although Jamesian or Jamean can also be used.

There are at least four specific individuals in the Apostolic Scriptures referred to as "James," some of whom could have been a legitimate author or originator of the material of the Epistle of James:

1. **James the son of Zebedee** was one of Yeshua's earliest disciples (Matthew 4:21; Mark 1:19). He was the brother of John, and the two of them together were given the title of "Boanerges" or "B'nei-Regesh" (CJB), meaning "Sons of Thunder" (Mark 3:17). Their mother's name was Salome (Matthew 27:56; Mark 15:40), and the two of them, along with their father, and Peter and Andrew, were partners in a fishing business along the Sea of Galilee (Luke 5:10; Matthew 4:18-21). This James was in the inner circle of Yeshua's Disciples along with his brother John and Peter, having witnessed both the Transfiguration (Matthew 17:1; Mark 9:2; Luke 9:28) and Yeshua's agony in the Garden of Gethsemane (Matthew 26:37; Mark 14:33). It is widely discounted that James the son of Zebedee could have been the author of this epistle, because of how Herod Agrippa "had James the brother of John put to death with a sword" (Acts 12:2) very early on, making him the first apostolic martyr.

2. **James the son of Alphaeus** was another of the Twelve Disciples of Yeshua (Matthew 10:3; Mark 3:18; Luke 6:15; Acts 1:13). Other than a reference to him as one of the Disciples, no other information is given about him in the Gospels or the Book of Acts. Some think that since Levi is described as being "the *son of*

---

[7] It does have to be observed how the adjective "Jacobean" can be easily confused with the Jacobite rebellion period in Eighteenth Century British history.

Alphaeus" (Mark 2:14), that the two of them were brothers. James the son of Alphaeus is the traditional author of this epistle in Roman Catholicism,[8] a position also adhered to by the Reformer John Calvin.[9]

There is some discussion in more recent scholarship, identifying a person as **James the son of Mary**, whose parents were likely Mary and Cleopas (Matthew 27:56; Mark 15:40; 16:1; Luke 24:10; John 19:25). Some choose to identify him as being James the son of Alphaeus, but others do not.[10]

3. **James the father of Judas** is listed in Luke 6:16 and Acts 1:13. Whether or not this James was actually the father of an apostle, making there be a father-son combination in the list of Apostles, has been debated. It "depends on the interpretation of the genitive [case indicating possession] (Gk. *Ioudas Iakōbou*)," even though "Nothing of special import is said of this James in the Gospels" (*ISBE*).[11] One could expect that if this James were the author of this epistle there would be more said about him.

4. **James the brother of the Lord**, known in early Christian writings as James the Just (*Iakōbos ho dikaios*), was presumably the oldest of the half-brothers of Yeshua (Matthew 13:55; Mark 6:3; cf. Jude 1), although it is observed how Yeshua's own brothers did not believe in Him (John 7:3-5). It was apparently only after Yeshua's resurrection that He appeared to James, and then the other Apostles, and James believed (1 Corinthians 15:7). James had a definite place of importance, as the main leader of the Jerusalem assembly (Acts 12:17; 21:18; Galatians 2:9; 1 Corinthians 9:5), and was the voice who issued the Apostolic decree regarding the inclusion of the non-Jewish Believers in the Body of Messiah at the Jerusalem Council (Acts 15:13-21). Much Christian tradition throughout history, adhered to by many conservative evangelicals of our time, has regarded James the Just as being the author or originator of the material in the Epistle of James.

---

[8] Duane F. Watson, "James, Letter of," in David Noel Freedman, ed., *Eerdmans Dictionary of the Bible* (Grand Rapids: Eerdmans, 2000), 670.

[9] John Calvin, *Calvin's New Testament Commentaries: A Harmony of the Gospels Matthew, Mark & Luke and James & Jude*, trans. A.W. Morrison (Grand Rapids: Eerdmans, 1972), 260.

[10] Cf. Donald A. Hagner, "James," in David Noel Freedman, ed., *Anchor Bible Dictionary*, 6 vols. (New York: Doubleday, 1992), 3:618; Robert E. Van Voorst, "James," in *EDB*, 669.

[11] R.L. Harris, "James," in Geoffrey Bromiley, ed., *International Standard Bible Encyclopedia*, 4 vols. (Grand Rapids: Eerdmans, 1988), 2:958.

Liberal examiners have been those tending to doubt genuine Jamean authorship of this letter,[12] in various degrees. Some liberals do espouse genuine Jamean origin of the sayings which appear in this letter, which would later have been composed into an epistle by either a student or admirer or James, a view which is followed by some conservatives.[13] A fair number of conservatives, though, continue to espouse genuine Jamean authorship of this epistle, or composition via an amanuensis or secretary, during James' own lifetime.[14] Various conservatives espouse a two-stage composition of the Epistle of James, involving (1) materials or sermonic messages originating during the lifetime of James the Just, with (2) a composition being written a generation or so later by a redactor, using it for the needs of his own community.[15]

Some of the main arguments against Jamean authorship of this letter, espoused by either liberals who consider the epistle to be widely pseudepigraphal, with some of them also appealed to by conservatives who espouse a two-staged composition,[16] include:

1. The Epistle of James demonstrates a high competency in Greek, and familiarity with classical moral philosophies.
2. The Epistle of James appears to misrepresent or misunderstand the teachings of Paul.
3. The Epistle of James has no real concern with the purity laws and rituals of the Torah, such as the debate over circumcision, necessitating a later time in the First-Second Centuries C.E. when these were not substantial issues.
4. The Epistle of James had a slow, canonical acceptance among the writings of the Apostolic Scriptures.

Some of the reasons proposed for denying genuine Jamean authorship and/or involvement with the letter, such as a misunderstanding of Paul's letters, or issues like circumcision not being addressed, are theological. Others, such as the high Greek competency of the Epistle of James, which was apparently a product of a Jerusalem Jew, are historical. There are good reasons for these sorts of claims, denying Jamean authorship of the epistle, to not have that strong a basis.

Ralph P. Martin, who is relatively conservative in his theology, is one who adheres to a two-stage composition for the Epistle of James. He explains his position more on linguistic grounds, less so on theological grounds:

---

[12] A.E. Barnett, "James, Letter of," in George Buttrick, ed. et. al., *The Interpreter's Dictionary of the Bible*, 4 vols. (Nashville: Abingdon, 1962), 2:795; Bo Ivar Reicke, *The Anchor Bible: The Epistles of James, Peter, and Jude* (Garden City, NY: Doubleday, 1964), 4.

[13] R.W. Wall, "James, Letter of," in Ralph P. Martin and Peter H. Davids, eds., *Dictionary of the Later New Testament & its Developments* (Downers Grove, IL: InterVarsity, 1997), pp 547-548; Johnson, in *NIB*, 12:183.

[14] W.W. Wessel, "James, Epistle of," in *ISBE*, 2:965-964.

[15] Davids, pp 12-13, 22.

[16] Cf. Sophie Laws, "James, Epistle of," in *ABD*, 3:622; Richard Bauckham, "James," in James D.G. Dunn and John W. Rogerson, eds., *Eerdmans Commentary on the Bible* (Grand Rapids: Eerdmans, 2003), 1483.

"The array of objections seems formidable, and on the several grounds of the letter's style, its Jewishness in tone and content, its post-Pauline ambience, and the suspicions it engendered among the church fathers and canon makers, it seems hardly to have been written *as it stands* by James of Jerusalem....[A]ssuming a two-layered stage in the production of the letter, the presence of hellenistic idioms and the polishing of the material ascribed to James the Jerusalem martyr with stylistic traits and literary flourishes such as the diatribe and repartee would be the work of an enterprising editor. He published his master's work in epistolary form as a plan to gain for it credibility as an apostolic letter. And in doing so, he aimed to address a situation of critical pastoral importance in his region."[17]

While a two-staged hypothesis for the composition of James is to be preferred from that of this letter being a total psuedegraph, written a generation or two after James' death, perhaps almost three-quarters of a century from the 40s-early 60s C.E. into the Second Century C.E. (and which raises some important ethical questions),[18] many conservatives are not at all convinced that reasons given against Jamean authorship—including the Greek of James and the slow acceptance of the letter into the canon—necessitate that this epistle did not mainly come from him directly. As Donald Guthrie observes in his *New Testament Introduction*,

"It is, of course, conceivable, that someone recognized the general value of James' homilies and was prompted, therefore, to edit them into a kind of circular under the name of James who, after all, was the true author of the material used. But a thing is not true because it is conceivable, but because the evidence requires it, and this can hardly be said in this case. If the editor was working under the supervision of James himself, this would amount almost to the traditional view. But if he is editing some time later than James' lifetime the problem of motive becomes acute, for why a later editor should suddenly have conceived such a publication plan when the great majority of the intended readers must have known that James was already dead is difficult to see, and it is even more difficult to understand how the letter came to be received."[19]

Douglas J. Moo, a more recent commentator on the Epistle of James (1999), remarks on how "we possess little evidence that pseudepigraphical epistles in the ancient world were accepted as authentic and truthful."[20] He further states, "The very fact that James was accepted as a canonical book...presumes that the early Christians who made this decision were sure that James wrote it."[21] Dan G. McCartney informs us how "virtually all scholars

---

[17] Martin, pp lxiii, lxxvii.

[18] Witherington, 396 rightly asserts how,

"We cannot a priori rule out the possibility of a pseudonymous document in the canon since it was a known practice in antiquity—even in Jewish and Christian contexts—but there are good reasons to doubt that such a practice would be seen as simply an accepted literary device that raised no moral issues in regard to plagiarism."

[19] Guthrie, 746.

[20] Moo, 20.

[21] Ibid., 21.

acknowledge that this prominent leader of the church in Jerusalem is the James referred to in James 1:1,"[22] even though many doubt whether the material originated from such a James directly or indirectly.

As far as people in today's broad Messianic movement are concerned, most will be highly inclined to accept genuine Jamean authorship of the letter, sometime during the lifetime of James the Just of Jerusalem. It is possible, that as Messianic engagement and scholarship diversifies, some may decide to entertain alternatives such as a two-staged composition of the epistle, or James being a compilation of genuine sayings of James assembled later by an student or admirer. While I think that the Epistle of James was a product of the Lord's half-brother himself, composed during his lifetime, that a secretary or amanuensis was there to assist, is something likely.

This commentary accepts genuine Jamean authorship of the Epistle of James, that the letter originated from James the Just, half-brother of Yeshua, and leader of the Jerusalem congregation. We will be engaging with various resources that do deny this, in various degrees, including those who adhere to a two-stage hypothesis (Davids, Martin), or some more liberal voices unsure about James' message and theology.

WHO WAS JAMES?

James, the half-brother of Yeshua, was likely too young to feature in Yeshua's teaching and healing ministry, and was not among His original disciples (Matthew 12:46-50; Mark 3:31-35; Luke 8:19-21). It is likely, as John 7:5 notes how "For not even His brothers were believing in Him," that James was among those who had his doubts about Yeshua. However, the risen Yeshua appeared to James—"He appeared to James, then to all the apostles" (1 Corinthians 15:7; cf. Acts 1:14)—and as a result of this James had to have believed, and following this quickly arose to take over the leadership of the Jerusalem assembly of Messiah followers. While James was an apostolic figure and leader for certain, he is generally not called an apostle, because the role and office he occupied may be regarded as a bit higher than that of an apostle. James presided over the Jerusalem Council of Acts 15, and was acknowledged as a leader by the Apostle Paul (Galatians 2:9). In both conservative and liberal scholarship, James the Just is widely recognized as being the main representative of the Jewish Believers in Jerusalem and Judea, as his writings do widely represent a more Jewish-specific approach to issues, rather than the more metropolitan, Mediterranean approach of those like Paul.

The first instance where James the Lord's brother is mentioned in the Book of Acts is in **Acts 12:17**, in the context of Peter being broken out of Herod's imprisonment by the angels, and then his showing up at the house of Mary, the mother of John Mark, as those gathered prayed for his release. It is recorded, "But motioning to them with his hand to be silent, he described to them how the Lord had led him out of the prison. And he said, 'Report these

---

[22] McCartney, 14.

things to James and the brethren.' Then he left and went to another place." James the son of Zebedee had just been martyred at the hands of Herod in Acts 12:2, and so by default the James mentioned in Acts 12:17 would have to be James the half-brother of Yeshua. While the Apostle Peter likewise played an important role in the leadership of the First Century *ekklēsia*, this is a Biblical indication that James had already assumed, perhaps as Yeshua's half-brother, an important role in the Jerusalem assembly (cf. Eusebius *Ecclesiastical History* 2.1.2-3).[23]

In **Galatians 2:1-10** the Apostle Paul mentions that he, Barnabas, and Titus made a visit to Jerusalem, to present the good news, as he preached it among the nations, to the Jerusalem leaders. In his letter, Paul specifically acknowledged how "James and Cephas and John...were acknowledged pillars" (Galatians 2:9, NRSV). There is disagreement among examiners, across the spectrum, as to whether or not the Galatians 2:1-10 meeting is the Acts 15 Jerusalem Council, **or** whether it is the relief visit, as is seen in Acts 11:28-30. If it is the relief visit, than the meeting between Paul and the Jerusalem leaders was widely a private visit, as he reported to them some of the preliminary work among the nations. The fact that Paul would make a point to acknowledge James as a key leader, especially as following his own Damascus road salvation encounter, "I did not see any other of the apostles except James, the Lord's brother" (Galatians 1:17), is important not only for an historical framework for reading the New Testament—but for a theological framework of not trying to think that James the Just and the Apostle Paul are at significant odds.[24] This especially concerns how one reads **Acts 21:16-26**, and the rumor about Paul, acknowledged as such by James, that Paul apparently taught the Jewish Believers in the Diaspora to abandon the Torah.

The second instance where James the Lord's brother appears in the Book of Acts is in **Acts ch. 15**, where the Jerusalem Council assembles to discuss the matter of what to do about the new, non-Jewish Believers coming to faith in Yeshua. Did they have to be circumcised as proselytes, and be ordered to keep the Torah, to be saved (Acts 15:1, 5)? The council decisively ruled against this, given the testimony of the Apostle Peter (Acts 15:8-9). The ruling of James the Just was that Tanach prophecy was in the process of taking place (Acts 15:15), specifically the inclusion of the nations within the Tabernacle of David (Acts 15:16-18; Amos 9:11-12, LXX)—a vision of not only a restored Twelve Tribes of Israel, but also of an expanded Kingdom realm of Israel welcoming in God's faithful remnant from all

---

[23] "Then also James, called the brother of our Lord, because he is also called the son of Joseph...This James, therefore, whom the ancients, on account of the excellence of his virtue, surnamed the Just, was the first that received the episcopate of the church at Jerusalem...Clement, in the sixth book of his Institutions, represented it thus: 'Peter, and James, and John after the ascension of our Savior, though they had been preferred by our Lord, did not contend for the honor, but chose James the Just as bishop of Jerusalem'" (*Ecclesiastical History* 2.1.2, 3).

Eusebius of Caesarea: *Ecclesiastical History*, trans. C.F. Cruse (Peabody, MA: Hendrickson, 1998), 35.

[24] For a review of Galatians 2:1-10, consult the relevant sections of the author's commentary *Galatians for the Practical Messianic*.

humanity. The Apostolic decree, mandating the non-Jewish Believers to abstain from idolatry, sexual immorality, strangled meat, and blood (Acts 15:20, 29), would decisively cut the new Greek and Roman Believers off from their old, pagan spheres of influence—making Jewish Believers, and by extension the Jewish community, their new sphere of social and spiritual involvement (Acts 15:21). There was no need to order such people to keep the Torah of Moses, as Tanach prophecy anticipated the nations coming to Zion to be taught God's Law (Micah 4:1-3; Isaiah 2:2-4), and the fact that the Holy Spirit was to write the Torah's instructions onto the hearts and minds of people via the promised New Covenant (Jeremiah 31:31-34; Ezekiel 36:25-27).[25]

There are some important attestations, made of James the Just, seen in early Christian writings.[26] Christians of the Second and Third Centuries saw James as a very pious and devout man, dedicated to the Torah, the Temple, and Judaism, but also one who was extremely kind, gentle, and loving. Hegesippus, a Christian leader from the Second Century C.E., is recorded by Eusebius' *Ecclesiastical History* to bear the following testimony of James:

> "James, the brother of the Lord, who, as there were many of this name, was surnamed Just by all, from the days of our Lord until now, received the government of the church with the apostles. This apostle was consecrated from his mother's womb. He drank neither wine nor fermented liquors, and abstained from animal food. A razor never came upon his head, he never anointed with oil, and never used a bath. He alone was allowed to enter the sanctuary. He never wore woolen, but linen garments. He was in the habit of entering the temple alone and was often found upon his bended knees, and interceding for the forgiveness of the people; so that his knees became as hard as camel's, in consequence of his habitual supplication and kneeling before God. And indeed, on account of his exceeding great piety, he was called the Just, and Oblias (or Zaddick and Ozleam) which signifies justice and protection of the people; as the prophets declare concerning him" (*Ecclesiastical History* 2.23.4-6).[27]

Generally speaking, conservative examiners have been accepting of Hegesippus' sentiments regarding James the Just.[28] Given the traditional predilection to James having been one, most often in prayer for people, such service is often associated with how Acts 6:7 records, "The word of God kept on spreading; and the number of the disciples continued to increase greatly in Jerusalem, and a great many of the priests were becoming obedient to the faith." James is widely thought to have had some kind of positive relationship with many of the priests and Temple authorities, at least offering some kind of secondary service in

---

[25] For a review of the deliberations of the Acts 15 Jerusalem Council, and Acts 21:16-26, consult the author's commentary *Acts 15 for the Practical Messianic*.

[26] Martin, pp xlvii-lxi offers an excellent summation of ancient traditions about James, but is uncertain, and expresses doubts, about how many of them are historically accurate.

[27] *Ecclesiastical History*, pp 59-60.

[28] Martin, pp lxvi-lxvii is one who doubts what Hegesippus says of James, as he thinks it inappropriately "turns James into a Nazirite."

prayer and liturgical worship. This is something which eventually caused the death of James, though, not only because of his Messiah faith, but also because of his genuine piety in contrast to the empty religion of many of his contemporaries. The historical record of Eusebius informs us,

> "[T]here were many therefore of the rulers that believed, [and] there arose a tumult among the Jews, Scribes, and Pharisees, saying that there was a danger, that the people would now expect Jesus as the Messiah. They came therefore together, and said to James, 'We entreat thee, restrain the people, who are led astray after Jesus, as if he were the Christ. We entreat thee to persuade all that are coming to the feast of the Passover rightly concerning Jesus; for we all have confidence in thee. For we and all the people bear thee testimony that thou art just, and thou respectest not persons'" (*Ecclesiastical History* 2.23.10).[29]

It appears that while various scribes and Pharisees had some problems with James, because of him declaring Yeshua as the Messiah, they still respected him. Eusebius' record continues, describing how things did reach a critical point, and James was beaten publicly for not renouncing his faith or denouncing Yeshua publicly. While being stoned and clubbed to death, James still prayed to God that those murdering him would be forgiven:

> "Persuade therefore the people not to be led astray by Jesus, for we and all the people have great confidence in thee. Stand therefore upon a wing of the temple, that thou mayest be conspicuous on high, and thy words may be easily heard by all the people; for all the tribes have come together on account of the Passover, with some of the Gentiles also. The aforesaid Scribes and Pharisees, therefore, placed James upon a wing of the temple, and cried out to him, 'O thou just man, whom we ought all to believe, since the people are led astray after Jesus that was crucified, declare to us what is the door to Jesus that was crucified.' And he answered with a loud voice, 'Why do you ask me respecting Jesus the Son of Man? He is now sitting in the heavens, on the right hand of great Power, and is about to come on the clouds of heaven.' And as many were confirmed, and gloried in this testimony of James, and said, 'Hosanna to the son of David,' these same priests and Pharisees said to one another, 'We have done badly in affording such testimony to Jesus, but let us go up and cast him down, that they may dread to believe in him.' And they cried out, 'Oh, oh, Justus himself is deceived,' and they fulfilled that which is written in Isaiah, 'Let us take away the just, because he is offensive to us; wherefore they shall eat the fruit of their doings.' (Isa. 3:10) Going up therefore, they cast down the just man, saying to one another, 'Let us stone James the Just.' And they began to stone him, as he did not die immediately when cast down but turning round, he knelt down saying, 'I entreat thee, O Lord God and Father, forgive them, for they know not what they do.' Thus they were stoning him, one of the priests of the sons of Rechab, a son of the Rechabites, spoken of by Jeremiah the prophet, cried

---

[29] *Ecclesiastical History*, 60.

out saying, 'Cease, what are you doing? Justus is Praying for you.' And one of them, a fuller, beat the brains out of Justus with the club that he used to beat out clothes. Thus he suffered martyrdom, and they buried him on the spot where his tombstone is still remaining, by the temple. He became a faithful witness, both to the Jews and Greeks, that Jesus is the Christ" (*Ecclesiastical History* 2.23.11-18).[30]

Many of the Jewish leaders, who do not appear to be Believers in Yeshua, were greatly offended that this barbarous action took place, and they informed the Roman authorities about this, as being most unlawful, placing much of the blame at the Sadducees (Eusebius *Ecclesiastical History* 2.23.21-23; Josephus *Antiquities of the Jews* 20.197-203). Even with various Jewish religious leaders not totally in agreement with James' belief in Yeshua as Messiah, they still ably recognized James' piety, and how no one deserved to be taken out and murdered like he was.

WHO WAS THE TARGET AUDIENCE OF THIS LETTER?

It is important to appropriately deduce the audience of the letter of James, which is needed to then ascertain the date of the epistle, and where its author was located while composing it. The Epistle of James is classified among the General Epistles of the Apostolic Scriptures, not only because of its rather general or basic spiritual themes—not addressing a specific issue or crisis in an ancient congregation—but also because no specific audience, in a geographical location, is provided for the reader. Examiners are not entirely sure if there was a specific assembly, assemblies, or informal fellowship(s) of Believers in view.

More conclusions can be drawn from internal clues seen in James, about the demographics of the letter's audience. James' discussion on faith and works was necessitated by many not providing for the needy among them, via essentials such as food and clothing (2:14-26). There are woes issued by the author upon wealthy landowners, who fail to pay their workers an adequate wage (5:1-6). The need for caring for the poor, and a denunciation of the rich, indicates that there was a tension between the lower and higher classes among James' audience.[31] The reference to agricultural conditions (5:4, 7) suggests a more rural environment, although with trading activity also mentioned (4:13-15), those who were somewhat metropolitan cannot be excluded.

One important component of the identity of James' audience, regards the author's reference to not only suffering (5:10), but to trial (1:12) and the crown of life (*ton stephanon tēs zōēs*). It can be thought that James' primary audience was composed of Jewish Believers who had fled the Land of Israel following the martyrdom of Stephen. Because Stephen was a Hellenistic, Greek-speaking Jew (Acts 6:5-9), James' primary audience may have been Hellenistic Jews living in the Diaspora, with a substantial part of them living in "Phoenicia and Cyprus and Antioch" (Acts 11:19). Donald W. Burdick is one who observes, "It is most

[30] Ibid, pp 60-61.
[31] Cf. Wall, "James, Letter of," in *Dictionary of the Later New Testament & Its Developments*, pp 549-550.

reasonable to assume that James, the leading elder of the Jerusalem church, would feel responsible for these former 'parishioners,' and attempt to instruct them somewhat as he would have done had they still been under his care in Jerusalem...he writes with the note of authority expected of one who had been recognized as a spiritual leader in the Jerusalem church."[32]

The only specific information, regarding the audience of James, is seen in the opening greeting, "James, a servant of God and of the Lord Jesus Christ, To the twelve tribes in the Dispersion" (1:1, RSV), *en tē diaspora*. **A Jewish audience for the Epistle of James is assumed by all readers, regardless of additional details.** Some of the additional factors to consider are noted by D.A. Carson and Douglas J. Moo, in *An Introduction to the New Testament*,

"The word translated 'scattered among the nations' [NIV]—diaspora, (*diaspora*, 'Diaspora')—was used to denote Jews living outside of Palestine (see John 7:35) and, by extension, the place in which they lived. But the word also had a metaphorical sense, characterizing Christians generally as those who live away from their true heavenly home (1 Peter 1:1). The early date and Jewishness of James favors the more literal meaning. Like other Jewish authors before him, James sends consolation and exhortation to the dispersed covenant people of God."[33]

That Jewish Believers, and even descendants of the exiled Northern Kingdom of Israel, who had been displaced into the immediate area just north of the Land of Israel many centuries earlier by Assyria, and were connected to the Jewish community, can be concluded as those among James' audience. While it is not difficult for modern readers to recognize ethnic Israelites among James' audience, it can be difficult for some readers to think that those entirely of the nations, could have been among James' audience as well. Whether or not non-Jewish Believers, mainly Greeks and Romans and various others, were among James' audience, is (1) theologically determined not only by James' greeting in 1:1, but James' intention in Acts 15:15-18 regarding the Tabernacle of David. It is (2) also determined by various appeals to classical philosophy embedded in James' exhortations, which would indicate a more diverse audience than just First Century Jews. And (3) the later James' epistle is dated, the likelihood that non-Jews were a part of the intended audience of the letter, as well, necessarily increases.

Recognizing that James himself made light of Amos 9:11-12 at the Jerusalem Council (from the Septugaint, no less), the identity of this letter's audience as "the twelve tribes," can definitely take on an eschatological dynamic. While there should be no doubting the fact that ethnic Israelites, of both Jews and descendants of the exiled Northern Kingdom who were part of the Jewish community, were among James' audience, Carson and Moo note how "After the exile, the twelve tribes no longer existed physically," meaning as distinct groups,

---

[32] Donald W. Burdick, "James," in Frank E. Gaebelein, ed. et. al., *Expositor's Bible Commentary*, 12 vols (Grand Rapids: Zondervan, 1981), 12:162-163.
[33] Carson and Moo, 628.

"but the phrase became a way of denoting the regathered people of God of the last days (see Ezek. 47:13; Matt. 19:28; Rev. 7:4-8; 21:12)."[34] If this factor bears some merit, then God's restored people in the eschaton is to include all Twelve Tribes of Israel recognizable (Isaiah 11:11-16; Zechariah 10:6-12), and concurrent with this, incorporate the righteous from the nations into an expanded Kingdom realm of Israel, as James testified in Acts 15:15-18 (cf. Amos 9:11-12, LXX).

Even though James' primary audience was Jewish Believers in Yeshua, this does not discount the possibility at all that non-Jews were also included among some of its original readers. James' reference "To the twelve tribes in the Dispersion" (1:1, RSV), may be viewed is (1) a reference to his Jewish brethren outside the Land of Israel, but (2) also a reference to the restored Kingdom of God at large, welcoming in those from the nations who have believed in the God of Israel. While a presumed dating of James' composition in the early 40s suggests that various numbers of non-Jews were only just starting to receive Yeshua, James' writing and distinctively Jewish character by no means excludes these people from also being some readers of his letter. McCartney expresses how, "we know from Acts that some Gentiles were being converted even before the Pauline mission and certainly before the controversy of circumcision arose. Since James is addressing churches outside Palestine, it is likely that some of them had Gentile converts."[35]

The Epistle of James does follow a style consistent with some kind of sermon or homily, and its words do tend to speak generally to the condition of God's people, not really taking on as situation-specific a message, compared to other Apostolic compositions. Conservative examiners will recognize how it is entirely possible, if not probable, that much of the transcribed material in the Epistle of James originated out of some kind of oral sermon or message.[36] The high quality of Greek, in the Epistle of James, has caused various liberals to doubt genuine Jamean authorship,[37] and as previously described, others think that a follower of James the Just took his sayings and compiled them into an epistle, to honor him and preserve his legacy, after his death, someone who is thought to have high Greek skills.

The language issue, surrounding the composition of James, does have some bearing on the identity and makeup of James' audience. There are certainly those within today's Messianic movement, who have tried to suggest that James, primarily writing to his fellow Jews, would have written his letter in Hebrew or Aramaic. Yet, if much of James' intended audience were in the Diaspora, dispersed following Stephen's martyrdom, this argument holds little weight. Greek would have been the international language of business that they would have understood, and it would have been the language that would have gained the

[34] Ibid., fn#35.

[35] McCartney, 33.

[36] Cf. J.A. Motyer, *The Message of James* (Downers Grove, IL: InterVarsity, 1985), pp 11-13; Witherington, 389 makes some observations on the oratory style of the epistle.

[37] Herbert Basser, "The Letter of James," in Amy-Jill Levine and Marc Zvi Brettler, eds., *The Jewish Annotated New Testament*, NRSV (Oxford: Oxford University Press, 2011), pp 427.

largest readership—especially if a substantial part of James' audience was in "Phoenicia and Cyprus and Antioch" (Acts 11:19).

Also to be considered, is whether or not a First Century Jewish person, from the Land of Israel, would have even had competence in Greek. While this is a debate for many of today's Messianic people, it is not a debate for those in contemporary Biblical Studies, who recognize the Land of Israel and/or Roman province of Judea as being a multi-lingual place. Among the many potential quotations which could be offered, R.W. Wall asserts the following, from his entry on the letter of James in the *Dictionary of the Later New Testament & Its Developments*,

"One need only appeal to the mounting evidence that demonstrates a fairly active social intercourse between Hellenistic and Palestinian cultures during the late Second Temple period. Religious Jews, especially in Galilee, may well have been anti-Hellenistic during the days immediately before and after the fall of Jerusalem in A.D. 70...however, Jew and Greek intermingled, if a little uneasily. Thus Acts describes a Jerusalem congregation that included Greek-speaking Jews and a pastor (James) who cites the Greek translation (LXX) of Scripture when instructing them (Acts 15:17-18; cf. Jas 4:6). Sharply put, James grew up in a Hellenized Jewish culture where Greek was used and perhaps learned well enough to write this book."[38]

James the Just, being bilingual in Hebrew or Aramaic *and* Greek, at the very least, is not something that can be dismissed—if he was truly the leader of the Jerusalem assembly, and as such regularly interacted with Believers from all over the Mediterranean, who were visiting Jerusalem.[39] Ben Witherington III observes on the language of James' letter, how "it is the kind of Greek that someone who has learned it well and is proficient, though not usually eloquent in it, would produce. The Semitic tinges suggest an author whose native tongue is another language or at least knows such a language."[40] It is fair to conclude, especially given James' appeal to the Septuagint reading of Amos 9:11-12 in Acts 15:15-18, that the style of the epistle's Greek is influenced by the Septuagint translation of the Hebrew Tanach, and hence has an Hebraic or Semitic quality to it.[41] What this would mean is that in various sayings which appear from James, it would be insufficient for readers to only examine a Greek definition of a term, when a well known Hebrew term or concept sits behind it (i.e., the different nuances between *shalom* and *eirēnē*). And it should go without saying, that the biggest source of Hebrew material which sits behind James, will actually be

---

[38] Wall, "James, Letter of," in *Dictionary of the Later New Testament & Its Developments*, 546; cf. Guthrie, pp 734-736; Johnson, in *NIB*, 12:183; Carson and Moo, 624; McCartney, pp 27-28; McKnight, pp 31-34.

[39] Cf. Moo, pp 15-15.

[40] Witherington, pp 399-400; cf. McCartney, pp 5-7.

[41] Wessel, "James, Epistle of," in *ISBE*, 2:962-963; Laws,"James, Epistle of," in *ABD*, 3:627; Witherington, pp 387-388.

For a broader view, consult R. Timothy McLay, *The Use of the Septuagint in New Testament Research* (Grand Rapids: Eerdmans, 2003).

the concepts and ideas quoted from, or at least embedded from, the Tanach or Old Testament.

WHEN DID JAMES WRITE THIS LETTER?

The martyrdom of James the Just is estimated by most scholars as having occurred in 61-62 C.E., which would require—if James the half-brother of Yeshua is the author of this letter—that his epistle be composed before this date. There is no appeal seen in the letter to the rulings of the Jerusalem Council, or it ever having occurred, which itself is estimated to have taken place in the late 40s or early 50s C.E. The content of James' message does not focus on issues like circumcision, which dominated the Jerusalem Council, which may indicate that it had not yet taken place.[42] Acts 11:28 records how that "a severe famine [had] spread over the entire Roman world" (NIV), which is estimated as having occurred in 43 C.E. This event is likewise not referenced in the letter, and could have some bearing on its date.

There are references made to persecutions which were facing some of the early Believers (1:2-4), they were being oppressed by some who were rich (5:1-6), and they were being discriminated against (2:1-13). This would seem to point to James' letter being probably written in the early-to-mid 40s. James' epistle was likely circulated following Stephen's martyrdom, and many Jewish Believers being driven out of the Land of Israel. If James' letter were composed later by James himself, it could reflect on a broad series of negative and unfortunate circumstances for a wide variety of ancient Believers. If James the Just is the genuine author, then it could be written no later than 61-62 C.E.,[43] allowing for a broad period of composition anywhere from 40-62 C.E.

Those who adhere to a non-Jamean or pseudepigraphal origin of the Epistle of James, often think that it was written in the late First Century C.E., perhaps sometime in the 90s.

As a letter, James was in usage by the Second Century C.E., as is attested by some early Christian materials, such as *1 Clement* or the *Shepherd of Hermas.*[44] It did, however, take the Epistle of James much longer, than some of the other books of the Apostolic Writings, to gain widespread canonical acceptance. But this was more on theological grounds than on compositional grounds.

WHERE WAS JAMES WHEN HE WROTE THIS LETTER?

Because James' letter falls into the classification of being one of the General Epistles to a broad audience, and because the author does not mention his location when writing it, examiners have to make some assumptions. As noted, some have suggested that the audience of this letter included Jews who were forced to leave Jerusalem following the

---

[42] Carson and Moo, 627.
[43] Guthrie, pp 752-753.
[44] Cf. Martin, pp xlvii-li; Witherington, 398; McCartney, pp 20-24.

martyrdom of Stephen, given the various references to persecution (1:2-4). Acts 8:1 describes, "And on that day a great persecution began against the [assembly] in Jerusalem, and they were all scattered throughout the regions of Judea and Samaria, except the apostles." They were not only scattered into Judea and Samaria, but Acts 11:19 further states, "those who were scattered because of the persecution that occurred in connection with Stephen made their way to Phoenicia and Cyprus and Antioch."

With James the Just assumed to be the author of this letter, and there being no extant tradition of him ever traveling outside of the Land of Israel to visit other Believers, we may safely assume that James was in or around the vicinity of Jerusalem when he wrote his epistle. A geographical location of the Land of Israel may be safely assumed when one considers things like the scorching east wind (1:11), the tossing waves of the sea (1:6), and "the early and late rains" (5:7)—all features of the region.[45]

WHAT IS THE THEOLOGICAL MESSAGE OF JAMES?

Throughout religious history, the Epistle of James has been associated with some controversy, as it was accepted rather late into the Apostolic canon by emerging Christianity, it has been viewed with much skepticism because of its emphasis on works, and it has been tended to be ignored by too many people in preference to the Pauline letters. A potential mistrust of the Epistle of James has also passed into much academic examination of the letter, as well as the Bible reading of many laypersons. Yet, among those who have sought to have a holistic reading of Scripture, those who appreciate texts which describe the practical wisdom of God's people, and those whose faith is focused on matters of holiness and piety—the Epistle of James has been a major source of guidance and inspiration. So, while it may be said that James is ignored by many, those who have paid attention to James have benefited greatly from it.

In his Fourth Century *Ecclesiastical History*, Eusebius had to acknowledge how the Epistle of James was "Among the disputed books, although...known and approved by many" (3.25.3).[46] Eusebius would also record, "These accounts were given respecting James, who is said to have written the first of the epistles general (catholic) but it is to be observed that it is considered spurious" (*Ecclesiastical History* 2.23.25).[47] "Eusebius himself regarded James, the Lord's brother, whom he calls an apostle, as the author, but he clearly knew the status of the letter was debatable because of uncertainly regarding its authorship" (*IDB*).[48] While there were doubts among many Christians of the Second-Third Centuries concerning the authorship of James, Moo details some of the other factors which contributed to the epistle's late canonical acceptance:

---

[45] Cf. McCartney, pp 24-26.
[46] *Ecclesiastical History*, 91.
[47] Ibid., 62.
[48] Barnett, "James, letter of," in *IDB*, 2:794.

"Early Christians tended to accord special prominence to books written by apostles; and James was such a common name that many probably wondered whether the letter had an apostolic origin or not. Moreover, James is filled with rather traditional and quite practical admonitions: it is not the kind of book that would figure prominently in early Christian theological debates. At the same time some early Jewish-Christian groups misrepresented some of the teaching of James in support of their own heretical agendas. Knowledge of this use of James among orthodox theologians may well have led them to look askance at James."[49]

The lack of seeing any specific reference to the sacrifice of Yeshua, and perhaps even some kind of declared "gospel message" of the salvation available in Him, has also contributed to people being skeptical of the Epistle of James. However, much of this perception only comes from **a surface level reading of the text,** as a careful and detailed examination of the Epistle of James will reveal anything but this. Moo asserts how, "while Jesus' person and work might be generally absent, his teaching is not. No NT document is more influenced by the teaching of Jesus than James."[50] Guthrie further attests, "there are more parallels in this epistle than in any other New Testament book to the teaching of our Lord in the gospels."[51] Some quite notable connections, which are seen between James and Yeshua's teaching in the Sermon on the Mount, include:

- 1:2: Joy in the midst of trials (cf. Matthew 5:10-12).
- 1:4: Exhortation to perfection (cf. Matthew 5:48).
- 1:5: Asking for good gifts (cf. Matthew 7:7ff).
- 1:20: Against anger (cf. Matthew 5:22).
- 1:22: Hearers and doers of the Word (cf. Matthew 7:24ff).
- 2:10: The whole law to be kept (cf. Matthew 5:19).
- 2:13: Blessings of mercifulness (cf. Matthew 5:7).
- 3:18: Blessings of peacemakers (cf. Matthew 5:9).
- 4:4: Friendship of the world as enmity against God (cf. Matthew 6:24).
- 4:10: Blessing of the humble (cf. Matthew 5:5).
- 4:11-12: Against judging others (cf. Matthew 7:1-5).
- 5:2ff: Moth and rust spoiling riches (cf. Matthew 6:19).
- 5:12: Against oaths (cf. Matthew 5:33-37).[52]

---

[49] Moo, 4.

One of the most notable, errant views of James the person, is seen in the Gnostic *Gospel of Thomas*: "The disciples said to Jesus, 'We know that you will depart from us. Who is to be our leader?' Jesus said to them, 'Wherever you are, you are to go to James the righteous, for whose sake heaven and earth came into being'" (logion 12; Thomas O. Lambdin, trans., "The Gospel of Thomas," in James M. Robinson, ed., *The Nag Hammadi Library* [San Francisco: HarperCollins, 1990], 127).

[50] Moo, 27.
[51] Guthrie, 729.
[52] Cf. Ibid, pp 729-730.

Other important parallels with the teachings of Yeshua include:

- 1:6: Exercise of faith without doubting (cf. Matthew 21:21).
- 2:8: Love to one's neighbor as a great commandment (cf. Matthew 22:39).
- 3:1: On the desire to be called teacher (cf. Matthew 23:8-12).
- 3:2ff: On the dangers of hasty speech (cf. Matthew 12:36-37).
- 5:9: The Divine Judge at the doors (cf. Matthew 24:33).[53]

The Epistle of James undeniably parallels the teachings of Yeshua the Messiah,[54] particularly His Sermon on the Mount. James focuses the obedience of God's people onto the same, foundational and imperative ethical matters, which can be quite easy for many religious people—who are used to going through some kind of mere "motions"—to dismiss. There are also parallels and connections which can be made between the Epistle of James and the Wisdom literature of both the Tanach and Apocrypha (i.e., Proverbs, Sirach, Wisdom of Solomon).[55] This contributes to the main thrust of James on teaching his readers how to act properly in the circumstances in which they found themselves.

Even though James makes many allusions to the Torah or Law of Moses, his focus is not so much on the ritual of various commandments, as it is on the Torah's moral message to human beings.[56] In addition to emphasizing the love that God's people are commanded to have toward one another (2:8-9), James warns about sins such as adultery and murder (2:11), the proper handling of the tongue in speech (3:8-10), an emphasis on godly wisdom (3:17), how one is to be humble and pure before God (4:8-10), and to be very cautious when speaking against or judging other brothers or sisters (4:11). James also goes to great lengths to explain the perseverance that God's people are to have (5:7), and how they are not to complain against one another (5:9). James' message, although delivered to a First Century audience with First Century concerns, is widely universal for just about any time.

Among the noticeable themes discussed in James, poverty-piety is affluent in various places (2:2-6).[57] This has a definite association with various parables and teachings about wealth seen in the words of Yeshua, as well as some kind of significant connection to admonitions appearing the Torah and Tanach (Deuteronomy 10:16-19; Ezekiel 16:49; Amos 2:6-7; Psalm 86:1-2).

The history of interpretation of the Epistle of James is noticeably struck by the fact that the Reformer Martin Luther rejected the canonicity of the letter, calling James an "epistle of straw." Luther, and various others following him, have concluded that the letter of James

---

[53] Ibid., 730.
[54] Davids, 48; Bauckham, in *ECB*, 1484; McCartney, pp 50-51; McKnight, pp 25-27.
[55] Witherington, pp 394-395; cf. Moo, 8.
[56] Wessel, "James, Epistle of," in *ISBE*, 2:960.
[57] Davids, pp 41-47; McCartney, pp 37-38.

derided the Pauline doctrine of justification by faith. At the same time, many Christians throughout more recent religious history, Protestant and Catholic, have tended to value the Epistle of James on various levels. Piety movements especially, and others tending to emphasize the value of good works, have highly regarded James. Contrary to Luther, the Reformer John Calvin more adequately summarizes the position of a great number of Protestants in approaching the Epistle of James:

"I am fully content to accept this epistle, when I find it contains nothing unworthy of an apostle of Christ. Indeed, it is a rich source of varied instruction, of abundant benefit in all aspects of the Christian life. We may find striking passages on endurance, on calling upon God, on the practice of religion, on restraining our speech, on peace-making, on holding back greedy instincts, on disregard for this present life—these, and such like, which we shall deal with duly in their proper places."[58]

Given the importance of Martin Luther, though, as one of the first major Reformers, modern commentators such as Moo have tried to offer some explanations as to why he held James in such low regard. Perhaps in the Sixteenth Century, Luther was attempting to reform a Catholic system which considered works—specifically works as defined by the Roman Catholic Church—as a means to justification and salvation. Moo observes, "Luther, faced with forms of Roman Catholic medieval theology that placed great emphasis on works in salvation, naturally focused on Paul in his preaching."[59] Luther did consider James to have many good things to say, but in his theology had extreme difficulty reconciling it with the writings of Paul, which emphasized the grace of God.

In the wake of Luther not quite knowing what to do with the Epistle of James, many Protestant leaders of note have had various degrees of success and difficulty, in seemingly having to reconcile this letter with the writings of Paul, which largely emphasize grace.

Moo mentions the activities of John Wesley in the Eighteenth Century, as he was "confronting...a church largely indifferent to the moral imperatives of the gospel."[60] Wesley would use a text like James to tell his parishioners to attain "Christian perfection,"[61] detailing in his *A Plain Account of Christian Perfection*,

"I tell you, as plain as I can speak, where and when I found this. I found it in the oracles of God, in the Old and New Testament; when I read them with no other view or desire but to save my own soul. But whosoever this doctrine is, I pray you, what harm is there in it? Look at it again; survey it on every side, and that with the closest attention. In one view, it is purity of intention, dedicating all the life to God. It is the giving God all our heart; it is one desire and design ruling all our tempers. It is the devoting, not a part, but all our soul, body, and substance to God. In another view, it is all the mind

---

[58] John Calvin, *Calvin's New Testament Commentaries: A Harmony of the Gospels Matthew, Mark & Luke and James & Jude*, trans. A.W. Morrison (Grand Rapids: Eerdmans, 1972), 259; cf. Moo, pp 5-6.
[59] Moo, 43.
[60] Ibid.
[61] Ibid., 37.

which was in Christ, enabling us to walk as Christ walked. It is the circumcision of the heart from all filthiness, all inward as well as outward pollution. It is a renewal of the heart in the whole image of God, the full likeness of Him that created it. In yet another, it is the loving God with all our heart, and our neighbour as ourselves."[62]

Whether ancient or more modern, the challenge that many have had when examining James, is what appears to be his preoccupation with the works of God's people (2:14-26). He attests "that a man is justified by works and not by faith alone" (2:24). This has been confusing for many, especially in light of Paul's word, which is that salvation comes "not as a result of works, so that no one may boast" (Ephesians 2:9). Are James and Paul at theological and spiritual odds—or do James and Paul need to be placed in a better context, on their own merits? If the latter is to be the preferred choice of action, then not only does an interpreter have to consider James and Paul as possibly having different vantage points in describing "justification," but also the different dynamics of "justification" themselves, ranging from a forgiveness and remittance from sin to being recognized as a member of God's covenant people.

The theological debate surrounding the Epistle of James, for many centuries, has been: How can James, and his emphasis on works, be reconciled to the words of Paul, which largely emphasize grace? Moo offers the perspective, "Works, claims Paul, have no role in getting us into relationship with God. Works, insists James, do have a role in securing God's vindication in the judgment. Paul strikes at legalism; James at quietism. Each message needs to be heard."[63] J.A. Motyer is a bit more to the point, in his publication, *The Message of James*: "disagreement between James and Paul is in fact artificially produced by wrenching James' words out of their context."[64] One is identified as expositing on saving faith (Paul), and another is identified as expositing on the life required by faith (James). Some interpreters have thought that parts of the Epistle of James were composed to engage with a garbled form of Pauline teaching on faith, and that had James and Paul actually been able to interact in person more frequently, that presumed differences between them could have been easily ironed out.[65] Paul himself was not at all opposed to good works flowing from genuine saving faith (i.e, Ephesians 2:10); he was opposed to people thinking that their good works provided saving faith (i.e., Ephesians 2:8-9). *ISBE* summarizes,

"The best-known passage in which faith is mentioned is 2:14-26, and here faith and works are contrasted. A study of this passage reveals that the author is not attempting to refute Paul. The two stand basically in agreement. For both James and Paul faith finds its object in the Lord Jesus Christ, and both are agreed that the first thing to do with faith is to

[62] John Wesley, *A Plain Account of Christian Perfection* (Kansas City: Beacon Hill Press, 1966), 117.
    The reader is referred to some of the useful notes and observations in Joel B. Green, "The Letter of James," in Joel B. Green, ed., *The Wesley Study Bible* (Nashville: Abingdon, 2009), pp 1500-1504.
[63] Ibid, 37.
[64] Motyer, 19.
[65] Carson and Moo, pp 625-626.

live by it. The 'faith' of which James speaks in 2:14-26 is really not faith at all, in the true Hebraic sense of confidence and trust in God that elicits appropriate action."[66]

A reasonable examination of the text of James' letter will not prove his writing to be in conflict with Paul's words about justification by grace. James was concerned about a life of faith manifested in works, as he stated, "You have faith and I have works; show me your faith without the works, and I will show you my faith by my works [*ek tōn ergōn mou tēn pistin*]" (2:18). For a figure such as James, works are to be the external evidence of one's faith in God, and are to show that a man or woman actually has faith. What is interesting, of course, is that James' words on the works of a Believer were widely written before much of Paul's teaching on human actions. In the Epistle of James, it is possible that there were those who misinterpreted some of Paul's preliminary teachings on works, and James had to issue some correction. Wall addresses how one has to appreciate the letter of James as being complimentary to Paul:

"[Many] have come to depend upon the book's wise solutions to everyday situations, which insist that a fully biblical religion requires more than mere confessions of orthodox faith. In this sense James offers a complementary 'check and balance' to the accents of the Pauline letters, helping to form a biblical witness that commends a firm trust in the saving work of the Lord Jesus (Pauline) and a practical wisdom patterned after his life (James)."[67]

The Apostle Paul himself recognized the authority and calling of James as a servant of the Lord. In 1 Corinthians 15:7, James is mentioned by name, before "all the apostles." Martin indicates how "He recognized James as a leader who was prominent in the mother church. He appealed to James' authority as a witness of the resurrection, and claimed himself to be a member of that company."[68] Yet Martin also draws the conclusion, remarking that "He was reluctant to state plainly that James was, in Paul's own estimation, an apostle—according to what is perhaps the best conclusion we can reach on the ambiguous wording of 1 Cor 15:7."[69] Of course, we have to note that in 1 Corinthians 15:7, James is mentioned by name, while the rest are reserved only the category of "apostles." While some have used this as a way to downplay James, James mentioned by name, as the half-brother of Yeshua and leader of the Jerusalem assembly, could be taken as a recognition that he was in a slightly higher status than that of the Apostles.

The importance of James the Just for the First Century Body of Messiah was quite significant, given the spurious involvement of his name in the incident at Antioch (Galatians 2:11-14), with what many conservative interpreters feel was an inappropriate appeal by some Jewish Believers to stir up trouble by somehow appealing to him, when they

---

[66] Wessel, "James, Epistle of," in *ISBE*, 2:960-961.
[67] Wall, "James, Letter of," in *Dictionary of the Later New Testament & Its Developments*, 545.
[68] Martin, xxxviii.
[69] Ibid.

were, in fact, unauthorized.[70] McKnight actually says, regarding the importance of James as a leader, "I am a Protestant and not in direct fellowship with the See of Rome, but if asked who was the 'first pope,' I would choose James. He was at the center of the church, the whole church, because the whole church had its start in Jerusalem."[71] Even if the Epistle of James is said to be a bit "primitive," as it were, in comparison to later theological issues and controversies which would erupt in the First Century Body of Messiah, James is a pretty important letter to be considered in terms of the absolute essentials of faith. It is the product of the half-brother of Yeshua, and should be studied and probed for worthwhile applications for serving God in our hurting world.

The Epistle of James offers Bible readers some of the most practical theology, which many modern Christian examiners appropriately recognize is well-needed for our times. James is one of the most frequently read letters in the Bible by people, but can be misunderstood because of its high emphasis on works. Many of today's evangelical Christians, in reviewing James' letter, have made great progress in trying to restore a greater appreciation of it for contemporary Believers. This does not only concern responsible Bible reading, but also in stirring Believers to action in the world, and in having an understanding of doctrine which is not stale in spiritual value. McCartney summarizes much of this:

"Our Western Christian heritage has vigorously stressed the importance of doctrine, focusing on propositional truth as crucial for Christian identity, because ideas and thoughts make a difference in actions and relationships, particularly our relationship to God. But James reminds us that the ultimate purpose of Christian instruction, the goal of doctrine, is a godly character and righteous behavior. This purpose is also found in Jesus's teaching and even in that of Paul...but it has tended to become lost in our battles over precise doctrinal formulation. James reminds us that genuine faith is more than a matter of simply acknowledging the right concepts; it is right living in accordance with those concepts."[72]

Motyer also makes some observations, which he directs toward modern Christian readers of James:

"As we look around us today...the abandonment of the old reactive separatism from the world has led to a forgetfulness of the concept of separation, and for very many Christians what goes in the world goes in the church. If everyone does it, why should not the Christian? We need to discover and live by positive Christian standards—not reacting against the world around us, but by responding obediently to the Word of God within the world around us. James wrote his letter just for us."[73]

---

[70] Moo, 17 astutely observes, "Did James himself send these people with his blessing? Or were they simply claiming to represent James without his authority?" Moo opts for the latter view.
[71] McKnight, 12.
[72] McCartney, 3.
[73] Motyer, 15.

While more Western Christians in the past have had difficulty relating to the various groups within James' First Century audience,[74] in our global world and economy, where the plight of those in undeveloped countries where poverty runs rampant can be readily seen on television or the Internet—James' words about those in need should be more impactful. For Twenty-First Century evangelicals, James presents a perspective of works required of Messiah followers, which are most relevant and highly significant, as a demonstration of the love of God toward human beings.

HOW DOES JAMES RELATE TO MESSIANIC BELIEVERS TODAY?

Unlike some of the varied challenges that either older or more contemporary Christian traditions have had with the Epistle of James, today's Messianic movement tends to have a very high appreciation of James. In much Messianic teaching, James' words about the works of Messiah followers tend to be emphasized, on different levels, in connection with Messianic Believers' Torah observance. Yet, while the Epistle of James is often valued by many Messianic people, there is some definite room for improvement. There is a need for Messianic readers to be a bit more text-conscious about all of the various issues seen in the letter, for them to pay a little closer attention to the nature of the works James has in mind, and most especially to not make the reverse error of many Christians, overplaying the Epistle of James at the expense of the letters of Paul.

How are today's Messianic Believers to approach the Epistle of James? An unnecessary amount of debate actually surrounds the common English title of this letter, which the 2011 *Tree of Life Messianic Family Bible—The New Covenant* rendered as "Jacob"[75] (the Complete Jewish Bible has "Ya'akov"). While it is useful for readers to be informed about the issues of *Iakōbos* and *Ya'akov*, there are some petty diatribes that can be witnessed among Messianics, which can take readers away from the much bigger issues of the actual contents and applications of the letter itself. There have been some Messianic Jewish attempts to address the Epistle of James, beyond David H. Stern's *Jewish New Testament Commentary*,[76] including the remarks appearing in Arnold G. Fructenbaum's *Ariel's Bible Commentary*,[77] and the volume *James the Just Presents Applications of Torah* by David Friedman, with D.B. Friedman.[78] (This second publication is not a verse-by-verse analysis of the epistle, as much as it is a series of essays presenting some proposed connections between James and ancient Rabbinical perspectives.)

---

[74] Ibid., 16.

[75] *Tree of Life Messianic Family Bible—New Covenant* (Shippensburg, PA: Destiny Image, 2011), 403.

[76] David H. Stern, *Jewish New Testament Commentary* (Clarksville, MD: Jewish New Testament Publications, 1995), pp 725-742.

[77] Arnold G. Fructenbaum, *Ariel's Bible Commentary: The Messianic Jewish Epistles* (Tustin, CA: Ariel Ministries, 2005), pp 205-313.

[78] David Friedman, with D.B. Friedman, *James the Just Presents Applications of Torah* (Clarksville, MD: Lederer, 2012).

Immediately jumping into the Epistle of James, there are various quarters of the Messianic community, where some rather caustic emotions are probable to erupt, when the intended authorship of this letter is considered. James identifies his audience as "the twelve tribes who are dispersed abroad" (1:1), and no reader or interpreter across a broad spectrum denies that Jewish people were his primary audience. Tension arises in conjunction with the issue of the corporately exiled Northern Kingdom of Israel/Ephraim, as pockets of people to the immediate north of Israel, in Syria and Lebanon, would have been among their descendants—and this is a likely location for much of James' audience (Acts 11:19). The real debate is not whether ethnic Israelites are an intended audience of James' letter, but whether any people entirely of the nations, are also intended. This is a definite place where if non-Jewish Believers are included as recipients of James' letter as well, an examiner has to stay, as far as possible, away from appropriating any themes of supersessionism, where the so-called "Church" is now the "New Israel."[79] Instead, a Kingdom of God known by a restored twelve tribes of Israel, should be in view, in conjunction with James' own words at the Jerusalem Council about Israel's Kingdom realm expanding to incorporate those of the nations (Acts 15:15-18; Amos 9:11-12).

Much of the issue regarding a wider audience than just First Century Jewish people, for the Epistle of James, is actually going to be determined from the author's appeal to classical philosophy and moralism (3:6),[80] and many in the Messianic movement struggle with classical Mediterranean background issues in the Apostolic Scriptures. No reader of James doubts that there are parallels between this letter and the Tanach or Old Testament, particularly its Wisdom literature. However, connections with classical philosophy indicate that there were Diaspora Jews among the letter's recipients, and among Diaspora Jews inevitably came those proselytes and God-fearers who would also come to Messiah faith.

While Messianic readers will necessarily be tuned in to connections made between the Tanach, and other ancient bodies of Jewish literature, and what is communicated in James—Johnson actually draws the conclusion that the letter of James' worldview, is closest to that of the Pauline letters:

"Of all the compositions from the first-century Mediterranean world, in fact, James most resembles the letters of Paul in its style and outlook. The resemblance is not restricted to the disputed lines in 2:14-26, nor is it due to the dependence of one writer on the other. Rather, despite the obvious differences between the extant literature of each author, James and Paul share a range of convictions and perceptions that is best explained by the hypothesis that both are first-century Jewish members of the messianic movement with significant roots in the world of Palestinian Judaism."[81]

---

[79] Barnett, "James, Letter of," in *IDB*, 4:796; Wessel, "James, Epistle of," in *ISBE*, 2:964; Guthrie, pp 747-748; Wall, "James, Letter of," in *Dictionary of the Later New Testament & Its Developments*, 548; Moo, 23.

[80] Cf. Carson and Moo, 624.

[81] Johnson, in *NIB*, 12:180.

While Bible readers, surveying the Epistle of James and the Pauline letters, can make some broad connections between the similarities between them—theologically speaking, Messianics, as much as many Christians, can have a tendency to think that James and Paul disagree on some issues. Messianic people today can demonstrate some difficulties, in sorting out the relationship between faith and works—and more frequently than some leaders and teachers probably want to know, in the minds of many individuals, James and Paul are pitted as adversaries, rather than dealing with different situations. James' audience has dismissed the proper actions attendant with faith, and Paul's audiences have often placed human activity as a cause for earning salvation. And, not enough are informed about how different components of "righteousness" or "justification" are in play,[82] which may not always involve being cleared from sin. A good approach for sorting through James' letter and Paul's writings is offered by the introduction to James (Jacob) in the TLV:

"Some wonder if there is a conflict between Jacob and Paul: Paul teaches that we are set right before God, justified by our faith, while Jacob says that this happens from our works (2:24). Actually Paul and Jacob compliment each other. God declares us to be righteous because of our faith, while our faith witnesses to others through our deeds. A true faith will show itself in how we live. Paul and Jacob would both be quick to agree to that. We say we have faith in *Yeshua*; now, let's live like it!"[83]

James the Just was not someone who believed that the Torah or Law of Moses had been abolished for Messiah followers. Even among examiners who do believe that the Torah has been abolished for the post-resurrection era, such as Moo, he still has to conclude, "James maintains the continuing authority of the OT law for Christians only insofar as it has been 'fulfilled' by Jesus. James's appeal to the 'love command' as *the* royal law forges a direct link with Jesus; and James, of course, alludes to the teaching of Jesus throughout his letter."[84] Given the many connections between James' letter and Yeshua's Sermon on the Mount, many of the Torah-prescribed or related actions that James discusses, will be related to acts of kindness, mercy, and heart attitude.

For James, obedience to God is not something that is crafted out of some kind of legalistic duty, but rather the completeness or the perfection of the individual. The term *teleios* appears in this epistle multiple times (1:4, 17, 25; 3:2), to describe the proper character of the Believer. *TDNT* describes it, in relation to James' writing, as a "sense" of being "'whole' or 'complete'...Those are who do the whole work and whose steadfastness works itself out fully. This means looking into the 'entire' law of liberty (1:25) and doing it. This law brings liberty with its observance. It finds fulfillment in love but also in self-control, for the whole

---

[82] Carson and Moo, 633; Moo, pp 37-43; Walter C. Kaiser, *The Promise-Plan of God: A Biblical Theology of the Old and New Testaments* (Grand Rapids: Zondervan, 2008), 253.

[83] *Tree of Life Messianic Family Bible—New Covenant*, 403.

[84] Moo, 33.

person bridles the whole body, including the tongue (3:2ff)."[85] In its ancient classical usage as a philosophical term, "*téleios* carries the sense of full humanity with an orientation to what is worthwhile and ethically good."[86] Consequently, when James admonishes his readers to attain to "perfection," all of these excellent qualities are being alluded to. Believers in Messiah Yeshua are to strive for a maturity that engulfs their entire being, and is to be evidenced in good ethics, morality, and spiritual steadfastness. James addresses a fair amount of inter-personal and inter-congregational related issues, and being perfect—meaning striving for the goal of excellence—is an overriding theme throughout James' epistle. The introduction to James (Jacob) in the TLV astutely concurs,

"Jacob focuses on ethics—how to live out the life of faith. This resonates with the emphasis of many modern Jews for whom ethics is often at the front of the agenda. The difference is that Jacob says that our life flows from our faith in *Yeshua* (2:1). He speaks to such issues as dealing with suffering; handling temptation; treating people fairly rather than playing favorites; showing the reality of one's faith through deeds; and using one's tongue properly (avoiding what modern Judaism calls *lashon ha-ra*, hurtful speech or gossip)."[87]

Recognizing that the good works, based in the Torah, which James emphasizes—**largely concern ethics and morality**—there should be no surprise how some significant connections have been proposed between his epistle and the Holiness Code of Leviticus ch. 19:

JAMES AND THE TORAH OF GOD[88]	
LEVITICUS 19:12-18	THE EPISTLE OF JAMES
You shall not swear falsely by My name, so as to profane the name of your God; I am the LORD (19:12).	do not swear...so that you may not fall under judgment (5:12).
You shall not oppress your neighbor, nor rob *him*. The wages of a hired man are not to remain with you all night until morning (19:13).	Behold, the pay of the laborers who mowed your fields, *and* which has been withheld by you, cries out *against you*... (5:4).

---

[85] G. Delling, "*téleios*," in Geoffrey W. Bromiley, ed., *Theological Dictionary of the New Testament*, abrid. (Grand Rapids: Eerdmans, 1985), 1164.

[86] Ibid.

[87] *Tree of Life Messianic Family Bible—New Covenant*, 403.

[88] This chart has been adapted from Walter C. Kaiser, *The Promise-Plan of God: A Biblical Theology of the Old and New Testaments* (Grand Rapids: Zondervan, 2008), 254.

You shall not curse a deaf man, nor place a stumbling block before the blind, but you shall revere your God; I am the LORD (19:14).	*no parallel*
You shall do no injustice in judgment; you shall not be partial to the poor nor defer to the great, but you are to judge your neighbor fairly (19:15).	My brethren, do not hold your faith in our glorious Lord Yeshua the Messiah with *an attitude of* personal favoritism (2:1).
You shall not go about as a slanderer among your people, and you are not to act against the life of your neighbor; I am the LORD (19:16).	Do not speak against one another, brethren. He who speaks against a brother or judges his brother, speaks against the law and judges the law; but if you judge the law, you are not a doer of the law but a judge *of it* (4:11).
You shall not hate your fellow countryman in your heart; you may surely reprove your neighbor, but shall not incur sin because of him (19:17).	let him know that he who turns a sinner from the error of his way will save his soul from death and will cover a multitude of sins (5:20).
You shall not take vengeance, nor bear any grudge against the sons of your people (19:18a).	Do not complain, brethren, against one another, so that you yourselves may not be judged; behold, the Judge is standing right at the door (5:9).
but you shall love your neighbor as yourself; I am the LORD (19:18b).	If, however, you are fulfilling the royal law according to the Scripture, "YOU SHALL LOVE YOUR NEIGHBOR AS YOURSELF," you are doing well (2:8).

When was the last time that any of us, in our own personal reading of the weekly Torah portions, or in a *Shabbat* service, have seen connections made between Leviticus 19:12-18 and the Epistle of James? Probably not as frequently as we should, because in a letter like

James, we see how important these principles are to be followed by men and women of faith in everyday life and interactions.

Not only have many Jewish Believers entered into the Messianic movement, and as a result have been reconnected to their Jewish heritage—but so have many non-Jewish Believers also entered into the Messianic movement, having started a diligent pattern of Torah study. But many of us *all wonder* where this Torah study and observance will lead us, and how we are to really practice it in the world. For Messianic Believers, the Epistle of James offers us a great venue, as we consider the faith required of the Believer, the works required of the Believer, and the right heart attitude toward one another in the community of faith and the world at large.

A lost emphasis on the works of the Believer is something that is being restored to those in today's Messianic community. Unfortunately, various teachers who examine James, can fall into the trap of emphasizing the works of a Believer over the grace of God—without a proper balance of the two. We do not come to faith in Messiah Yeshua solely for the sake of demonstrating our devotion to God by our works. After we come to faith in Yeshua we are to obey our Heavenly Father because we love Him and because we want to please Him, and we are to love one another. This is something clearly emphasized by James in his comments concerning "the royal law" (2:8).

Everyone in the Messianic movement today needs to hear James' message regarding perfection. While none of us may be able to be entirely perfect this side of eternity, we still nevertheless need to strive for greater and greater excellence. We can definitely see many non-Jewish Believers, in particular, who enter into the Messianic movement not because they are spiritually convicted that they need to be following the Torah and hence live as Messiah Yeshua lived, but because they are trying to prove themselves superior to others. This is evidenced in the attitudes of those who unwarrantedly criticize our Christian brothers and sisters, and rather than reason with them constructively on various issues, condemn them mercilessly. As a movement, all of us need to have a mature attitude instilled within us, whereby we are never having to prove how we are "better than everyone else." *James addresses how the Messianic movement today needs a heart check.*

James delivers a very strong message to the Messianic community today. We are a still-developing movement, as well as a maturing movement. *No one should be under any allusions that bringing together Jewish and non-Jewish Believers, and making a difference in the world together, is an easy thing.* James admonishes us about the personal piety and holiness that we should all be striving for, while we must also be ethical, moral, and above all loving toward our fellow human beings. These are lessons that should be second nature to all of us, especially if we claim that we follow the Torah. Paul A. Cedar validly writes, "I believe that James should be one of the first books read and mastered by the new Christian. Too often the church has mastered the art of informing people regarding what they *should* be doing, but has failed to teach them *how* to do it!"[89] **How much more so does this apply to us as Messianic Believers who need to know how to properly live the Torah in modern society, positively impacting others with the truth?** What are some of the areas, described by James, where we need to seriously improve?

There is a widespread tendency among many Messianics for them to think that the "works" James primarily expects are those of keeping the Sabbath, the appointed times of Leviticus 23, or eating kosher—when this is not only the case. An honest reading of the Epistle of James demonstrates how its author is much more concerned about those required actions of people of faith that help instill a sense of human wholeness in others. As James summarizes, "Pure and undefiled religion in the sight of *our* God and Father is this: to visit orphans and widows in their distress, *and* to keep oneself unstained by the world" (1:27).

Messianic Believers today should know the appropriate place that works play in their lives. They follow the Torah's commandments because the Messiah Yeshua did. They cannot just have "faith in their faith"; our faith in the God of Israel must be evidenced by good conduct in the world, and the standard that the Lord has set forth in His Torah. James, the half-brother of Yeshua, continued to live by this standard, and instructed others to live by it as well. He emphasizes the ethics and morality that all Messiah followers *and* emulators should have, as they live forth God's love in the world.

On the technical side as you prepare to read this commentary on James, note that I have purposefully refrained from overly using Hebraic terminology, other than the name "Yeshua the Messiah" for Jesus Christ, and on occasion "Torah" instead of Law, for the familiarity of most readers, and those who can be easily confused by unfamiliar words. The 1995 New American Standard, Updated Edition is the base English translation used in these studies, because of its literalness and widespread usage among many conservative evangelical Christians. Other major English versions I consult include the Revised Standard Version and New International Version.

References to the Greek Apostolic Scriptures are from United Bible Societies' 1998 Greek New Testament, Fourth Revised Edition, the same basic text as the Nestle-Aland Novum Testamentum Gracae, 27th Edition. If you have any competency in Greek, an excellent resource to employ in examining our text is the Nestle-Aland Greek-English New Testament, which includes the 27th Edition GNT and a parallel RSV.

ABBREVIATED OUTLINE OF JAMES

    I.   Greeting (1:1)
    II.   Trials and how to meet them (1:2-4)
    III.   Wisdom and how to obtain it (1:5-8)
    IV.   Wealth and how to regard it (1:9-11)
    V.   Temptation and trial distinguished (1:12-15)
    VI.   Good gifts (1:16-18)
    VII.   Hearing and doing (1:19-27)

---

[89] Paul A. Cedar, *The Preacher's Commentary: James, 1&2 Peter, Jude* (Nashville: Thomas Nelson, 1984), 9.

VIII.   Against partiality (2:1-13)
IX.   Against a barren faith (2:14-26)
X.   Qualities required in teachers (3:1-18)
     a.   Control of speech (3:1-12)
     b.   True wisdom (3:13-18)
XI.   Dangers (4:1-17)
     a.   Human passions (4:1-10)
     b.   Evil speaking (4:11-12)
     c.   Rash confidence (4:13-17)
XII.   Warnings to wealthy oppressors (5:1-6)
XIII.   Encouragements to the oppressed (5:7-11)
XIV.   Against oaths (5:12)
XV.   The power of prayer (5:13-18)
XVI.   Help for the backslider (5:19-20)[90]

BIBLIOGRAPHY FOR INTRODUCTION

Basser, Herbert. "The Letter of James," in *The Jewish Annotated New Testament*, pp 427-435.

Barabas, Steven. "James, Letter of," in *NIDB*, pp 494-495.

Barnett, A.E. "James, Letter of," in *IDB*, 2:794-799.

Bauckham, Richard. "James," in *ECB*, pp 1483-1492.

Beardsless, W.A. "James," in *IDB*, 2:790-794.

Burdick, Donald W. "James," in *EXP*, 12:161-205.

Carson, D.A., and Douglas J. Moo. "James," in *An Introduction to the New Testament*, pp 619-635.

Davids, Peter. "Introduction," in *NIGTC: The Epistle of James*, pp 1-61.

Gillman, Florence Morgan. "James, Brother of Jesus," in *ABD*, 3:620-621.

Gundry, Robert H. "The Catholic, or General, Epistles," in *A Survey of the New Testament*, pp 431-453.

Guthrie, Donald. "The Epistle of James," in *New Testament Introduction*, pp 722-759.

Hagner, Donald A. "James," in *ABD*, 3:616-618.

Harris, R.L. "James," in *ISBE*, 2:958-959.

Johnson, Luke T. "The Letter of James," *NIB*, 12:177-225.

Kaiser, Jr., Walter C. "James: The Perfect Law of God," in *The Promise-Plan of God*, pp 250-255.

Laws, Sophie. "James, Epistle of," in *ABD*, 3:621-628.

Martin, Ralph P. "Introduction," in *WBC: James*, 48:xxxi-cix.

McCartney, Dan G. "Introduction to James," in *Baker Exegetical Commentary on the New Testament: James*, pp 1-76.

McKnight, Scot. "Introduction," in *NICNT: The Letter of James*, pp 1-55.

Moo, Douglas J. "Introduction," in *Pillar New Testament Commentary: The Letter of James*, pp 1-46.

Motyer, J.A. "Introduction," in *The Message of James*, pp 11-22.

Perkins, Pheme. "The Letter of James," in *New Interpreter's Study Bible*, pp 2171-2179.

Reicke, Bo Ivar. "The Epistle of James: Introduction," in *The Anchor Bible: The Epistles of James, Peter, and Jude*, pp 3-10.

Stern, David H. *Jewish New Testament Commentary*, pp 725-742.

---

[90] Adapted from Guthrie, *New Testament Introduction*, pp 757-759.

Tree of Life Messianic Family Bible—New Covenant, pp 403-411.

Van Voorst, Robert E. "James," in *EDB*, pp 669-670.

Wall, R.W. "James, Letter of," in *Dictionary of the Later New Testament & Its Developments*, pp 545-561.

Ward, R.B. "James, Letter of," in *IDBSup*, pp 469-470.

Wessel, W.W. "James, Epistle of," in *ISBE*, 2:959-966.

Witherington, III, Ben. "Introduction to James," in *Letters and Homilies for Jewish Christians: A Socio-Rhetorical Commentary on Hebrews, James and Jude*, pp 385-415.

JAMES 1
COMMENTARY

1 James, a bond-servant of God and of the Lord Yeshua the Messiah, to the twelve tribes who are dispersed abroad: Greetings.

1:1a The author of this epistle identifies himself as James, or "Jacob" (TLV), *Iakōbos* being a Greek equivalent of the Hebrew *Ya'akov*. While James the half-brother of Yeshua the Messiah is not stated specifically, it was on the assumption that this was the James who composed this material, or was its originator, that the letter has been deemed canonical.[1] There have certainly been debates as to whether or not James is a pseudepigraphal epistle, as adhered to by various liberals, or perhaps with the Epistle of James going through a two-staged composition, first as a series of genuine Jamean sayings, and secondly edited later by a follower or admirer into the present letter. Various conservatives, although not including this writer, may adhere to the latter theory. Dan G. McCartney makes light of some good reasons as to why this letter should not, though, be accepted as a pseudegraph:

"Were this letter pseudepigraphal, one would have expected the author to have made more of James's unique relationship with Jesus, as indeed was done in certain quarters of the church in centuries following. However, this James identifies himself not as Jesus's brother but as Jesus's servant, thus classifying himself along with all his readers."[2]

James specifies his vocation as being a "servant" or *doulos*, which may also be translated as "slave." *Doulos* is frequently used in the Septuagint to render the Hebrew *eved*, a title which itself is used for a wide number of important Tanach figures, such as Moses (Deuteronomy 34:5; Daniel 9:11) and King David (Jeremiah 33:21). *Doulos* is also a common title employed by figures such as Peter (2 Peter 1:1) and Paul (Romans 1:1; Galatians 1:20; Philippians 1:1; Titus 1:1). The position of an *eved*, or *doulos*, was one of being associated with a long line of leaders of the community of Israel, often with, although not always, some kind of important leadership or prophetic duties.

James affirms that he is a servant "of God and of the Lord Yeshua the Messiah." Here, there is a close association of the titles "God" (*Theos*) and "Lord" (*Kurios*), with the latter used to refer to the Messiah, although in the Septuagint the title *Kurios* would most often render the Divine Name YHWH/YHVH. It may be safely assumed that with titles used to

[1] Cf. McKnight, 62.
[2] McCartney, 79.

describe God the Father applied to Yeshua the Son, that the Divine Lordship of Yeshua is affirmed.[3] This is perhaps something that most closely mirrors that of the Apostle Peter's dynamic preaching in Acts 2:36, "Therefore let all the house of Israel know for certain that God has made Him both Lord and Messiah—this Yeshua whom you crucified."

1:1b In his greeting, James directs his epistle "To the twelve tribes in the Dispersion" (RSV), *tais dōdeka phulais tais en tē diaspora*. While no interpreter, generally on any side of the conservative-liberal divide, denies that there was a Jewish audience, to some degree, intended for the Epistle of James—there are some details regarding what "the twelve tribes" actually encompasses, or is intended to represent, which need not escape readers' notice.

There is no doubting the fact that there have been numerous Christian interpreters throughout history, who have viewed James' reference to "the twelve tribes"—not as a reference to the Kingdom of Israel—but have instead totally allegorized it as the so-called "Church" being a "New Israel," per supersessionism or replacement theology.[4] On the exact opposite side of this, however, it has also been witnessed that James' reference to "the twelve tribes" has been used, by various Christians and Messianic Jews, to claim an exclusively Jewish audience for the letter. This is probably a bit too convenient, especially given James' own perspective on the people of God and the restored Kingdom of Israel, which *includes* those from the nations at large who recognize Israel's Messiah (Acts 15:15-18; Amos 9:11-12).

Going back at least to the time of John Calvin, the audience of v. 1 and the issue of the exiles from the fallen Northern Kingdom of Israel/Ephraim, taken away by Assyria, has been admittedly an uncomfortable topic for examiners to consider, but one which has had to be weighed into discussions. Calvin's remarks on the issue are rather general:

"When the ten tribes were led away, they were exiled by the Assyrians in various regions. As later empires rose and fell over the years, no doubt they wandered yet further afield, this way and that. Jews were dispersed over virtually the entire world. Thus all the number whom he could not address face to face, for the distances that lay between them, [James] calls up by written word."[5]

At least up until the rise of the Nineteenth Century and negative phenomenon like British-Israelism—the descendants of the exiles of the Northern Kingdom were believed to exist in pockets of people groups, here and there, within the sphere of influence of the old Assyrian, Babylonian, and Persian Empires. The traditional places where such people have been sought have been Southeast Asia, the Indian sub-continent, the Middle East, the Eastern Mediterranean, and into Central Africa. Various exiles in the Middle East, who had

---

[3] Motyer, pp 27-28; Moo, 49; McCartney, 78.

[4] Davids, 63; Motyer, 24; Johnson, in *NIB*, 12:186; N.T. Wright, *The Early Christian Letters for Everyone: James, Peter, John, and Judah* (Louisville: Westminster John Knox, 2011), 4.

Cf. A. Casurella, "Israel, Twelve Tribes," in *Dictionary of the Later New Testament & Its Developments*, pp 542-544.

[5] Calvin, 261.

not assimilated into the local cultures, did join the wider Jewish community which had been exiled by Babylon, with many returning back to the Land of Israel when Babylon was conquered by Persia, or just staying in the Diaspora. That such people of the "twelve tribes" were among James' audience, were his audience mainly in places to the immediate north of Israel, is certain.

Also important to be sure, with a wider Diaspora of people from both the Northern and Southern Kingdoms of Israel present in the world, the terminology "twelve tribes" would have probably taken on a dynamic of eschatological restoration via the Messiah. Scot McKnight summarizes it as much:

"...[T]he expression 'twelve tribes' could have been seen as almost *per definitionem* metaphorical: ten of those tribes have been lost since the Assyrian captivity. But it is not that easy: Jews with plausible connections back to the eighth-century deportation were present in the Diaspora in the first century, and the hope of their return was a routine feature of Jewish eschatology. So, since that return is expected but has not yet occurred in the ethnic sense, 'twelve tribes' must be a reference to all of Israel, and this expression probably also included the eschatological hope of reunion. This is how Jesus used 'twelve' (Mark 3:13-19; Matt 19:28), and for Jesus there is a reconstitution of that twelve-tribe group for those who follow him and his apostles. Which means, in light of our comments about James stemming from a messianic community shaped by a messianic hermeneutic, it is highly likely that he is writing to the 'twelve tribes' in the sense of those ethnic Jews who are part of the apostolically-led messianic community."[6]

McCartney similarly observes,

"The 'twelve tribes in the Diaspora' is, of course, a reference to Israel. Although many Jews had some knowledge of their tribal connections (e.g., Paul the Benjamite, Symeon the Levite), the twelve tribes as distinct and discernible units or clans within Judaism were a thing of the past, especially the 'northern' tribes (though the Samaritans probably were largely derived from northern Israelites). But the OT and later Jewish writings sometimes speak of the twelve tribes as an aspect of the restored Israel (Ezek. 47:13; T. Benj. 9.2)...Since early Christians (Acts 26:7), following Jesus's lead (Matt. 19:28), regarded the community of believers in Christ as the fulfillment of the promises of restoration, James does not hesitate to apply this OT designation of restored Israel (cf. Ezra 6:17) to his hearers."[7]

---

[6] McKnight, pp 66-67.

Ibid., pp 67-68 leans personally toward the community addressed being a sub-group of Jewish Believers, in the Diaspora, within a larger Jewish community.

[7] McCartney, 79.

Christian expositors, including Douglas J. Moo,[8] have been correct to draw the attention of readers to how James' reference to the "twelve tribes" can be representative of the restored Messianic Kingdom, and the prophetic fulfillment, or in-process fulfillment, of some key Tanach passages (i.e., Isaiah 11:11-12; Jeremiah 31:8-14; Ezekiel 37:21-22; Zechariah 10:5-12). Their challenge has been a general failure to stay away from replacement theology.

Non-Jewish Believers, who have no ethnic ancestry to Ancient Israel, cannot at all individually be regarded as part of the "twelve tribes"—although they can be regarded part of an enlarged Kingdom realm of Israel, noted by its restored twelve tribes, who are ethnic Israelites. They are a part of the Commonwealth of Israel (Ephesians 2:11-13), grafted-in by faith in Israel's Messiah (Romans 11:16-17), members of the Israel of God (Galatians 6:16).

The perspective of the Epistle of James having a principal Jewish audience—who are doubtlessly part of the Messianic restoration inaugurated by Yeshua—but also *not excluding* Messiah followers from the nations, is tempered by James' words at the Jerusalem Council. As James the Just appealed to the restoration of David's Tabernacle occurring (Acts 15:15-18; Amos 9:11-12), not only would this involve a restored twelve tribes of Israel at its center—but it would see Israel's Kingdom realm expand to incorporate the righteous from the nations. Those, especially among today's Messianic Believers, need not be proponents of supersessionism to posit a mixed Jewish *and* non-Jewish audience for the Epistle of James, if "twelve tribes" eschatologically represents an in-process restored Kingdom of Israel. It is interesting to note how a resource like *IDB* indicates how James might have seen the salvation of his Jewish people leading to the salvation of the nations, and Paul might have seen it occurring opposite:

"Perhaps James and many other Jewish Christians believed that the mission to the Jews would pave the way for the salvation of the Gentiles, as is suggested by Acts 15:16-18, quoting Amos 9:11-12 (LXX). Paul, on the other hand, believed that the salvation of the Gentiles would unexpectedly precede the conversion of the Jews (Rom. 10-11). It is difficult, however, to know James's thought in detail..."[9]

When one evaluates both the perspectives of James and Paul, that both the salvation of Israel proper would lead to that of the nations—and the salvation of the nations would then culminate in the grand salvation of Israel—are what is witnessed.

The involvement of non-Jewish Believers being among the audience of James, in addition to Jewish Believers, mainly involves factoring in James' own words at the Jerusalem Council (Acts 15:15-18), which would be representative of a restored Israel of twelve tribes, then expanding itself. Obviously, various proselytes and God-fearers were a part of the ancient Jewish community—especially in the Diaspora—and if any of them became Believers in Yeshua, then they were surely intended recipients of James' letter. Notably,

---

[8] Moo, pp 49-50.
[9] Barnett, "James, letter of," in *IDB*, 2:792.

however, there is nothing in James' letter—given its widely ethical and moral appeals—which would decisively discount Greeks and Romans from being directly intended.

While he incorrectly sees "the Church" as a kind of "New Israel," J.A. Motyer does take the audience of "twelve tribes" in an important direction, which readers should not overlook:

"Better than any other description could, *the twelve tribes* places the [audience] firmly within the pressures and persecutions of this life. We can think of [the]...tribes in the storm and stress of Egyptian slavery (Ex. 2:23), redeemed by the blood of the lamb (Ex. 12:13), on pilgrimage with God through 'the great and terrible wilderness' (Dt. 8:15; *cf.* Ex. 15:22), battling to enter into what the Lord had promised (Jos. 1:2) and struggling ever after to live in holiness amid the enticements of a pagan environment. These are the experiences through which James would have his readers understand their pilgrim path."[10]

In order to understand many of the concepts seen in the Epistle of James, no Messianic Believer today can deny that some level of identification with, and/or understanding of, the accounts of Ancient Israel in the Tanach, is needed. Debates over ecclesiology, the study of God's elect, are certainly raging at present in the broad Messianic world. For many of today's Messianic Jews, identifying James' audience of "twelve tribes" as representing a restored Messianic Kingdom of Israel, which would necessarily have to factor in James' own words of Acts 15:15-18, is too much. For many of today's Christians, the "twelve tribes" are only a metaphorical reference to the people of God, "the Church" as a "New Israel," with God no longer interested in ultimate restoring ethnic Israelites or Jews to their home country in *Eretz Yisrael*. We all have to do better, and acknowledge "twelve tribes" as representing a restored central Israel, which will then naturally expand its borders to incorporate the righteous from the nations (cf. Isaiah 49:6).[11]

2 Consider it all joy, my brethren, when you encounter various trials, 3 knowing that the testing of your faith produces endurance.

1:2 James' first instruction to his readers is, "My brothers and sisters, whenever you face trials of any kind, consider it nothing but joy" (NRSV). How much of this assertion will set the theme for the remainder of James' letter? Peter Davids suggests that "James is here, like Jesus in Matthew, instructing his readers to get the proper perspective, i.e. an eschatological perspective, on the situation in which they find themselves. One can easily picture a *Sitz im Leben* [Ger. 'situation in life']...in the early church as soon as the church

---

[10] Motyer, pp 24-25.

[11] For a further discussion, consult the author's publication *Are Non-Jewish Believers Really a Part of Israel?* Also consult the further, useful analysis in his book *Israel In Future Prophecy: Is There a Larger Restoration of the Kingdom to Israel?*

began to face social, economic, or physical persecution,"[12] with him then noting the martyrdom of Stephen (Acts 7). Moo also thinks, "By placing trials in this position of prominence in the letter, James suggests that the tough times the believers were facing were a key reason for his writing to them."[13] A connection between v. 2, and the word of Psalm 126:5, can be detected: "Those who sow in tears shall reap with joyful shouting." As bad as trials, afflictions, or tribulations can be, God usually does have an important purpose for them in the lives of His people (Romans 5:2-4; 1 Peter 1:5-7). Some of these things are doubtlessly intended to prepare Believers for what is to come in the future (5:8).

James notes the setting: *hotan peirasmois peripesēte poikilois*, "when you meet various trials" (RSV). The verb *peripiptō* can mean **"to encounter at hazard, *fall in with, fall into*"** (*BDAG*),[14] and is witnessed in the Apostolic Scriptures regarding a person encountering robbers and being beaten until almost dead (Luke 10:30), as well as a shipwreck (Acts 27:41). McKnight is correct to describe how *"peripiptō* indicates an *unexpected encounter,"* often relating "with something that puts a person to the test by taking one to the end of and beyond one's means."[15] Suffice it to say, whatever the diverse difficulties were being faced by James' audience, these were things not of their own making or choosing. James' words in v. 2, parallel Yeshua's words in Matthew 5:12: "Rejoice and be glad, for your reward in heaven is great; for in the same way they persecuted the prophets who were before you."

In my Messianic experiences, I have seen v. 2 applied a wide variety of ways. Various English readers might take v. 2, "count it all joy when you fall into various trials" (NKJV), as being a widely passive action. There is no indication anywhere in the short statement of v. 2 that Believers are to cause trials; they merely encounter them when life circumstances manifest. It is unfortunate, though, that many of the "trials" today's Messianic Believers are thought to face—*are in actuality* self-induced *trials, followed by* self-victimization. This often comes about because of various insecurities about one's Messianic beliefs and practices, or uncertainties about people both inside and outside of the Messianic community (Jewish or Christian).

V. 2 cannot be used as substantiation for experiencing joy—or for an appeal for pity and sympathy by others—in self-caused afflictions, when people have not used wisdom (v. 5), tact, discernment, and above all love (vs. 19-20, 25), regarding a situation. In today's broad Messianic world, this often involves how we approach controversial spiritual and theological issues, and the temperament of various people. At present, the situations that Messianic Believers in the largely tolerant West face—pale in comparison to the difficulties encountered by the First Century Believers.

---

[12] Davids, 67.

[13] Moo, 53.

[14] Frederick William Danker, ed., et. al., *A Greek-English Lexicon of the New Testament and Other Early Christian Literature*, third edition (Chicago: University of Chicago Press, 2000), 804.

[15] McKnight, 74.

1:3 If James' audience can understand the necessity of demonstrating joy in difficult trials, then they will be able to "know that the testing of your faith develops perseverance" (NIV), "steadfastness" (RSV), or "endurance" (NASU). *Hupomonē* is "**the capacity to hold out or bear up in the face of difficulty, *patience, endurance, fortitude, steadfastness, perseverance***" (*BDAG*).[16] Those who possess this great virtue guiding their lives are surely those who can perform God's purposes in the Earth.

James speaks of how "the proving of your faith worketh patience" (American Standard Version), *to dokimion humōn tēs pisteōs katergazetai hupomonēn*. It can be recognized how *dokimion*, "*a test, means of testing*" (*LS*),[17] could have the image of the refiner's fire in view, as *dokimion* is used in the Septuagint version of Proverbs 27:21: "Fire is the trial [*dokimion*] for silver and gold; and a man is tried [verb *dokimazō*] by the mouth of them that praise him. The heart of the transgressor seeks after mischiefs; but an upright heart seeks knowledge" (LXE). Some of this sentiment may have made its way into the Moffat New Testament rendering of v. 3: "the sterling temper of your faith produces endurance."

It cannot go unnoticed, from reading v. 3, how there is a definite emphasis on the "faith" (*pistis*) of James' audience. Many readers and examiners of the Epistle of James do pay a great deal of attention to the letter's emphasis on "works." **But let it never be said that James has no emphasis on faith.** Those who are adequately tried by life circumstances, if they believe and trust in God, will have their faith in Him processed into something grand and mature. McCartney summarizes some of the different variables present, which readers of James have to all consider:

"The term 'faith' is complex. In Jewish contexts it carries many of the features of the Hebrew word '*ĕmûnâ*, which implies not just belief in something but also fidelity, commitment, and truth. James sometimes is considered to be a book about 'works,' but in fact James's great concern with faith is what drives the entire book. His concern with works results from his concern with genuineness of faith, precisely because faith is so important."[18]

Because James' audience was facing serious tests—most probably because of their belief in Yeshua—they were to be joyful through those tests, because the tests will prove to be the making of them.

4 And let endurance have *its* perfect result, so that you may be perfect and complete, lacking in nothing.

1:4 While the term *hupomonē* might be rendered with some variance among English translations, James' intention in v. 4 is largely not complicated for English readers to

---

[16] *BDAG*, 1039.

[17] H.G. Liddell and R. Scott, *An Intermediate Greek-English Lexicon* (Oxford: Clarendon Press, 1994), 208.

[18] McCartney, 86.

comprehend: "let steadfastness have its full effect, that you may be perfect [mature, NRSV] and complete, lacking in nothing" (ESV). As the faith of Messiah followers is tested, the perseverance, or endurance that will come, will experience *ergon teleion*, its "perfect work" (KJV). The NLT paraphrases v. 4a with, "your endurance is fully developed."

This is the first instance in James' writing where he uses the word *teleios*, which has an important background, largely via the Septuagint. It is widely recognized how behind much of the application of *teleios* sits the Hebrew word *tamim*.[19] It is used to speak of the blamelessness of people like Noah (Genesis 6:9), as well as the high quality of various animals intended for sacrifice (Exodus 12:5; Leviticus 1:10; 3:6; et. al.). While often associated with "perfection," the concept of *teleios* is more readily associated with completion and maturity of an individual, as some of the main definitions provided by *BDAG* indicate: "**pert. to meeting the highest standard**," "**pert. to being mature, *full-grown*, mature, adult**," "**pert. to being fully developed in a moral sense**."[20] And, the tenor of James' communication in vs. 3-4 is that such completion/maturity/perfection is not something attained by a man or woman all at once. Motyer concludes, "Without losing sight of the ultimate aim, here is our present target: maturity of personality—and to this, just as to the heavenly fulfillment, the path is the same, namely, testings, endurance and perseverance."[21]

Not to be ignored is how the Greek term *teleios* did have some importance in classicism. "In philosophy *téleios* carries the sense of full humanity with an orientation to what is worthwhile and ethically good. In Plato this entails the attainment of insight by recollection and the resultant achievement of true being. Whereas the perfection of the cosmos is its completeness, the *téleion* in the ethical sphere is intrinsic goodness or the absolute good...In Aristotle perfection is present with right ethical choice, i.e., with the choice for its own sake of the good in an absolute sense" (*TDNT*).[22] While James would probably have been more interested in concepts of *teleios* associated with the Hebrew *tamim*—and how a verse like Deuteronomy 18:13 commands, "You shall be blameless [Heb MT: *tamim*; Grk. LXX: *teleios*] before the LORD your God"—one cannot totally discount some of the classical views of *teleios* being present among his audience, which represent some degree of high excellence to be present in people.

Of all the sentiments to be considered, regarding *teleios* or *tamim*, is how Yeshua Himself instructed, "**Therefore you are to be perfect, as your heavenly Father is perfect**" (Matthew 5:48). This is a completion/maturity/perfection that can only come about by people submitting themselves to the will of God, and His perfect character. The importance of perfection, for those who are in Yeshua, is something that the Apostle Paul considered rather important (Philippians 3:15; Colossians 4:12). He especially instructed in 1

---

[19] Davids, pp 69-70.
[20] *BDAG*, pp 995-996.
[21] Motyer, 33.
[22] Delling, "*téleios*," in *TDNT*, 1164.

Corinthians 14:20, "Brethren, do not be children in your thinking; yet in evil be infants, but in your thinking be mature [*teleios*]."

Not only is *hupomonē*/endurance/steadfastness supposed to produce *teleios*/completion/maturity/perfection in people; it is also to produce a state of completeness. *Holoklēros* means, "*complete in all parts, entire, perfect*" (LS),[23] a fuller definition "**being complete and meeting all expectations, with integrity, whole, complete, undamaged, intact, blameless**" (BDAG).[24] Those who are able to demonstrate patient endurance via the power of the Lord, will not only be mature, but they will be "complete [and] lacking in nothing." This can, at times, pertain to physical health, as in Acts 3:16 the related term *holoklēria* is used to describe "this man whom you see and know; and the faith which *comes* through Him has given him this perfect [*holoklēria*] health in the presence of you all." More importantly, *holoklēros* pertains to a level of sustenance where all aspects of the human person are affected, the type that is seen in 1 Thessalonians 5:23: "Now may the God of peace Himself sanctify you entirely; and may your spirit and soul and body be preserved complete [*holoklēros*], without blame at the coming of our Lord Yeshua the Messiah."

James would certainly have wanted his ancient audience, and all Messiah followers, to take his words of being "mature and complete" (NIV) seriously, and see people motivated to action. But how this involves trial (v. 3), as well as how it is to be actually implemented, has understandably provoked some deep responses. Ralph P. Martin, in particular, offers some thoughts that need to be considered:

> "Three ideas are to be seen in the use of [*teleios*] in our verse: (1) it is primarily a statement about a person's character, not simply a record of his or her overt acts...(2) the achieving of a 'perfect work' of moral character is not simply a human endeavor writ large as in the Stoic ideal...but is modeled on the divine pattern which sets the standard and inspires the believer, as the subsequent verses will illustrate (1:5, 17-18)...(3) 'the "perfection" of James is eschatological'...that is, it looks ahead to its fullest maturity at the end time when God's purposes have been achieved. Until then, the believer has to endure trials en route to the goal and to strive to attain the fulfillment of God's plan, not excusing himself or permitting any failure to block the way thereto."[25]

It should not be difficult for any of us to consider that the *teleios*/perfection being described in v. 4, is something that is lifelong, and will not reach its climax, until Earthly life is relatively over for the individual. What is a bit difficult, perhaps, are Martin's interjections that the *teleios*/perfection James wanted to see manifested among God's people, would not be totally present until the end-times and consummation of the age. Obviously in

[23] *LS*, 552.
[24] *BDAG*, 703.
[25] Martin, 17.

the Twenty-First Century, we are much closer to the Messiah's return than James' original audience was. And, for those of us in the emerging Messianic movement, we believe that our very presence on the scene of history is something prophetic and most significant. What aspects of the *teleios*/completion/maturity/perfection—either elaborated on by James or others in the Scriptures—do we need to seriously see integrated into our distinct Messianic spirituality and worldview? McKnight, focusing on the place of James' original First Century audience, observes,

"For James...we may safely conclude that he believes the messianic Jewish community is to strive for a level of morality (character and behavior) where particular forms of sin are not manifested and that this morality derives from a perfect God, who gives perfect gifts, not least of which is new birth (1:18), and from a royal, perfect Torah, so that the messianic community can be noted for its Torah observance."[26]

The aspects of Torah observance in view here are not necessarily keeping the Sabbath or eating kosher (as important as they are)—but will instead specifically pertain to attitudes, ethics, and things such as conflict resolution. When any of us face trials (v. 3), we are to learn things that enable us to mature in our faith, and consequently provide us the means to demonstrate good works. Today's Messianic community, compared to other religious movements, is still very much in the early days of its development. People across the Messianic spectrum have made many mistakes in such early days. Yet, it is not at all too late for us to learn from those mistakes, and be committed to a better course of perfection and wholeness. Even if the Second Coming is probably some time away, texts like the Epistle of James should still be molding and shaping our thoughts, ideas, and ideology (both corporate and individual)—as we steadily approach the ultimate, eschatological perfection God intends.

5 But if any of you lacks wisdom, let him ask of God, who gives to all generously and without reproach, and it will be given to him. 6 But he must ask in faith without any doubting, for the one who doubts is like the surf of the sea, driven and tossed by the wind.

1:5 Requesting wisdom of God is one of the most important things that any one of His people can do. James directs his audience, "If any of you lacks wisdom, let him ask of God, who gives to all liberally and without reproach, and it will be given to him" (NKJV). Wisdom as a concept (Heb. *chokmah*; Grk. *sophia*) is something which features prominently in the Book of Proverbs (i.e., 1:1-7; 2:6-8, 10-15; 4:5-9). Proverbs 9:10 is likely one of the most important verses in the Tanach about wisdom: "The fear of the LORD is the beginning of wisdom, and the knowledge of the Holy One is understanding." More immediate to what James has just stated, in vs. 3-4 about trials and perfection, are some sentiments expressed

---

[26] McKnight, 82.

in the Apocrypha. Sirach 4:17 indicates how wisdom is needed in order to endure trials,[27] and Wisdom 9:6 expresses how wisdom is needed for genuine perfection.[28] Given the plentitude of possible connections and associations that can be made, N.T. Wright's conclusions, on the composition of James most closely mirroring the Wisdom literature of the Tanach, are widely accurate:

"James is the most obvious representative in the New Testament of what in the ancient Israelite scriptures (the Old Testament) we think of as 'wisdom literature': the sifted, tested and collected wisdom of those who learned to trust God for everything and to discover how that trust would work out in every aspect of daily life. How should I cope with this situation, with that tricky moment? You need wisdom—and you should ask for it."[29]

In terms of actually implementing what James communicates in his epistle, Davids makes the point, "in the NT wisdom is closely associated with understanding the divine plan and responding to it...Wisdom...is the possession of the believer given by the Spirit that enables him to see history from the divine perspective."[30] While much of James' letter will focus on daily themes of a Believer's life, there is no doubting the fact that daily occurrences have to be enjoined by a comprehension of the greater plan of God—a plan that can only be understood if a person petitions Him for His wisdom. James says that God will provide wisdom to those who ask rather generously. Yeshua Himself said in Matthew 7:7, "Ask, and it will be given to you; seek, and you will find; knock, and it will be opened to you." The manifestation of wisdom, in the spiritual experiences of the Messiah's followers, is to serve as evidence of their maturity in Him, as indicated by Paul:

"[A]nd my message and my preaching were not in persuasive words of wisdom, but in demonstration of the Spirit and of power, so that your faith would not rest on the wisdom of men, but on the power of God. Yet we do speak wisdom among those who are mature; a wisdom, however, not of this age nor of the rulers of this age, who are passing away" (1 Corinthians 2:4-6).

"We proclaim Him, admonishing every man and teaching every man with all wisdom, so that we may present every man complete in Messiah" (Colossians 1:28).

1:6 The importance of asking God for wisdom, without doubt, is expressed by James: "let him ask in faith without doubting. For the doubter is like the surging sea, driven and tossed by the wind" (HCSB). While simply reading this straight through James' epistle, would surely emphasize how a person who doubts is compared to a rough sea or ocean

---

[27] "For at first she will walk with him on tortuous paths, she will bring fear and cowardice upon him, and will torment him by her discipline until she trusts him, and she will test him with her ordinances" (Sirach 4:17).

[28] "[F]or even if one is perfect among the sons of men, yet without the wisdom that comes from thee he will be regarded as nothing" (Wisdom 9:6).

[29] Wright, 5.

[30] Davids, 72.

current, when this is decompressed just a bit, we should be able to appreciate how important it is for Messiah followers not to doubt. Isaiah 57:20-21 can be immediately considered: "'But the wicked are like the tossing sea, for it cannot be quiet, and its waters toss up refuse and mud. There is no peace,' says my God, 'for the wicked.'" There are also some related statements in ancient Jewish literature, and elsewhere in the New Testament.

Sirach 33:1-2, in the Apocrypha, expresses how a person who is hypocritical is like a boat tossed around in a storm: "No evil will befall the man who fears the Lord, but in trial he will deliver him again and again. A wise man will not hate the law, but he who is hypocritical about it is like a boat in a storm." Philo allegorized the Israelites' entry into Canaan, and described an unstable scene as people being tossed about by the surf:

"[N]ow the most suitable time is when God shall lead thee into fluctuating reason, that is to say, into the land of the Canaanites, not in any chance manner, but in the manner in which he himself swore that he would; not in order that being tossed about hither and thither in the surf and tempest and heavy waves, you may be deprived of all rest or stability, but that having escaped from such agitation you may enjoy fine weather and a calm, and reaching virtue as a place of refuge, or port, or harbor of safety for ships, may lie in safety and steadiness" (*The Sacrifices of Abel and Cain* 90).[31]

V. 6 can be said to definitely parallel Paul's word of Ephesians 4:14, where "we are no longer to be children, tossed here and there by waves and carried about by every wind of doctrine, by the trickery of men, by craftiness in deceitful scheming." Evil people are asserted by Jude 13 to be "wild waves of the sea, casting up their own shame like foam." Some have tried to even compare the imagery of the ocean waves in v. 6, with the lack of faith demonstrated by Peter on the Sea of Galilee (Matthew 14:28-32), but this has been disputed.

Martin observes how for v. 6, "The point to be reinforced is that the doubter is as insecure and unsteady as a boat rocked in turbulent seas. The allusion draws on a familiar theme in Jewish literature, denoting the wicked or heretical or hypocritical people as those who are at the mercy of an unruly ocean."[32] Being the Almighty Creator of the universe, God certainly does not lack wisdom, and all His people have to do is ask for it. But this wisdom must be asked for with the proper attitude and motivations, "ungrudgingly" (NRSV). Those who do so with doubt are like a violent sea which can be cast aside to and fro. Moo's conclusion is that "The picture here is not of a wave mounting in height and crashing to shore, but of the swell of the sea, never having the same texture and shape from moment to moment, but always changing with the variations in wind direction and strength."[33] So too are limited mortals, who ask God for wisdom, but do not have the confidence that they need,

---

[31] Philo Judeaus: *The Works of Philo: Complete and Unabridged*, trans. C.D. Yonge (Peabody, MA: Hendrickson, 1993), 105.

[32] Martin, 19.

[33] Moo, 61.

either in Him or in His plans for the world. If they were to acquire any degree of wisdom, these would be the people who would abuse it for their own ends.

7 For that man ought not to expect that he will receive anything from the Lord, 8 *being* a double-minded man, unstable in all his ways.

1:7-8 James says that the person who doubts, "must not suppose that he will receive anything from the Lord" (v. 7, ESV). Those who are unstable "waver back and forth in everything they do" (v. 8, NLT). The person who doubts is asserted by James to be "double-minded" or "two-souled" (YLT). *Dipsuchos* "**pert. to being uncertain about the truth of someth., doubting, hesitating**" (BDAG).[34] The Phillips New Testament represents it as "a man of divided loyalty." Davids describes how "The term [*dipsuchos*], which does not appear in Greek literature earlier than James, has its background in Jewish theology. In the OT one finds that the person is to love God with an undivided heart, a perfect or whole heart (Dt. 6:5; 18:3)."[35] 1 Chronicles 12:33 references soldiers from Zebulun, serving in David's army, "who could draw up in battle formation with all kinds of weapons of war and helped *David* with an undivided heart [*b'lo-lev v'lev*]." Contrary to this is how Psalm 12:2 references evil people, "With flattering lips and with a double heart they speak."

Anyone who is "double-minded" or "two-souled" is divided in his or her devotion to God. One should consider how Deuteronomy 26:16 directs, "This day the LORD your God commands you to do these statutes and ordinances. You shall therefore be careful to do them with all your heart and with all your soul." The Lord expected the Ancient Israelites not to waver in their dedication to Him, and to devote their entire beings to Him. When a person is double-minded, he or she will think and act from *both a godly and a worldly perspective*. This can manifest itself by people speaking out of both sides of their mouth, as it were, saying one thing and doing another—or saying one thing to one person, and something totally different to another person. No one who claims to follow the ways of God needs to find themselves serving the will of God on one hand, but following their own will on another.

Messiah followers are not to be changing their ways left and right, but demonstrate consistency in their approach to God and in obedience to Him. Believers should be on a single road, and that road should be the road of eternal life. Yeshua Himself said, "Enter through the narrow gate; for the gate is wide and the way is broad that leads to destruction, and there are many who enter through it" (Matthew 7:13). Sadly, too many people, who think they are serving God, do frequently find themselves deviating between the road to life and the road to death—and do not even realize it.

---

[34] *BDAG*, 253.
[35] Davids, 74.

As many can testify from events in our still-developing and maturing Messianic community over the past two to three decades, there has been a documentable phenomenon of large ministries of note flip-flopping on some major theological issues—and/or having leaders who themselves are unsure about major theological issues, which in some cases relate to salvation. *This is hardly fine-tuning one's perspective on issues, and being able to better or more fully explain oneself.* Various teachers and leaders you will encounter in the Messianic movement are caught in the trap of being double-minded. Where we should see spiritual stability and people being edified to the betterment of their relationship with God, we can sometimes see leaders who pander to the crowd, or to other leaders. Their motivation is not to give the people the solid teaching and instruction that they need in God's Word, but rather to impress others with their so-called "nuggets of insight" (which often have no spiritual or intellectual value whatsoever), or even to service a market to sell their wares. The result is that there is no consistent teaching or theology or spirituality. This is something that Messianic people need to get beyond, but given the fact that there will be false teachings in the Last Days (1 Timothy 4:1-2), it seems unlikely that this problem will entirely go away.[36]

9 But the brother of humble circumstances is to glory in his high position; 10 and the rich man *is to glory* in his humiliation, because like flowering grass he will pass away. 11 For the sun rises with a scorching wind and withers the grass; and its flower falls off and the beauty of its appearance is destroyed; so too the rich man in the midst of his pursuits will fade away.

1:9 James' words in vs. 9-11 are debated by some readers and interpreters, as the circumstances of the one who is humble, the one who is rich, and what will happen to those who fail to follow the will of God are considered. There are many, many passages in the Tanach which speak against oppression of the poor (i.e., Amos 2:7; 8:6), so it is not surprising how in this early point of the epistle, a commentator like Ben Witherington III thinks, "James sounds much like an Old Testament prophet, excoriating the 'fatted calves' who are among and associate with and claim allegiance to Israel and its God....James is...mainly speaking about and to those wealthy ones who claim faith but do not live out its implications."[37]

James begins this segment with the assertion, "Believers in humble circumstances ought to take pride in their high position" (TNIV). The verb *kauchaomai* more readily means "*to boast or vaunt oneself*" (LS),[38] with the RSV/NRSV/ESV renderings all having "boast." The

---

[36] For a further review, consult the author's book *Confronting Critical Issues: An Analysis of Subjects that Affects the Growth and Stability of the Emerging Messianic Movement.*

[37] Witherington, 430.

[38] *LS*, 424.

Kingdom New Testament has a unique presentation of v. 9: "Brothers and sisters who find themselves impoverished should celebrate the fact that they have risen to this height." Given James' high reliance on the Tanach, it would seem that the sort of boasting he has in view for poor people is one which is surely rooted in the fact that these people are high in faith and in the Lord. As Jeremiah 9:23-24 says,

"Thus says the LORD, 'Let not a wise man boast of his wisdom, and let not the mighty man boast of his might, let not a rich man boast of his riches; but let him who boasts boast of this, that he understands and knows Me, that I am the LORD who exercises lovingkindness, justice and righteousness on earth; for I delight in these things,' declares the LORD."

A major element in James' audience was poor, and was subject to some oppression by the rich. *The **height** of the poor is found in their trusting God, possession of His wisdom, and in their spiritual course of maturity.* In contrast to this, the lowness of the rich is self-evident (vs. 10-11). Davids describes how for the poor person, "This [Believer] must overlook the present circumstances in which it is the rich who boast...and see life from an eschatological perspective in which the one who really has the exalted position and who is really rich is the [Believer], the poor person."[39] Suffice it to say, even with some First Century circumstances for James' audience likely in view, that people who are rich have a difficult time in matters of faith, is something which is generally universal to those trying—in some cases quite poorly—to serve God.

1:10 The NASU rendering of v. 10 has notably added some words, "the rich man *is to glory* in his humiliation," with the source text having *ho de plousios en tē papeinōsei autou*, "and~the rich one in the humiliation of him" (Brown and Comfort).[40] The RSV/ESV simply has, "and the rich in his humiliation," and the NRSV with, "and the rich in being brought low." The addition of "*is to glory*," on the part of the rich, can be contested. What cannot be contested, though, is how "like the flowering grass he will pass away." Yet what is also contested, is how not all interpreters are agreed if the rich person described in v. 10 is an actual Believer or a pretending Believer.[41]

Biblically speaking, wealth is meaningless in view of human death (Job 15:29-30; Matthew 6:19-21; 19:21), and wealth is frequently a cause for moral corruption (1 Timothy 6:9). As Sirach 10:22 explains, both rich and poor equally are to seek after God: "The rich, and the eminent, and the poor—their glory is the fear of the Lord." Paul directed Timothy, "Instruct those who are rich in this present world not to be conceited or to fix their hope on the uncertainty of riches, but on God, who richly supplies us with all things to enjoy" (1 Timothy 6:17).

---

[39] Davids, 76.

[40] Robert K. Brown and Philip W. Comfort, trans., *The New Greek-English Interlinear New Testament* (Carol Stream, IL: Tyndale House, 1990), pp 795-796.

[41] Davids, pp 76-77; Martin pp 25-26; Moo, 68.

James says in v. 10, "like flowering grass [the rich] will pass away." This description and its language are derived from the Tanach. The following are some passages to consider, where this terminology appears:

"A voice says, 'Call out.' Then he answered, 'What shall I call out?' All flesh is grass, and all its loveliness is like the flower of the field. The grass withers, the flower fades, when the breath of the LORD blows upon it; surely the people are grass. The grass withers, the flower fades, but the word of our God stands forever" (Isaiah 40:6-8).

"You turn man back into dust and say, 'Return, O children of men.' For a thousand years in Your sight are like yesterday when it passes by, or *as* a watch in the night. You have swept them away like a flood, they fall asleep; in the morning they are like grass which sprouts anew. In the morning it flourishes and sprouts anew; toward evening it fades and withers away" (Psalm 90:3-6).

"As for man, his days are like grass; as a flower of the field, so he flourishes. When the wind has passed over it, it is no more, and its place acknowledges it no longer" (Psalm 103:15-16).

Those who rely on their wealth, or themselves, are going to wither away like grass or flowers. One gets the impression in v. 10 that it is not the wealth which is transitory, even though that will be seen further on (5:2-3); it is the wealthy people who are transitory! Connecting this to James' previous comments about people being double-minded (v. 8), Yeshua says that "No one can serve two masters; for either he will hate the one and love the other, or he will be devoted to one and despise the other. You cannot serve God and wealth" (Matthew 6:24). It is extremely difficult for those who put their trust in their wealth to enter into the Kingdom. In fact, one of the Messiah's most difficult words was, "it is easier for a camel to go through the eye of a needle, than for a rich man to enter the kingdom of God" (Matthew 19:24). This is impossible in and of itself—and that is how difficult it often is for rich people, who have physical means, to be humbled enough to come to saving faith.

Those of "humble circumstances" (v. 9), because they lack great financial means, are to rejoice because through their faith and service to the Lord, their wealth is being stored up in Heaven. Yeshua promises, "store up for yourselves treasures in heaven, where neither moth nor rust destroys, and where thieves do not break in or steal; for where your treasure is, there your heart will be also" (Matthew 6:20-21). When James says "Let the lowly brother boast in his exaltation" (v. 9, RSV), the boasting is to be in the temporal nature of a low estate, because the poor person will be exalted in Heaven. Proverbs 13:7 is quite keen to explain, "There is one who pretends to be rich, but has nothing; *another* pretends to be poor, but has great wealth." James is no doubt relying on his readers' knowledge of the Tanach and Yeshua's teachings to focus on an important point: **those who are poor are free to be spiritually wealthy.** Those who store up things only for themselves and do not serve the

Lord, sadly may find themselves judged by Him. James warns against this in his letter. Yeshua likewise issues some stern words to the wealthy, teaching,

"But God said to him, 'You fool! This *very* night your soul is required of you; and *now* who will own what you have prepared?' So is the man who stores up treasure for himself, and is not rich toward God" (Luke 12:20-21).

Did Yeshua or James decisively speak against having wealth? No. They did not teach that having wealth is something that is always bad. Money as a tool can be used to benefit others—and there are those who are called by God to go make money, and use it for the benefit of the Body of Messiah. Paul said of the rich in 1 Timothy 6:18, "*Instruct them* to do good, to be rich in good works, to be generous and ready to share." But equally so, for those who improperly use or approach their possession of money, **it can take them away from God.** And more often then not, wealth takes people away from God.

1:11 James says this about the rich people, who are actually to be regarded as low (v. 10): "up comes the sun with the scorching wind and withers the grass, its flower drops off, and the splendour of it is ruined: so shall the rich fade away amid their pursuits" (Moffat New Testament). Even though such people on the outside may look beautiful or attractive, they are judged—the same way as elements such as the sun and wind damage the common grass, "even while [the rich person] goes about his business" (NIV). Unless repentant, it is assured that just as the sun rises and wind blows, that those wealthy in v. 11 will meet condemnation. While it is debated as to whether or not the wealthy person is an immature Believer, v. 11 does not give an indication that the rich in view are genuinely saved, but instead are pretenders to Messiah faith.

> **12 Blessed is a man who perseveres under trial; for once he has been approved, he will receive the crown of life which *the Lord* has promised to those who love Him.**

1:12 James tells his audience, "Blessed is anyone who endures temptation. Such a one has stood the test and will receive the crown of life that the Lord has promised to those who love him" (NRSV). Related to the noun *hupomonē* (vs. 3, 4), the verb *hupomenō* is defined by BDAG to mean, "**to maintain a belief or course of action in the face of opposition, *stand one's ground, hold out, endure*.**"[42] While the difficulties faced by the poor in James' audience would challenge their faith, we do not really get the impression that they will be challenged to the point of denying their belief in Yeshua, as much as having to endure through difficult circumstances and demonstrate proper character throughout them.

The theme of receiving a crown at the consummation of the age, when the Messianic Kingdom is inaugurated, is one seen throughout the Apostolic Scriptures (1 Corinthians 9:25; 2 Timothy 2:5; 4:8; 1 Peter 5:4; cf. Wisdom 5:15-16). One admonition, that of Yeshua the Messiah, could be considered in relation to v. 12: "Be faithful until death, and I will give you

---

[42] BDAG, 1039.

the crown of life [*ton stephanon tēs zōēs*]" (Revelation 2:10). By using the term *stephanos*, "*crown, wreath, garland, chaplet*" (*LS*),[43] James does employ some very important language, which has some classical significance. Moo describes, "people in the Greco-Roman world would probably have thought more often of the laurel wreath given to the victors in athletic contests...James probably also has the imagery in view, since the victory of a trained and disciplined athlete in a race is a fitting image for the reward that God bestows on those who remain faithful to him over the often long and difficult race of life."[44] The language of *ton stephanon tēs zōēs*, given its significance to First Century Greco-Roman classicism, should be taken as a partial indication of an inclusive, mixed Jewish *and* Greek and Roman audience for the epistle. Perhaps more to be noted, though, even with many in James' immediate audience likely not facing death—is how it has been suggested by some, at least in passing, that the reference to *stephanos*, or crown/laurel, plays off the name of the Hellenistic Jewish Believer Stephen (*Stephanos*), the first Messianic martyr.[45]

13 Let no one say when he is tempted, "I am being tempted by God"; for God cannot be tempted by evil, and He Himself does not tempt anyone. 14 But each one is tempted when he is carried away and enticed by his own lust. 15 Then when lust has conceived, it gives birth to sin; and when sin is accomplished, it brings forth death.

1:13 While having just described the circumstances of life that cause and produce trial (v. 12), James interjects how, "No one undergoing a trial should say, 'I am being tempted by God.' For God is not tempted by evil, and He Himself doesn't tempt anyone" (HCSB). From the source language, whether it be the Hebrew *nasah*[46] or Greek verb *peirazō*,[47] either verb as seen in the Holy Scriptures can mean "to test" or "to tempt"—and are obviously contingent on context. Vs. 13-15 make it clear that the action in view regards a temptation to sin/perform evil. So, while those among James' audience may experience difficulties, no one can claim that an Eternal God is actually tempting people to sin, and then use it as an excuse for bad behavior. A God whose character is infinitely and entirely pure, cannot even remotely be lured by sinful evil, and nor does He provoke sinful behavior. A sentiment seen in Sirach 5:11-12 in the Apocrypha astutely says, "Do not say, 'Because of the Lord I left the right way'; for he will not do what he hates. Do not say, 'It was he who led me astray'; for he had no need of a sinful man."

---

[43] *LS*, 745.

[44] Moo, 70.

[45] Cf. Martin, 33.

[46] Francis Brown, S.R. Driver, and Charles A. Briggs, *Hebrew and English Lexicon of the Old Testament* (Oxford: Clarendon Press, 1979), 650; Ludwig Koehler and Walter Baumgartner, eds., *The Hebrew & Aramaic Lexicon of the Old Testament*, 2 vols. (Leiden, the Netherlands: Brill, 2001), 1:702.

[47] *LS*, 616; *BDAG*, pp 792-793.

It is true, however, that in the course of human history—as certainly evidenced by the actions of the Ancient Israelites in the wilderness (Exodus 17:7; Numbers 14:22)—that people have tempted God to inappropriate action, decisively placing Him in the situation of being tempted. Yet, God's nature is such that He can never succumb to temptation, nor be swayed by it. Motyer's observations on v. 13 are excellent:

> "*God cannot be tempted with evil.* The divine nature is of such unmixed holiness that it is impossible for him to be enticed to plot to harm us. There is nothing within his whole nature to which that or any other temptation could appeal, or which would respond to that or any other base suggestion. Secondly (and consequently) *he himself tempts no one.* He is of such unmixed goodness in his attitudes and actions that there is no room in motive, will or deed for that which would bring disaster, great or small, on any of his people. To be sure, he places tests in our pathway...But there is never an ulterior motive in all this, for his holiness offers no lodging-place for evil within his nature; neither is there the least impulse to trip us up, for his goodness forbids that he should seek our hurt. When he tests, it is so that we may pass the test and inherit the blessing. When the reverse happens, the blame lies elsewhere than in the God of all grace."[48]

1:14 The blame for temptation to sin does not rest on God (v. 13), but here on people themselves: "each person is tempted when he is lured and enticed by his own desire" (RSV), and how "by his own evil desire, he is dragged away and enticed" (NIV). The negative impulse that has to be recognized and opposed is seen in the term *epithumia*, noted by *TDNT*, in a classical context, to relate to "desire, especially for food or sex. This desire is morally neutral at first, but philosophy, holding aloof from the sensory world, regards it as reprehensible." For the Apostolic Scriptures, the same *TDNT* entry remarks, "Desire is a manifestation of sin...it discloses our carnality, our apostasy from God, and our subjection to wrath (Gal. 5:16; Rom. 1:18ff)."[49] *Epithumia* is rendered as "lust" (KJV/NASU) in some other English versions, and is something that James will pick up again in his letter (4:1-2).

It is thought among various commentators, that James probably relies on his readers' knowledge of Rabbinic opinions regarding the nature of people, associated with the concept of the "evil impulse" or the *yetzer ha'ra*. Martin is one who concludes, "The lessons the author draws are dependent on the Jewish-rabbinic discussion of the 'evil impulse'....Our author locates the source of the trouble in the seat of the human psyche, specifically in the

---

[48] Motyer, 51.

It cannot go overlooked that sometimes James 1:13 is used by proponents of a low Christology, as proof against the Divinity of Yeshua, as the Messiah was tempted by Satan in the wilderness. It cannot be avoided how the Holy Scriptures record the fact that God the Father was directly tempted in the Torah by the Israelites. Does this at all, of a sudden, make Him something less than an Eternal and Supreme Creator? The point of James 1:13 is not that God cannot be in the situation of being tempted by some party; the point is that God can never succumb to temptation.

Consult the author's publication *Confronting Yeshua's Divinity and Messiahship.*

[49] F. Büchsel, "*epithymía, epithyméō,*" in *TDNT*, pp 339-340.

arrogant desire to achieve ambition independently of God....the rabbinic doctrine of the 'evil impulse'...goads men and women into sin...The point of emphasis here is to fasten moral responsibility on the individual."[50] Frequently, as is witnessed in a great course of mortal experience, human beings are responsible for tempting themselves to sin. Hence because of their baseness, people are far too frequently carried away by their own evil desires or lusts. Davids validly remarks how, "Each person is put to the test [*hupo tēs idias epithumias*]...This fact, as well as the whole flow of thought, indicates the meaning which the phrase has for James. What puts a person to the test is the evil impulse (*yēṣer hārā'*) within."[51]

Some ancient Jews may have thought that the evil impulse was not entirely evil—as it could produce some positive human traits—but that it just needed to be controlled.[52] The controlling element introduced by God was His Torah, to be followed by people (b.*Berachot* 5a; 61b). While a debated passage to be sure, the proverbial "I" sinner of Romans 7:19[53] expresses an internal conflict between good and bad: "For the good that I want, I do not do, but I practice the very evil that I do not want." Ultimately, the only decisive answer to overcoming temptation, lust, and sin, **is for people to have the eternal forgiveness and salvation available in Yeshua,** and to be transformed by the Holy Spirit via a life of discipleship and maturity (Romans 7:25-8:1). With James' emphasis on perfection, this is a definite thrust of his epistle. Moo appropriately recognizes, "throughout our time on earth...maturity [of Believers] is not indicated by the infrequency of temptation but by the infrequency of succumbing to temptation."[54] Paul emphasized maturity as well, and his writings are not in conflict with James on this. McKnight summarizes some useful points here:

"If the rabbis find the resolution to the *yetzer hara'* in the study of the Torah and Paul finds it in the indwelling presence of the Holy Spirit, James seems to find it in three interlocking ideas: the necessity of Torah observance and obedience (the *yetzer*), rebirth

---

[50] Martin, 30, 31, 36.

[51] Davids, 83.

[52] Cf. "Yetzer Ha-Ra," in David Bridger, ed. et. al., *The New Jewish Encyclopedia* (West Orange, NJ: Behrman House, 1976), pp 527-528.

This entry describes how, "the significance of the so-called evil inclination was recognized...[as] without it, the rabbis say, there would be no passion, no ambition, no building of cities, no civilization. Intrinsically the Yetzer ha-Ra is not necessarily bad. The manner in which a man responds to it determines its ethical value."

[53] There is a great deal of discussion and debate, as to whether or not the sinner of Romans ch. 7 is the Apostle Paul himself, or is a hypothetical person, internally wrestling with the effects of sin and fallen behavior.

Cf. J.M. Everts, "Conversion and Call of Paul," in Gerald F. Hawthorne, Ralph P. Martin, and Daniel G. Reid, eds., *Dictionary of Paul and His Letters* (Downers Grove, IL: InterVarsity, 1993), 158.

Do note that while many Romans commentators today recognize the strong possibility that the "I" in Romans 7 is not Paul speaking about himself, there are many different conclusions drawn as to what is being specifically communicated if this is not autobiographical material. For a further evaluation, consult the author's commentary *Romans for the Practical Messianic*.

[54] Moo, 76.

through the Word (1:18), and (only possibly) the indwelling Spirit and work of God (4:5-10)."[55]

1:15 The consequences, of people allowing themselves to be tempted and guided by sin, are quite serious according to James: "desire when it has conceived gives birth to sin; and sin when it is full-grown brings forth death" (RSV). That sin, offenses against the Law of God and His will, result in a condition of death and removal from Him, is a Biblical constant (Genesis 2:17; Ezekiel 18:4; Romans 5:12; 6:12; 7:7-12). Sin is conceived in the heart and mind of a person, before it is "fully grown" (NRSV) or "reaches maturity" (Kingdom New Testament). Before anyone decides to go ahead with a sinful act, an individual must first conceive of the offense in his or her mind. This is why James will appeal to his audience putting aside all sinful behavior, and receiving the gospel of God in their hearts for salvation (v. 21).

16 Do not be deceived, my beloved brethren. 17 Every good thing given and every perfect gift is from above, coming down from the Father of lights, with whom there is no variation or shifting shadow. 18 In the exercise of His will He brought us forth by the word of truth, so that we would be a kind of first fruits among His creatures.

1:16-17 While no specific sins are stated in vs. 13-15 preceding, given the theme of wealth and judgment of the rich (vs. 10-12), it is provoking to think that there may have been a temptation, on the part of some of the poor people in James' audience, to steal or pilfer from wealthy persons within the community. And, perhaps with the abundance that various, oppressive wealthy people had, contrasted to the poor, such poor people might have tried to dismiss sinful attitudes. Regardless of what sin might have been specifically in view, James is clear: "Do not be deceived, my dearly loved brothers and sisters" (v. 16, TLV). James will describe how the God they serve, is One who is most generous, and who graciously provides for His own.

James assures his audience, "all we are given is good, and all our endowments are faultless, descending from above, from the Father of the heavenly lights, who knows no change of rising and setting, who casts no shadow on the earth" (v. 17, Moffat New Testament). By telling his readers that "every perfect gift is from above, coming down from the Father of lights," we see an emphasis on the majesty of God, "with whom there is no variation or shadow due to change" (RSV). Immediately, readers should consider how James is likely appealing to some Tanach concepts, which indicate God's supremacy over His Creation or the universe at large (Genesis 1:14-18; Isaiah 40:22; Jeremiah 31:35; Psalm 136:4-9). One of the descriptions that the Qumran community gave the Lord, as seen in the Dead

---

[55] McKnight, 119.

Sea Scrolls, is how "The authority of the Prince of Light extends to the governance of all righteous people" (1QS 3.20).[56]

That v. 17 indicates how with God there is no *parallagē*, *"variation, change"* (LS),[57] one can surely consider not only God's sovereign control of the cosmos, but also His immutable character. Malachi 3:6 tells us, "For I, the LORD, do not change; therefore you, O sons of Jacob, are not consumed." Moses admonished the Ancient Israelites, "Be strong and courageous, do not be afraid or tremble at them, for the LORD your God is the one who goes with you. He will not fail you or forsake you" (Deuteronomy 31:6). And also, as the author of Hebrews says, "Yeshua the Messiah is the same yesterday and today and forever" (Hebrews 13:8). So, if God is in control of a universe—which human beings even in the Twenty-First Century are still trying to understand, and First Century people understood far less[58]— should His people have enough faith to consider how He will provide gifts to them, taking care of their needs? And, should this not also mean that sinful activities, while evil, are ultimately quite petty in view of His awesomeness?

1:18 The great importance of acknowledging God's sovereignty, via something like His oversight of the the universe, is how significant the community of Believers in His Messiah is. James asserts, "Having purposed, He brought us forth by *the* Word of truth, for us to be a certain firstfruit of His creatures" (LITV), *tina tōn autou ktismatōn*. The view of one like McKnight is, "I suspect James is referring here to the messianic community as a harbinger of a universal ecclesial community—perhaps even the kingdom of God. This would include all of creation."[59]

Much is, of course, contingent on recognizing the Believers in Yeshua, here as "first fruits," as constituting the first generation of many more generations to come. If the Epistle of James is dated early, to sometime in the early-to-mid 40s C.E., then there is no denying how "first fruits" should be more correctly focused on a smaller community of Messiah followers, which would steadily get bigger and bigger. This is consistent with how James' audience is noted by a Kingdom of God centered around a restored "twelve tribes" of Israel (v. 1), but how such a restored twelve tribes of Israel necessarily also involves the enlargement of Israel's Kingdom realm to incorporate the righteous from the nations—from James' own words, no less (Acts 15:15-18; cf. Amos 9:11-12)!

In describing the Believers in v. 18, James is alluding to descriptions seen in the Torah, describing the presentation of various first fruits offerings before the Lord (Exodus 23:16, 19; 34:22-26; Leviticus 23:10-14). Various first fruits offerings were ultimately received by the Levites: "All the best of the fresh oil and all the best of the fresh wine and of the grain, the first fruits of those which they give to the LORD, I give them to you" (Numbers 18:12). As

---

[56] Michael Wise, Martin Abegg, Jr., and Edward Cook, trans., *The Dead Sea Scrolls: A New Translation* (San Francisco: HarperCollins, 1996)., pp 129-130.

[57] *LS*, 599.

[58] Consult the useful observations in the FAQ, "Creationism."

[59] McKnight, 130.

first fruits were to be part of the sustenance of the Levitical priesthood and their families, Believers in Yeshua, being first fruits as well, can by extension be associated with a priestly calling (1 Peter 2:5, 9). The description of first fruits is also applied to those such as "the household of Stephanas...the first fruits of Achaia" (1 Corinthians 16:15), and the future 144,000 sealed witnesses (Revelation 14:4). The association of James' audience, as (some sort of) first fruits, should be an indication—at the very least—of how important the Epistle of James is for all Messiah followers in the successive generations, to read, pay attention to, meditate and reflect upon, and reason through, *for their own spiritual and theological edification.*

19 **This you know, my beloved brethren. But everyone must be quick to hear, slow to speak** *and* **slow to anger;** 20 **for the anger of man does not achieve the righteousness of God.**

1:19 James admonishes his audience with some very direct moral instructions, related to the proper conduct that Messiah followers are to demonstrate toward their fellow human beings: "My dear brothers and sisters, take note of this: Everyone should be quick to listen, slow to speak and slow to become angry" (TNIV). Those who are Believers are to be men and women who do not act rashly or unreasonably, but are rather those who think before speaking, and do not become angry too easily. Yet, how many times do people seeking to be holy in the Lord, need to be reminded of this? Calvin astutely observed, "Spiritual birth is not the work of a mere moment. Since some traces of the old humanity still remain, we must ever be re-fashioned, until the flesh is done away. Our violent behaviour, our arrogance, our apathy, greatly obstruct God from finishing His work in us."[60] For many people, being purged of irrational and unspiritual tendencies *can be a (long) process.* Many important parallels can be seen between v. 19, and various passages from the Book of Proverbs:

"When there are many words, transgression is unavoidable, but he who restrains his lips is wise" (Proverbs 10:19).

"He who despises his neighbor lacks sense, but a man of understanding keeps silent. He who goes about as a talebearer reveals secrets, but he who is trustworthy conceals a matter" (Proverbs 11:12-13).

"The one who guards his mouth preserves his life; the one who opens wide his lips comes to ruin" (Proverbs 13:3).

"He who restrains his words has knowledge, and he who has a cool spirit is a man of understanding" (Proverbs 17:27).

---

[60] Calvin, 271.

"A fool always loses his temper, but a wise man holds it back" (Proverbs 29:11).

We do not know some of the specific circumstances which may have prompted James to say this to his audience. Perhaps some of the relatively poor people had gotten very angry at the rich, and they would speak things—either among themselves or to their offenders—without thinking. Perhaps many of the Jewish Believers who had been forced out of Judea (Acts 11:19) were resentful of it, and were harboring bitterness. Although, the need for someone to be "quick to listen but slow to use his tongue, and slow to lose his temper" (Phillips New Testament), is fairly universal for human living. Moo observes,

"[The] concern with improper speech and the anger that can often cause such speech is a traditional theme of Jewish wisdom literature. But James appropriates the tradition because he recognizes that his readers are struggling in just this area."[61]

One such viewpoint, that James may be relying on, is seen in Sirach 5:11-13: "Be quick to hear, and be deliberate in answering. If you have understanding, answer your neighbor; but if not, put your hand on your mouth. Glory and dishonor come from speaking, and a man's tongue is his downfall."

Most significant for some of the background of James' word in v. 19, to be sure, would be Yeshua the Messiah's teaching in His Sermon on the Mount: "But I say to you that everyone who is angry with his brother shall be guilty before the court; and whoever says to his brother, 'You good-for-nothing,' shall be guilty before the supreme court; and whoever says, 'You fool,' shall be guilty enough to go into the fiery hell" (Matthew 5:22).

There are some important Rabbinic dictums in the Mishnah tractate Pirkei Avot, which concur with James' word in v. 19. Shammai is recorded as saying "Say little and do much" (m.Avot 1:15).[62] Later we see how "There are four sorts of personality: (1) easily angered, easily calmed—he loses what he gains; (2) hard to anger, hard to calm—what he loses he gains; (3) hard to anger and easy to calm—a truly pious man; (4) easy to anger and hard to calm, a truly wicked man" (m.Avot 5:11).[63] Similarly seen in the early Christian document, the Didache, is the sentiment, "Be not prone to anger, for anger leadeth the way to murder; neither jealous, nor quarrelsome, nor of hot temper; for out of all these murders are engendered" (3:2).[64]

Regardless of whether it was James' First Century audience, or Twenty-First Century Messianic Believers—**we must be careful with how we act**—hearing, speaking, and possibly getting angry. Messianics today, for a variety of possible reasons, and likely involving the newness and developing nature of our faith community—and the challenges

---

[61] Moo, 81.

[62] Jacob Neusner, trans., The Mishnah: A New Translation (New Haven and London: Yale University Press, 1988), 674.

[63] Ibid., 687.

[64] BibleWorks 7.0: Ante-Nicene Fathers. MS Windows XP. Norfolk: BibleWorks, LLC, 2006. CD-ROM.

of bringing Jewish and non-Jewish Believers together—are more affected by their base human instincts than many evangelical Christian Believers may be. It can be quite easy for today's Messianic people, particularly over doctrinal issues, to speak very loudly and quite angrily, but not demonstrate the humility of a figure like James *or* the love of the Messiah. Much of the spiritual and religious culture of the Messianic movement is not centered around someone winning an argument on the basis of logic, reason, and objectivity—but on who can be the most pushy, obnoxious, and manipulative. Moo's direction should be well taken:

"Psychologists will sometimes claim that emotions, since they are a natural product of the personality, cannot truly be controlled—only suppressed or ignored. But James's exhortation here (and many similar biblical exhortations) presume differently. Emotions are the product of the entire person; and, by God's grace and the work of the Spirit, the person can be transformed so as to bring emotions in line with God's word and will."[65]

While there can certainly be such a thing as righteous indignation (cf. Ephesians 4:26)—where God's people can legitimately be angry and mad at sinful behavior and at the schemes of the Adversary—a born again Believer **is not to be perpetually active in anger.** It might be advised that the next time one of us encounters a circumstance, or is told something where anger is likely to manifest—that being upset, disappointed, or distressed—and expressing displeasure toward the party committing the offense, is something better than getting mad. Usually, disappointment or distress can be turned into something constructive, as resolution to an issue or circumstance is sought.

1:20 The reason for James instructing his audience to be careful with hearing, speaking, and being angry, is how "human anger doesn't produce the righteousness of God" (TLV). The statement *orgē gar andros dikaiosunēn Theou ouk ergazetai*, might be more literally rendered along the lines of "for the anger of man does not work the righteousness of God" (RSV), as the verb *ergazomai*, "to work at, practise" (LS),[66] can be taken as representing bad works.

Theologically, it is important for readers to recognize how the term *orgē*, while often rendered as "anger" in various versions (RSV, NASU, NIV, NRSV, ESV, et. al.), is much better rendered as "wrath" (KJV/NKJV). *TDNT* describes how "In most instances [*orgē*] undoubtedly denotes the divine work of judgment, yet God's serious displeasure at evil is also implied."[67] **Wrath is rightly taken to be a quality of judgment reserved only for God Himself.** In the Torah, we see how the Lord says, "Vengeance is Mine, and retribution, in due time their foot will slip; for the day of their calamity is near, and the impending things are hastening upon them" (Deuteronomy 32:35).

The wrath of God is something that only He can distribute upon sinners—and God certainly does not need any person to somehow "help Him," as it were, to punish them, *via*

---

65 Moo, 83.
66 *LS*, 311.
67 G. Stählin, "anger, wrath," in *TDNT*, 723.

their own mortal limitations, no less! Those who are to be found in Yeshua, having repented of their sins and received forgiveness via His sacrifice—should not be operating in a mode of wrath or condemnation, but rather one of prayer, intercession, and supplication for those who do them wrong. That unrepentant sinners will experience the *orgē* of God, as eternal punishment, is a sober reality emphasized throughout the Apostolic Scriptures:

> "Never take your own revenge, beloved, but leave room for the wrath [*orgē*] *of God*, for it is written, 'VENGEANCE IS MINE, I WILL REPAY' [Leviticus 19:18], says the Lord" (Romans 12:19).

> "For it is because of these things that the wrath [*orgē*] of God will come upon the sons of disobedience" (Colossians 3:6).

> "[H]e also will drink of the wine of the wrath [*orgē*] of God, which is mixed in full strength in the cup of His anger; and he will be tormented with fire and brimstone in the presence of the holy angels and in the presence of the Lamb" (Revelation 14:10).

With "wrath" as a quality reserved exclusively for the Creator Himself to issue to sinners, His people must be steadfastly focused on His righteousness. When someone is wronged, passages such as Psalm 35:24 should come to mind: "Judge me, O LORD my God, according to Your righteousness [*k'tzid'qekha*], and do not let them rejoice over me." The Lord's decree of Isaiah 46:13 is also useful for Believers to consider: "I bring near My righteousness [*tzid'qati*], it is not far off; and My salvation will not delay. And I will grant salvation in Zion, *and* My glory for Israel." Yeshua's words at His immersion by John the Baptist are also important: "Permit *it* at this time; for in this way it is fitting for us to fulfill all righteousness [*plērōsai pasan dikaiosunēn*]" (Matthew 3:15).

It is appropriate that readers be aware of how there are various components to the terms *tzedaqah* and *dikaiosunē*, often rendered in Bibles along the lines of "righteousness" or "justification." The 2011 Kingdom New Testament breaks the mold a little, rendering v. 20 with, "Human anger, you see, doesn't produce God's justice!"

Commentators are aware of how *dikaiosunēn Theou* can be viewed from some multiple angles. Davids summarizes his thoughts, "what does James mean by 'the righteousness of God'? Several possibilities suggest themselves: (a) God's righteous standard, (b) the righteousness God gives, (c) righteousness before God, or (d) God's eschatological righteousness." Davids goes on to state, "It is obvious on this point that one cannot interpret James by Paul," concluding that what is in view in v. 20, is "the type of righteousness which reflects God's standard."[68] Moo only says, "James's very simple point is that human anger does not produce behavior that is pleasing to God."[69] More reflective of something than just

---

[68] Davids, 93.
[69] Moo, 84.

proper character being described, McKnight thinks, "'righteousness/justice of God' refers to the inability on the part of humans to use 'anger' to bring about God's saving action as these same humans seek to establish God's will in society."[70] Such activity might be detectable in James' later word, "And the seed whose fruit is righteousness is sown in peace by those who make peace" (3:18).

While most readers of v. 20, myself included, will be inclined to view *dikaiosunēn Theou* from the perspective that the appropriate, righteous character of God is what is mainly intended—no one can overlook the fact that such character is to be reflective of an ethos that brings His justice and goodness to others, making His Kingdom power be manifest to the world.

Anyone who is a Messianic Believer, who is most likely to claim adherence to the morality of the Torah, is to be operating in love, grace, and mercy, and impacting others for the Lord by a positive spiritual example. Unfortunately over the past decade or more, a word like v. 20, **"for a person's anger does not accomplish God's righteousness!"** (CJB), has been too often ignored. There are teachers and leaders of note within the broad Messianic movement, who operate via a wrathful or vindictive demeanor. There are those who condemn our evangelical Christian brothers and sisters mercilessly for their shortcomings toward the Torah, and others who condemn non-Jewish Messianic Believers who try to keep the Torah as somehow trying to replace or displace Messianic Jews. There is a great deal of venom and bile which should not be present in the hearts and minds of too many people. And in the latter half of the 2000s and now into the 2010s, there has been a huge amount of abuse via the blogosphere and online social media, which have revealed not only in writing—but for the entire public to see—much of the baseness of both the clergy and laity of many sectors of our faith community. *Will James' direction be at all heeded and implemented?*

21 Therefore, putting aside all filthiness and *all* that remains of wickedness, in humility receive the word implanted, which is able to save your souls.

1:21 The correct action which James prescribes, to avoid wrath (v. 20), is quite profound and significant: "put away all filthiness and rank growth of wickedness and receive with meekness the implanted word, which is able to save your souls" (RSV). One can see a similar exhortation in Hebrews 12:1: "let us also lay aside every encumbrance and the sin which so easily entangles us, and let us run with endurance the race that is set before us." More significant to v. 21 might be how the high priest Joshua, in Zechariah 3:3-4, was commanded to change his clothes, from dirty to clean:

"Now Joshua was clothed with filthy garments and standing before the angel. He spoke and said to those who were standing before him, saying, 'Remove the filthy garments from

---

[70] McKnight, 139.

him.' Again he said to him, 'See, I have taken your iniquity away from you and will clothe you with festal robes.'"

James the Just, half-brother of Yeshua, and leader of the Jerusalem assembly, was entirely right to require Messiah followers to "put aside all filthiness and superabundance of evil" (YLT). While people often do struggle with ungodly attitudes and behavior—especially given the condition of our fallen world—God's people are not to be "clothed," as it were, with wickedness. *Rhuparia* is "**a state of moral defilement or corruption, *moral uncleanness, vulgarity***" (BDAG),[71] which the NIV renders as "moral filth," and The Message with "cancerous evil." While much of James' message in his epistle relates to the obedience that God requires of His people, James' major emphasis, as certainly seen in v. 21, is on the attitudes of people.

As filth and the defilements of sin are removed from men and women, they are to "welcome with meekness the implanted word that has the power to save your souls" (NRSV). The power of redemption is found in "the word implanted," *ton emphuton logon*, and is rightly regarded here as being synonymous with the gospel message, **and** all that such a message involves, in changing and transforming lives. The presence of "the implanted word" has been most appropriately compared to the salvific power of the prophesied New Covenant in the Tanach (Jeremiah 31:31-34; Ezekiel 36:25-27), by various commentators. Not only would this involve a permanent forgiveness and cleansing from sins, but the implantation of a new heart, *and* the supernatural compulsion to obey the Lord's commandments by His Spirit. Moo, who actually does believe that the Torah has been abolished in the post-resurrection era, still makes some astute remarks on v. 21 that need to be seriously considered:

> "James likely draws this striking concept of the implanted word from the famous new covenant prophecy of Jeremiah 31. The prophet, noting the failure of Israel to live up to the terms of the Mosaic covenant, announces on behalf of God a new covenant that God would enter into with his people. As a prominent component of that new covenant arrangement, God promises to put his law within his people, to write it on their hearts (Jer. 31:33). The repeated failures of Israel to obey the law that God gave to them had made it clear that the human heart was not capable of submitting to external rules. A new, interior work would have to be done, giving people a 'new heart' (see the somewhat parallel passage in Ezek. 36:24-32) so that they could respond truly and obediently to God's word. James's language reminds his readers that they have experienced the fulfillment of that wonderful promise. But it also reminds them that the word that has saved them cannot be dispensed with after conversion. God plants it within his people, making it a permanent, inseparable part of the believer, a guiding and commanding presence within."[72]

---

[71] *BDAG*, 908.
[72] Moo, 87.

McCartney is a bit more concise in his words, drawing the same basic conclusion:

"Jeremiah prophesied of a time when God would write his law upon people's hearts (Jer. 31:33). Here is evidence that James implicitly shares the redemptive-historical perspective of other NT writers who saw Jeremiah's prophecy of a new covenant fulfilled in the coming of Jesus Christ (Matt. 26:28 and pars.; Rom 11:27; 2 Cor. 3:6; Heb. 8:8-12; 10:16)."[73]

While "the implanted word" involves the message of salvation in Yeshua and the implementation of the New Covenant in the hearts and minds of the redeemed, salvation is by no means *only* to be regarded as redemption from sin. Salvation also involves a way of life and a process of sanctification, as men and women in Yeshua are to be enduring and persevering and continuing in faith. Not only is obedience to God's Word expected and required of His own, but with His word/gospel being implanted within them, the power and influence of sin is to be greatly reduced. *In fact, sin is to be regarded as something most repugnant and putrid to those born again!* McCartney, noting how "the implanted word...is able to save," thinks that it has more of a futuristic aspect, as "The implanted word, if it is received, has the ability to deliver lives because of the development of the word of God within a person removes that person from the power of evil and produces, in place of the abundant harvest of evil, the abundant harvest of good fruit (cf. Matt. 13:23)."[74] That salvation is a process which begins with forgiveness, and is to grow more maturely, is something laid forth in 1 Peter 1:22-2:2:

"Since you have in obedience to the truth purified your souls for a sincere love of the brethren, fervently love one another from the heart, for you have been born again not of seed which is perishable but imperishable, *that is*, through the living and enduring word of God. For, 'ALL FLESH IS LIKE GRASS, AND ALL ITS GLORY LIKE THE FLOWER OF GRASS. THE GRASS WITHERS, AND THE FLOWER FALLS OFF, BUT THE WORD OF THE LORD ENDURES FOREVER' [Isaiah 40:6-8]. And this is the word which was preached to you. Therefore, putting aside all malice and all deceit and hypocrisy and envy and all slander, like newborn babies, long for the pure milk of the word, so that by it you may grow in respect to salvation."

22 But prove yourselves doers of the word, and not merely hearers who delude themselves.

1:22 Having "the implanted word" (v. 21) present in a Believer's life demands appropriate action. James says, "Be practitioners of the word, not mere self-deceiving listeners" (*Lattimore*). There is a definite strike issued against hypocrisy here, a problem present with many of those claiming the God of Israel throughout the Holy Scriptures. The word of Ezekiel 33:31-32 is especially poignant to review here:

---

[73] McCartney, 118.
[74] Ibid., 119.

"They come to you as people come, and sit before you *as* My people and hear your words, but they do not do them, for they do the lustful desires *expressed* by their mouth, *and* their heart goes after their gain. Behold, you are to them like a sensual song by one who has a beautiful voice and plays well on an instrument; for they hear your words but they do not practice them."

James says in v. 22, "be doers of the word, and not hearers only, deceiving yourselves" (RSV). *Vine* notes how the verb *paralogizomai* can mean, "'to reckon wrong,' [and] hence means 'to reason falsely'...or 'to deceive by false reasoning.'"[75] While in much Hebraic thought, "to hear" God (verb *shama*)[76] often means to obey Him as well, given the tenor of the *Shema* (Deuteronomy 6:4ff)—when trying to confront complacency or inaction, as v. 22 does, hearing is specifically enjoined with doing. A *poiētēs* is "a maker, producer, author," and "a doer, performer" (*Thayer*).[77] The "doing," that is required of those who have "the implanted word," is that Messiah followers demonstrate the proper actions of those who are diligently obeying God, both outwardly *and* inwardly. Yeshua Himself said, "blessed are those who hear the word of God and observe it" (Luke 11:28).

Contemporary Christians have definitely wrestled with v. 22, given the implication that the doing of God's Word, necessarily means obeying God's Torah or Law—at least in some way (v. 25). In the literature of the Dead Sea Scrolls, for example, those who are faithful to God are described as "obedient to the Law" (1QpHab 7.11) and "those who obey the Law" (1QpHab 8.1; cf. 12.4).[78] Some have tried to sidestep, to some degree, the implication that those who are "doers" (*poiētai*), and who have "the implanted word" (v. 21) within them per the New Covenant (Jeremiah 31:31-34; Ezekiel 36:25-27), is not as much the Torah or Moses' Teaching, per se, versus the gospel and the Messiah's teachings. Davids is reflective of such a position:

"The Jews...often spoke of doing the law (*'āśâ hattôrâ*: Dt. 28:58; 29:28; etc.), which the LXX translated literally [*poiētēs nomou*] (...Sir. 19:20; Rom. 2:13). The transition from law to word was easy for one who felt Christ's teaching was a new law...James calls the Christian to obey the gospel, which in this case means primarily the ethical teaching of Jesus."[79]

Martin, who acknowledges the language here as being derived from performing the Torah, draws the conclusion that primarily intended is that "Jesus redefined the practice of God's will as 'love for neighbor,' a theme to be picked up in 1:25 in James' comment on the 'perfect law' and in 2:8-11 on 'the royal law' (Lev 19:18)."[80]

---

[75] W.E. Vine, *Vine's Expository Dictionary of New Testament Words* (Nashville: Thomas Nelson, 1968), 58.

[76] Cf. *BDB*, pp 1033-1034.

[77] Joseph H. Thayer, *Thayer's Greek-English Lexicon of the New Testament* (Peabody, MA: Hendrickson, 2003), 527.

[78] Wise, Abegg, and Cook, 119.

[79] Davids, 96.

Ibid., 97 where he goes on to assert, "The hearing would parallel the listening to the listening to the law in the synagogue reading, but would in fact mean the learning of the traditions of Christ."

[80] Martin, 49.

No one in today's Messianic movement should ever be caught denying how being "doers of the word," involves a faithful response to the good news of salvation in Yeshua, and in emulating one's life after His example and teachings. It is most unfortunate, though, to witness Christian scholars widely dismissing the validity and relevance of God's Torah, as though somehow "the perfect law" (v. 25) of which James will later speak, is something not too related to Moses' Teaching, and hence should not be too well considered for spiritual instruction today. Even the Apostle Paul would claim, "*it is* not the hearers of the Law *who* are just before God, but the doers of the Law will be justified" (Romans 2:13). And, with various vantage points of *dikaiosunē* to be considered, such "justification" in Romans 2:13, should be regarded as representing membership among God's people, and not some vindication from sin (which human Torah keeping can never achieve).

James' statement about obedience in v. 22 cannot be taken as some assertion about the teaching of Yeshua somehow supplanting the instruction of the Torah—as opposed to Moses' Teaching finding its proper fulfillment and interpretation via the word of Yeshua (v. 21). On the contrary, v. 22 is one of the most forthright words **in favor of Torah observance** for Messiah followers in the entire Apostolic Scriptures. But for James, a true obedience to God involves being decisively purged from sin, evil attitudes, and immoral cravings.

Performing the Word of God for most of today's Messianic Believers is something multi-faceted. On the one hand, we should be outwardly Torah observant, and keep things such as the seventh-day Sabbath/*Shabbat*, the appointed times of Leviticus 23, the dietary laws, and other things as Messiah Yeshua did them. But, we are also steadfastly required to demonstrate love for God and neighbor. Being Torah observant is both an outward *and* an inward obedience, which God requires of us. If someone who claims to be "Torah observant" is only outwardly so, and treats other people with dishonor and disrespect, then James would still say, "Don't only hear the message, but put it into practice; otherwise you are merely deluding yourselves" (Phillips New Testament).

Too many Messianics examine James 1:22 thinking that they are following this verse because they keep outward things, not realizing that James' primary admonition here relates to morality and personal behavior. Let us not forget this, because a person who treats another one with hatred **is even more guilty** of violating the Torah, than a person who eats ham or bacon. Let none of us fall into the trap that James warns about, falsely reasoning with ourselves because we are "Torah observant" on the outside, whereas on the inside we have nothing but contempt for others.

23 For if anyone is a hearer of the word and not a doer, he is like a man who looks at his natural face in a mirror; 24 for *once* he has looked at himself and gone away, he has immediately forgotten what kind of person he was.

1:23 James describes the person who hears the Word of God, and does not do it: "if anyone is a hearer of the word and not a doer, he is like a man who looks intently at his natural face in a mirror" (ESV). The verb *katanoeō*, often rendered as "looks" or "observes" (RSV), can mean "'to immerse oneself in.' This may be in the field of sensory perception, but critical examination is also denoted" (*TDNT*).[81] James does not just describe the hearer as someone who just passively listens to a teaching from Scripture, but as someone who makes some effort as though gazing with detail into a mirror. One gets the definite impression that if nothing is done to heed the message of the Word, that various people may find themselves recipients of, at the very least, God's chastisement.

V. 23 actually employs the terminology *to prosōpon tēs geneseōs*. While often rendered as "natural," the actual word of note is *genesis*, "an origin, source, productive cause" (*LS*),[82] which technically allows for *to prosōpon tēs geneseōs* to be rendered a bit woodenly as, "the face of *genesis*." When the mirror of God's Word—something brought to its climax in the salvation work and atonement of Yeshua the Messiah—is placed in front of human beings, it should not only reveal who they really are, but it reveals the source of the problem: **our beginning nature,** or the sin nature all have inherited from Adam (Romans 5:12). The Jewish philosopher Philo employed the word *genesis* in a negative context, describing that people are unstable, compared to God who is stable because of His eternality:

"Now that which stands still without any deviation is God, and that which is moved is the creature [*to de kinēton hē genesis*], so that he who comes near to God desires stability; but he who departs from him, as by so doing he is approaching a creature easily overturned, is borne towards that which resembles it" (*Posterity and Exile of Cain* 23).[83]

Whether a person among James' original audience, or a presumed Believer today, either hears or reads Scripture—those who encounter and examine themselves thoroughly as a result, are going to see some major areas of life needing to be conformed to Biblical standards. When you look at the spiritual mirror that the Word of God is, an individual *is to be convicted to change.* James specifically targeted those who would carefully scrutinize themselves. Any disobedience after such a careful, critical examination, cannot be blamed because of a lack of understanding what the Scriptures say—but rather a willful defiance of God's Instruction. Donald W. Burdick observes, "In the Judeo-Christian context, knowledge is inseparably tied to experience. The believer gains knowledge through experience, and his knowledge is intended to affect subsequent experience."[84] Scripture is the touchstone of our

---

[81] E. Würthwein, "*katanoéō*," in *TDNT*, 639.

[82] *LS*, 162.

[83] *The Works of Philo: Complete and Unabridged*, 134.

[84] Burdick, in *EXP*, 12:175.

experiences, and is the ultimate test to determine how we have to change to be in compliance with what the Lord directs of us.

1:24 The danger that James warns about is those who look at themselves—and see their carnal, sin nature in light of God's Word—and then the person "goes away and at once forgets what he was like" (RSV). In other words, no matter how sinful some are exposed to be by Scripture, the individual knowing this does not care that much to change. Will this mean that a heavy weight of penalty, for failing to comply with God's intention, will then ensue? Thankfully, any final judgment of a person falls to God, and not to any human being. Yet, all would do well to heed James' warning; the person who rejects God's Word, "immediately...forgot of what kind he was" (LITV), when proven to be a sinner. There are various examples that we might consider, regarding either ancient Believers failing to keep some of the high imperatives of God's Word, or people today who fall into similar errors. But, the general knowledge of knowing that some people know quite well what God's Word says about sin, what the example of the Messiah is regarding such matters—and they go on and act like they have forgotten it—**is something most sober and most frightening to consider.**

25 But one who looks intently at the perfect law, the *law* of liberty, and abides by it, not having become a forgetful hearer but an effectual doer, this man will be blessed in what he does.

1:25 James the Just speaks to his audience of how, "the one who looks intently into the perfect *Torah*, the *Torah* that gives freedom, and continues in it, not becoming a hearer who forgets but a doer who acts—he shall be blessed in what he does" (TLV). Each Messiah follower is called to be a *poiētēs ergou*, "a doer of work," and so be blessed as a result of the doing.

Makarios, "blessed," is the same Greek term that appears in the source text of Yeshua's Sermon on the Mount teaching of Matthew ch. 5, where He tells His audience "blessed are" nine specific times (Matthew 5:3, 4, 5, 6, 7, 8, 9, 10, 11). The interconnectivity, between Yeshua's teaching and James' remark here, can definitely be seen. Notably in view is how the teachings and example of Yeshua, via His fulfillment of the Torah and Prophets (Matthew 5:17-19), are to compose what James calls *nomon teleion ton tēs eleutherias*, "the perfect law, the *law* of liberty" (NASU), or "the perfect law that gives freedom" (NIV). Walking in appropriate works, reflective of the high standard of God in His Torah, is certainly emulative of the Messiah Himself (John 10:25).

Once again, v. 25 is a place where various Christian interpreters have **significantly struggled** through the idea that "the perfect law" has really anything to do with the Torah of Moses. Bo Ivar Reicke, who does not adhere to genuine Jamean authorship of this letter, claims that "the 'law' here refers to the gospel or the word of salvation to which the writer has referred repeatedly in the foregoing passages (vs. 18-24). The fact that the gospel is called 'law' does not involve any attempt to reintroduce external observances..."[85] He goes on to suggest[86] that the Epistle of James instead should be read from the perspective of endorsing various Stoic ideals, and various other ideas seen in Philonic Jewish material—which has notably been spoken against by commentators like Davids,[87] who interestingly enough, holds to a two-stage composition of the letter (discussed previously in the **Introduction**). Other interpreters of James, though—by being a bit weary about Messiah followers keeping the Mosaic Law in the post-resurrection era—are more inclined to see James' reference to "the perfect law," as the Torah's ethical and moral instructions, as interpreted and applied by Yeshua,[88] perhaps as some kind of reworked "law of Christ" (cf. Galatians 6:2).[89] Among contemporary Christian examiners, McKnight is probably the closest to what the actual reality is: "James is Torah-observant in a Jesus kind of way."[90]

Some do believe that "the perfect law," referenced by James in v. 25, may not have a great deal to do with the Torah or Moses' Teaching. They will claim that any major keeping of the Law of Moses in the post-resurrection era is likely to bring bondage and legalism to people, and that what is intended is only following a series of instructions, rooted around the Messiah's teachings. Certainly, while none of today's Messianic Believers should find themselves in a situation denying the importance and centrality of Yeshua's teachings and example—a definite problem exists for those who do not understand that without God's Torah, **there is no definitive guideline concerning what sin is,** and what the Messiah Himself considered acceptable and unacceptable behavior.[91] David H. Stern validly states, "it is the *Torah* which, because it is perfect, gives freedom! Only rebellious antinomians seek to be free from rules and regulations; the wise understand that only within a framework of law is true freedom possible....The 'perfect' or 'completed' *Torah*, then, is the *Torah* which includes the New Covenant."[92] As born again Believers with the Holy Spirit resident inside of us, the Torah should be much easier to keep, not more difficult, especially as Messiah Yeshua has shown His followers how to live it through His example. For those who have

---

[85] Reicke, 23.

[86] Ibid., 24.

[87] Davids, pp 99-100.

[88] Davids, 100; Burdick, in *EXP*, 12:176; Moo, 94; McCartney, pp 123-124 reflects a more positive view from his Reformed perspective.

[89] Witherington, pp 445-446.

Galatians 6:2 we should think, is rightly understood as "the *Torah's* true meaning, which the Messiah upholds." For a further discussion, consult the author's commentary *Galatians for the Practical Messianic*.

[90] McKnight, 158.

[91] A most poignant example of this would be the fact that Yeshua Himself never *specifically* said anything about homosexuality, something that liberal Christians who think homosexuality is an acceptable lifestyle, grossly abuse. Yet, if Yeshua the Messiah upheld the Torah as valid instruction for His followers (Matthew 5:17-19), it is obvious that a reprehensible sin like homosexuality, which merited capital punishment in the pre-resurrection era, is still most sinful today, even if capital punishment is not to be issued against gays and lesbians.

[92] Stern, *Jewish New Testament Commentary*, 727.

recognized Yeshua as their Redeemer, their obedience to God's Torah is to be decisively fulfilled via His love (2:8).

Would James have agreed with a word such as Psalm 1:1-2? *"How blessed is the man who does not walk in the counsel of the wicked, nor stand in the path of sinners, nor sit in the seat of scoffers! But his delight is in the law of the LORD, and in His law he meditates day and night."* Would James have agreed with a word such as Psalm 19:7-11? *"The law of the LORD is perfect, restoring the soul; the testimony of the LORD is sure, making wise the simple. The precepts of the LORD are right, rejoicing the heart; the commandment of the LORD is pure, enlightening the eyes. The fear of the LORD is clean, enduring forever; the judgments of the LORD are true; they are righteous altogether. They are more desirable than gold, yes, than much fine gold; sweeter also than honey and the drippings of the honeycomb. Moreover, by them Your servant is warned; in keeping them there is great reward."* For far too many Christians today, these are irrelevant, if not non-spiritual, words—only relevant to the spirituality of the Ancient Israelites, but not really modern-day Believers in Jesus.[93]

Properly keeping God's commandments in the Torah—via the example of the Messiah, no less—is to bring liberty or freedom to God's people; it is not to bring bondage. Herbert Basser, in the relatively liberal *Jewish Annotated New Testament*, makes the useful indication, *"The perfect law* is later called 'the royal law' (2.8), the law that teaches compassion. B. Eruv. 54a, referring to Ex 32.16 describing the tablets of the law as God's writing 'engraved,' reads 'engraved' [Heb 'ḥarut'] law as if it said 'freedom' [Heb 'ḥeirut'] law, suggesting that the law of Sinai itself is a law of freedom."[94] The Talmudic reference in its entirety says,

"And said R. Eleazar, 'What is the meaning of the verse of Scripture: "Tables of stone" (Exo. 31:18)? If a man presents his cheeks as stone that is not easily worn away, his learning will endure in his possession, but if not, his learning will not endure in his possession.' *And said R. Eleazar, 'What is the meaning of the verse of Scripture: "Graven upon the tables"* (Exo. 32:16)? If the first tablets hadn't been broken, the Torah would never have been forgotten from Israel.' R. Aha bar Jacob said, 'No nation or language could have ruled over them: "graven"— read the word as though it bore vowels to yield "freedom"'" (b.*Eruvin* 54a).[95]

Richard L. Scheef remarks on v. 25, "By calling it **the law of liberty** [James] reflects the then current Jewish teaching that obedience to the law is true freedom."[96] This was primarily based around the idea that when God freed Ancient Israel from its bondage in Egypt, that He led the people to Mount Sinai to give them His Torah, so that they would be free and blessed. *The idea that keeping the Torah is some kind of legalistic "bondage," is one which*

---

[93] Consult the author's remarks in Chapter 1 of his book *The New Testament Validates Torah*, "Christian Misunderstanding of Antinomian Assault?"

[94] Basser, in *The Jewish Annotated New Testament*, 430.

[95] *The Babylonian Talmud: A Translation and Commentary*. MS Windows XP. Peabody, MA: Hendrickson, 2005. CD-ROM.

[96] Richard L. Scheef, "James," in Charles M. Laymon, ed., *The Interpreter's One-Volume Commentary on the Bible* (Nashville: Abingdon, 1971), 919.

has been improperly perpetuated by too much of Christianity, without a sound Biblical foundation. Thankfully, though, there are evangelical Christians like Motyer, whose viewpoint of v. 25 and what "the law of freedom/liberty" involves is something that most Messianics are not only likely to agree with, but find most enlightening and quite edifying to their walk of faith:

> "We shall begin to understand the link between law and liberty if we go back to the very moment of the law-giving at Mount Sinai. The Lord is speaking (Ex. 20:2a) to those whom he has brought out of Egypt. They have been redeemed (Ex. 6:6) and the means of their redemption was the blood of the lamb (Ex. 12:13). We see, then, that the Lord gives his law not as a means of salvation, but as a life-style for those who have already been saved. It is the way he wants his redeemed ones to live. But then he goes on to say that he is speaking to those whom he has brought out of bondage (Ex. 20:2b): not to those whom he is bringing into bondage by imposing his law upon them, but to those who are now (for the first time) enjoying liberty, and to whom he gives his perfect law in order to safeguard the freedom he has secured for them. True freedom is the opportunity and the ability to give expression to what we truly are. We are truly free when we live the life appropriate to those who are created in the image of God. The law of God safeguards that liberty for us. But it does even more, for obedience brings life and power (Lv. 18:5; Dt. 4:1a; Acts 5:32). The law of God is *the law of liberty* because it safeguards, expresses and enables the life of true freedom into which Christ has brought us. This is the blessing of which James speaks (25), the blessing of a full life, a true humanity. Obedience is the key factor in our enjoyment of it."[97]

The Jewish philosopher Philo said, "those who are under the dominion of anger, or appetite, or any other passion, or of treacherous wickedness, are in every respect slaves; and those who live in accordance with the law are free" (*Every Good Man is Free* 45).[98] These words do parallel what the Scriptures say. If God's people are keeping the Torah through the empowerment of His Holy Spirit, then they cannot be subject to the wills of the flesh, and of its terrible passions. As Paul so astutely says, "But the fruit of the Spirit is love, joy, peace, patience, kindness, goodness, faithfulness, gentleness, self-control; against such things there is no law" (Galatians 5:22-23). Those, who have "the implanted word" (v. 21) within them, will actually find themselves evidencing fruit and blessings, as they follow Moses' Teaching—with the goal of demonstrating a sound inward morality and fair outward observance, emulating the example of Yeshua, as well as key godly persons like James. Such an obedience must steadfastly keep in mind the interests of neighbor, and how born again Believers are called to serve the community of faith. Martin speaks to this:

"Freedom is not *from* the works {deeds/doing} of the law...but rather it connotes a release from one's self-interest and a new capacity to practice God's will in the interests of

---

[97] Motyer, 71.
[98] *The Works of Philo: Complete and Unabridged*, 686.

one's needy neighbor...James exploits this meaning of law but gives it a richer content from a Christian perspective by his recourse to the eschatological fulfillment of Jer 31 in the age of God's new creation."[99]

While there is variance, and while various scholars and commentators of note will wrestle with it—there are those who quantitatively have to acknowledge that "the perfect law" (NASU) or "the perfect *Torah*" (CJB), does involve the New Covenant promise (Jeremiah 31:31-34; Ezekiel 36:25-27), and *at least* the Torah's ethical and moral statutes as demonstrated by the Messiah. While today's Messianics might think that more than just moral principles in the Torah are involved, we cannot disagree with the importance of such injunctions for daily life, and in demonstrating our faith in a world that is hurting and needs a significant demonstration of God's love and mercy. If you can at all believe it, much of the wrestling over what "the perfect law" involves, is something that has been detected at least as early as the Sixteenth Century, as seen in Calvin's commentary on v. 25:

> "[H]is {James'} reasons for speaking of *the perfect law, the law of liberty*, have eluded exegetes, who have failed to observe the contrast he makes, with reference to other passages of Scripture. As long as the Law is preached by man's outward utterance, and not written in the heart with the finger and Spirit of God, it is a dead letter, it is like a lifeless corpse. The Law may reasonably be held to be impaired, until it finds a place in the heart. The same argument applies to its lack of freedom. Divorced from Christ, it bears children unto bondage (Gal. 4.24), and it can only affect us with profound apprehension and fear (Rom. 8.15). But the Spirit of regeneration, printing its message on our inmost being, confers in like manner the grace of adoption. It is as though James had said, Do not make a slavish thing of the Law's teaching, but rather a vehicle of liberty; don't be tied to the apron-strings, but reach out with it to perfection; you must receive it with whole-hearted affection, if you aim to find a godly and holy life. Further we may see from the witness of Jeremiah (31.33), and many others, and the re-fashioning which the Law of God will give us is a blessing of the new covenant. From this it follows that it could not be found, until the coming of Christ. He alone is the accomplishment and perfection of the Law. Hence James' addition of *liberty*, inseparably attached, for Christ's Spirit never gives us new birth without equally giving testimony and pledge to our adoption, so as to set our hearts free from hear and alarm."[100]

There is **an undeniable component** of doing/performing/obeying God's Word, following His Torah or Law, that is required of those who are Messiah followers, faithful to Him. While this would have been understood relatively easy for many of the First Century Jewish Believers—how might this relate to the reason for the Apostolic decree in Acts 15:21, and James' testimony that the salvation of the nations was according to Tanach prophecy

---

[99] Martin, 51.
[100] Calvin, pp 273-274.

(Acts 15:15-18; Amos 9:11-12, LXX; cf. Micah 4:1-3; Isaiah 2:2-4)? Given the many appeals to the Torah and Tanach's code of ethics and morality in this epistle, would James the Just, brother of Yeshua, have wanted the new, non-Jewish Believers to have access to Israel's Scriptures—so that they might be able to have a better idea about what a letter like this one communicates? There should be no denying the fact that the Apostolic decree (Acts 15:19-21, 29) was not always followed, and/or that Greek and Roman Believers were not always welcome among First Century Jews. Yet, the intention of the Apostolic decree was to surely get Greek and Roman Believers removed from their paganism, and latched onto a community where Moses was being taught every Sabbath (Acts 15:21), and which served the God of Israel and His intentions. Only when God's Word is decisively understood and implemented, in the lives of *all of His people*, can it then be manifested in blessings, and even greater blessings![101]

26 If anyone thinks himself to be religious, and yet does not bridle his tongue but deceives his *own* heart, this man's religion is worthless.

1:26 While proper obedience to the Torah or Law of God is expected of Messiah followers, one of the initial actions that can prove whether such obedience is genuine or fallacious, is seen in James' direct instruction, "If anyone thinks he is religious, without controlling his tongue but deceiving his heart, his religion is useless" (HCSB). Those who do not control their speech, or how they communicate, are to be reckoned as violators of God's Torah. In terms of "the perfect law" (v. 25), this should include not only the Torah or Moses' Teaching, but also the Tanach as a whole, as well as the teachings of Yeshua that demonstrate forth the maturity that men and women are to be attaining. James' words parallel Proverbs 10:31: "The mouth of the righteous flows with wisdom, but the perverted tongue will be cut out."

While traditionally rendered as "religion" in most English versions, *thrēskeia* might more fully mean, "**expression of devotion to transcendent beings,** esp. as it expresses itself in cultic rites, *worship*" (BDAG).[102] The actions performed by people in obedience to God are certainly to be regarded as some form of worship. While we commonly associate worship with singing songs, reciting Scripture, or repeating liturgy of praises to God—our daily speech in life is to also reflect the character of the Holy One we serve. This is an area where human beings, of all times, and of all shapes and sizes, have certainly committed a huge number of offenses. We are all guilty of profaning our Creator, in some form or fashion, by failing to bridle our tongue. In many ways, the tongue is like a wild horse that needs to be desperately tamed, lest it run rampant and cause all kind of damage. Today's Messianic movement, for a variety of complicated spiritual and sociological reasons, is a

---

[101] Consult the author's commentary *Acts 15 for the Practical Messianic*.
[102] *BDAG*, 459.

widespread offender of not controlling the tongue. As we steadily approach the return of the Lord, more and more Messianic people are going to have to learn how to speak and communicate via a demeanor of holiness, and not base human flesh.

27 Pure and undefiled religion in the sight of *our* God and Father is this: to visit orphans and widows in their distress, *and* to keep oneself unstained by the world.

1:27 The kind of action, reflective of Messiah followers adhering to "the perfect law" (v. 25), is elaborated by James: "Religion that is pure and genuine in the sight of God the Father will show itself by such things as visiting orphans and widows in their distress and keeping oneself uncontaminated by the world" (Phillips New Testament). Those who wish to really demonstrate their sincerity to the Lord, are those who have to enter into places, and deal with people, who are in serious distress. They also have to guard themselves "from being polluted by the world" (NIV). Witherington observes, on the thrust of v. 27, on how "The warning against self-deception is apt, especially for Jews in a Greco-Roman environment like the Diaspora, where religion was regularly associated with correct and exacting performance of religious ritual and not necessarily with various codes of ethical conduct."[103] Anyone taking the aim of v. 27 seriously has to recognize how outward religious motions are insufficient, if they are not joined with acts of kindness and mercy toward those in need.

The requirement for the community of God to take care of the poor and destitute among them, of whom widows and orphans are most to be pitied, is seen affluently throughout the Tanach.[104] Making note of a series of passages from Deuteronomy (10:17ff; 24:17ff, 20ff), Motyer draws a connection between Ancient Israel's slavery, the release from the slavery of sin found in Yeshua, and how such a release is to properly motivate Believers to care for others. He says, "The Deuteronomy references...link our concern for orphans and widows with the Lord's concern to redeem us from our Egyptian slavery. They therefore call to our minds the redeeming, Calvary-love of Jesus as the model for the caring Christian."[105] Seeing the Torah commandments and admonitions of the Prophets observed, so that Messiah followers take care of orphans, widows, the poor, the homeless, and others in need—is a definite component of true religion/worship to James.

Another major direction is that Believers are to be "unspotted from the world" (KJV), meaning contaminated by its most fallen and corrupt methods. The term *aspilos* **"pert. to**

---

[103] Witherington, 447.

Moo, 96 states the similar, "James is not polemicizing against religious ritual per se but against a ritual that goes no further than outward show and mere words. He is probably somewhat dependent on a widespread pagan and Jewish tradition that emphasized that proper cultic worship must be accompanied by ethical conduct."

[104] Exodus 22:22; Deuteronomy 10:17-18; 14:29; 24:17-22; 26:12; Isaiah 1:10-17; Jeremiah 22:3; Hosea 14:3; Zechariah 7:9-10; Psalm 10:14; 68:5; 146:9; cf. 4 Esdras 2:20.

[105] Motyer, 77.

being of untainted character, *pure, without fault* of inward condition" (*BDAG*),[106] and needs to be remembered by those seeking to do good works, so that they might be piqued to know that such good works are going to be genuine deeds produced by "the word implanted" (v. 21), guided and tempered by the love and grace of God. While this would have been beset with various challenges for James' First Century Diaspora audience, implementing this as Twenty-First Century Believers can be even more of a challenge. Motyer's detailed observations on v. 27 should not go unnoticed:

> "...James summons us to be *unstained from the world* (27b). 'The world' (see, especially, 4:4) has the same meaning for James as for Paul and John. It is the whole human scheme of things organized in terms of human wisdom to attain a human goal, without reference to God, his laws, his values or his ultimate judgment. The world is, in fact, anything and everything that is at odds with the Lordship of Jesus over our lives. If we are to live for him in the world, there is a constant issue of commitment, loyalty, to be faced: are we his or are we not? Are we his, not by virtue of a past decision allowed to grow stale, but in the daily pressure of the often small things by which our lives are besmirched? For it is more than likely true that, if life were all large decisions, few of us would go far wrong. Yet, faced with the world's ceaseless bombardment of our eyes, ears, thoughts, and imaginations, the world's insidious erosion of values and standards, and clamour for our time, money and energy, it is easy to adopt a general day of life which, though it avoids the open pitfalls of sin, yet is not discernibly different from the style of one who does not know Christ. We may well decide to belong to Jesus, yet fail to carry that decision through with the rigour which alone proves that it was a real decision. It is one thing to yield our lives unto him, but it is another to live each moment of the day on his side in the great divide from the world."[107]

There is a definite part of obedience to God—*a part of Torah observance, no less*—which involves what many might call "the social gospel." This requires Believers to be concerned about others' physical needs. In all of my time in the Messianic movement, I have found it most interesting that many, staunchly pro-Torah people, will quote from James' writing about being a doer (v. 22), but they often gloss over the fact that James largely emphasizes the morality, attitudes, and social actions that Believers are to perform. Evangelical Christians, who do not keep the seventh-day Sabbath, appointed times of Leviticus 23, or eat kosher—but who are concerned about humanitarian good works—are frequently the target of negative criticism, which does not help for fair-minded discussion with them. How we learn to implement a delicate balance, of proper attitudes and actions, is frequently not something that enough contemporary Messianic Believers do. Most unconsciously, many people in our faith community allow themselves to be stained and spotted with worldly

---

[106] *BDAG*, 144.
[107] Motyer, pp 77-78.

attitudes and temperaments. Too many of us, as we steadily approach the return of the Messiah, *have to learn to do better!*

JAMES 2
COMMENTARY

1 My brethren, do not hold your faith in our glorious Lord Yeshua the Messiah with *an attitude of* personal favoritism.

2:1 James the Just, having just completed some introductory remarks and observations about the problems his audience was facing, now begins to address some more specific issues, becoming much more direct and forthright. James emphasizes the fact that all are to have faith in Yeshua, demonstrating proper actions and attitudes, admonishing, "My brothers and sisters, do not hold the faith of our glorious Lord *Yeshua* the Messiah while showing favoritism" (TLV). Apparently, for a sector of James' audience, showing "snobbery" (Phillips New Testament) was an extreme problem, and it was disruptive for others trying to enter in. The NRSV has a unique rendering of v. 1, as it posits the question, "My brothers and sisters, do you with your acts of favoritism really believe in our glorious Lord Jesus Christ?" Practicing favoritism would be in direct disobedience to the royal Torah law of loving neighbor (v. 8; cf. 1:25), and could demonstrate some level of infidelity to the Lord. Given the tenor of some of the verses following (vs. 15-18), not all of James' audience was desperately poor, but it did include people who were impressed by the rich. As Leviticus 19:15 would warn: "You shall do no injustice in judgment; you shall not be partial to the poor nor defer to the great, but you are to judge your neighbor fairly."

James' emphasis on "faith" (*pistis*) regards far more than people having made some sort of affirmation to a series of beliefs. One could be reminded of Paul's later word in the First Century, on "keeping faith and a good conscience, which some have rejected and suffered shipwreck in regard to their faith" (1 Timothy 1:19). Those who keep faith with the Lord Yeshua, and who value their salvation—while surely affirming His supremacy—are also going to *be faithful* to His teachings and example. As Dan G. McCartney so ably describes, "There can be no separation between the trust component of faith and the faithfulness component, because to trust an authority entails a commitment to it. This is not to turn faith into some kind of work, but to point out that faith is a matter of commitment to relationship, not just the acceptance of some intellective truth."[1]

The object of faith and trust is *tou Kuriou hēmōn Iēsou Christou tēs doxēs*, "our glorious Lord Yeshua the Messiah." Associating Yeshua with the description of *doxa*, the Septuagint

---

[1] McCartney, 136.

equivalent of the Hebrew *kavod*, is Christologically important. *Kavod* appears in some critical Torah passages describing the Divine presence of God:

> "The glory of the LORD [*kevod-ADONAI*] rested on Mount Sinai, and the cloud covered it for six days; and on the seventh day He called to Moses from the midst of the cloud" (Exodus 24:16).

> "Then Moses said, 'I pray You, show me Your glory [*kevodekha*]!'" (Exodus 33:18).

> "Then the cloud covered the tent of meeting, and the glory of the LORD [*kevod ADONAI*] filled the tabernacle" (Exodus 40:34).

The term *kavod* literally means "heavy," and it has a wide variety of connotations. The most significant of these predominantly regards the presence of God manifested in the Tabernacle in the wilderness. *TWOT* describes the significance of the word *kavod:*

"The bulk of occurrences where God's glory is a visible manifestation have to do with the tabernacle (Ex 16:10; 40:34; etc.) and with the temple in Ezekiel's vision of the exile and restoration (9:3; etc.). These manifestations are directly related to God's self-disclosure and his intent to dwell with men, to have his reality and his splendor known to them. But this is only possible when they take account of the stunning quality of his holiness and set out in faith and obedience to let that character be manifested in them (Num 14:10; Isa 6:3; Ezr 10, 11)."[2]

When James uses the Greek term *doxa, doxa* carries with it the same understanding of *kavod*. While *doxa* is a title of honor to be sure, much more than just appropriate honor and reverence to be issued toward Yeshua was intended. McCartney's brief estimation is, "In calling Jesus 'glorious Lord,' James effectively ascribes the divine attributes and importance to Christ."[3] Peter Davids offers a much fuller thought on the title *doxa* ascribed to Yeshua, detailing how "this is not simply to say that 'our Lord' is most honorable or exalted, for to one who knew the LXX the term would immediately recall the OT use of [*doxa*] to translate the Hebrew *kāḇôḏ*, characteristically meaning, 'the luminous manifestation of God's person' particularly in bringing salvation to Israel (Ex. 14:17-18; Psa. 96:3; Isa. 60:1-2; Ezk. 39:21-22; Zc. 2:5-11...). Thus it is a term of exaltation, revelation, and eschatological salvation."[4] One important later usage of *doxa*, which need not escape any Bible reader, is how Titus 2:13 exclaims how Believers are to be "looking for the blessed hope and the appearing of **the glory of our great God and Savior, Messiah Yeshua** [*tēs doxēs tou megalou Theou kai Sōtēros hēmōn Iēsou Christou*]." Here, the glory in view is obviously the manifestation of God's greatness at the Second Coming—but especially not to be overlooked is how Yeshua Himself

---

[2] John N. Oswalt, *"kaveid,"* in R. Laird Harris, Gleason L. Archer, Jr., and Bruce K. Waltke, eds., *Theological Wordbook of the Old Testament,* 2 vols. (Chicago: Moody Press, 1980), 1:427.

[3] McCartney, 137.

[4] Davids, 107.

is labeled with the titles of "God and Savior," necessarily implying that the Messiah is, Himself, God.[5]

As is seen throughout the contents of ch. 2, James was absolutely concerned about the right demonstration of faith for Messiah followers, expressing a particular consternation for those who would show "partiality" (RSV) or "personal favoritism" (NASU), *prosōlēmpsia*. While the related verb *prosōpolēpteō* is commonly defined as *"to be a respecter of persons"* (LS),[6] it is often associated with the Hebrew *lo-tisa pnei* from Leviticus 19:15, as God's people are to "not lift up the face" (YLT; cf. Psalm 82:2; Proverbs 6:35; 18:5; 24:23; 28:21; Malachi 1:8; 2:9; also Sirach 7:6-7; 35:10-18). As Douglas J. Moo concludes, "To 'receive a face' means to make judgments about people based on external appearance. James applies this principle to differences in dress that reflect contrasting social/economic situations."[7] Discrimination based on outward appearance was a problem for many of James' readers, and it might be said that much of James' admonition about partiality is a summation of Deuteronomy 10:17-18:

"For the LORD your God is the God of gods and the Lord of lords, the great, the mighty, and the awesome God who does not show partiality nor take a bribe. He executes justice for the orphan and the widow, and shows His love for the alien by giving him food and clothing."

Concurrent with this, while demonstrating favoritism toward the rich is something that James finds to be quite deplorable (vs. 2-7), this does not mean that the legitimate spiritual concerns of more well to do people should be ignored, either. This is something which needs to be especially kept in mind, as more modern applications of v. 1 are considered by individual Believers, particularly in congregational environments (vs. 2-3). Ben Witherington III fairly observes,

"[James] is saying that one should *not* show favoritism to the rich, which is then unfair to the poor, nor should one slight the poor and so dishonor them. All persons should be treated fairly regardless of their socioeconomic status. Since there is an imbalance in a fallen world full of self-centered acquisitive persons, one can argue that God is concerned about balancing the scales, about justice for all, and in a fallen world this may appear to be partiality for the poor."[8]

---

[5] Consult the author's commentary *The Pastoral Epistles for the Practical Messianic*, for a review of Titus 2:13 and the Granville Sharp rule; also consult his publication *Confronting Yeshua's Divinity and Messiahship*.

[6] *LS*, 701.

[7] Moo, 102.

[8] Witherington, 454.

2 For if a man comes into your assembly with a gold ring and dressed in fine clothes, and there also comes in a poor man in dirty clothes, 3 and you pay special attention to the one who is wearing the fine clothes, and say, "You sit here in a good place," and you say to the poor man, "You stand over there, or sit down by my footstool," 4 have you not made distinctions among yourselves, and become judges with evil motives?

2:2 Vs. 2-4 describe the serious problem of showing partiality or favoritism inside the assembly, particularly for James' audience, as the poor were being issued a degree of disgust, even though this is something surely opposed by the Tanach and ancient Jewish literature (Proverbs 14:21; Sirach 10:19-11:6). The thought of 2 Corinthians 8:9 is also useful for consideration: "For you know the grace of our Lord Yeshua the Messiah, that though He was rich, yet for your sake He became poor, so that you through His poverty might become rich."

While sometimes skewed with the rendering "assembly" (RSV/NASU/ESV) or "meeting" (NRSV), the source text of v. 2 actually does describe how, "if there come into your synagogue a man with a gold ring, in fine clothing, and there come in also a poor man in vile clothing" (American Standard Version). In v. 2, James employs the term *sunagōgē* or "synagogue," which can also mean "gathering."[9] This is an indication from the Apostolic Scriptures, that at the very least, the early Believers in the First Century had no problem associating themselves with the common label of a Jewish assemblage of worship, and that being a **synagogue** extended not only to the Believers in the Land of Israel, but also in the Diaspora (cf. 1:1).[10] In the estimation of David H. Stern, from his *Jewish New Testament Commentary*, "This is a Messianic synagogue, a congregation of believers in Yeshua, predominantly Jewish, expressing their New Covenant faith in a way retaining most or all of the prayers, customs and style of non-Messianic synagogues."[11] More neutrally, per the content of v. 2 and what is being described, Scot McKnight details,

---

[9] As noted by *LS*, 166, the term *sunagōgē* has a wide range of meanings, which go beyond a Jewish assembly of worship or teaching:

- *a gathering in of* harvest, Polyb.
- *a drawing together, contracting,* [*s. stratias*] *a forming* an army *in column*, Plat.; [*s. tou prosōpou*] *a pursing up* or *wrinkling* of the face, Isocr.
- a collection of writings, Arist.
- a conclusion, inference, Id.

While for the Epistle of James, *sunagōgē* should be rightly understood as a Jewish assembly or house of worship, there are other places where additional meanings of *sunagōgē* need to be considered for appropriate balance (i.e., Revelation 2:9; 3:9). For a further review, consult the sub-section, "What is 'the Synagogue of Satan'?", in Chapter 3 of the author's book *Israel in Future Prophecy*, "Cross-Examining the Two-House Teaching."

[10] Against: Burdick, in *EXP*, 12:177-178 who simply takes *sunagōgē* in its most neutral sense as some kind of "gathering"; also McCartney, 138, although not as strongly.

[11] Stern, *Jewish New Testament Commentary*, 728.

"[I]t is reasonable to see 'assembly' or 'congregating place' (*synagōgē*) in 2:2 as a term referring to the messianic community's worship and learning center, which for whatever reasons visitors sometimes attended."[12]

I am personally inclined to think that the reference to the gathering of Messiah followers in v. 2, is labeled as a "synagogue," rather than an assembly (*ekklēsia*), as being an indication of how early James was composed. The later reference to Believers gathering more as an *ekklēsia* (commonly mistranslated in English Bibles as "church," but by specialty versions like YLT and LITV as "assembly"), would express commonality and continuance with the assembly of Ancient Israel in the Tanach, per how *ekklēsia* commonly rendered the Hebrew *qahal*, but would allow for some degree of difference with the establishment of the Jewish Synagogue which did not recognize Yeshua as Messiah.[13]

Some expositors, while choosing not to recognize that the early Believers did indeed conduct their worship services and protocol quantitatively similar to the First Century Synagogue, are instead inclined to think that James' comments might reflect that of a Jewish court of justice (b.*Shevuot* 31a). Ralph P. Martin indicates that the use of *sunagōgē* "could pertain either to a public worship service or a congregational gathering for the purpose of hearing a judicial case."[14] This could account for James' appeal to fair rulings and fair treatment of fellow Believers throughout his letter. Moo summarizes some of the different options regarding the gathering in view for v. 2:

"With most commentators in the past, we could assume that [James] is depicting a typical weekly worship gathering of the Christian community. The 'ushers,' perhaps with tacit approval from the leaders of the assembly, conduct the splendidly dressed person to a fine seat, while contemptuously ordering a poorly dressed person to sit on the floor. But an alternative suggestion about the scenario James describes has been gaining ground: that the situation is a meeting of the Christian assembly to sit in judgment over a dispute between two of its members."[15]

While it is useful for readers of James' letter to be aware of v. 2 perhaps pertaining to a Jewish court of justice, with disputes being resolved between people, Moo himself goes on and concludes, "On the whole...the possessive 'your meeting' in v. 2 seems to point to a definite, well-known gathering that better fits the worship service than a judicial assembly."[16] Discrimination toward one group of people in the assembly, either during a worship service, or during other sorts of gatherings, is not limited to James' letter. Paul

---

[12] McKnight, 183.

[13] Cf. Tim Hegg, *I Will Build My Ekklesia: An Introduction to Ecclesiology* (Tacoma, WA: TorahResource, 2009), 14.

Also see the section, "The Term Ekklēsia," in the author's publication *Are Non-Jewish Believers Really a Part of Israel?*

[14] Martin, 61.

[15] Moo, 99.

[16] Ibid., 100; also Witherington, pp 454-455.

chastised the Corinthians for not allowing the poor and needy among them from being among the first to eat at fellowship meals:

"But in giving this instruction, I do not praise you, because you come together not for the better but for the worse. For, in the first place, when you come together as [an assembly], I hear that divisions exist among you; and in part I believe it. For there must also be factions among you, so that those who are approved may become evident among you. Therefore when you meet together, it is not to eat the Lord's Supper, for in your eating each one takes his own supper first; and one is hungry and another is drunk. What! Do you not have houses in which to eat and drink? Or do you despise the [assembly] of God and shame those who have nothing? What shall I say to you? Shall I praise you? In this I will not praise you" (1 Corinthians 11:17-22).

James specifically mentions two types of people who may enter into the assembly: one who is dressed in fine clothes, and one who is dressed in dirty clothes. Seemingly, the person dressed in fine clothes and gold is rich, and likewise the one who is dressed in dirty clothes is poor. Typical to the First Century, and even into more modern times, gold rings worn by people can demonstrate a certain high social status.

While the rich and poor being present in a community of Messiah followers, could be the case in any First Century Mediterranean city, Bo Ivar Reicke speculates that the one wearing a gold ring may be a reference to rich Roman nobles. He comments, "In this connection the rich man is said to wear a gold finger ring, which indicates that he was of senatorial rank or a Roman nobleman. During the early years of the empire only such men had the right to wear a gold ring. When it is added that he wears a 'splendid garment,' this may indicate that he is seeking political office and adherents."[17] Some of these observations are likely affected by Reicke's late dating of the Epistle of James. Yet, regardless of whether or not the rich present were Roman officials, they nevertheless commanded quite a presence. The author could use these sentiments as a slight exaggeration, to point out how even if someone were finely dressed in such a manner, the poor still demanded attention.

Ignoring those who are poorly or shabbily dressed, showing favor and preference to those who are more finely dressed, would run entirely contrary to the Torah-demanded ethical imperative for God's people to service those in need. Perhaps most important to consider, if some kind of worship or fellowship gathering is indeed in view for v. 2, is whether or not the poor person entering into the assembly/synagogue is even a Believer (in Israel's God) himself. What testimony would it be to not treat such a person with care and respect? Most of the outside sojourners or *gerim* in the Torah, who would enter into Ancient Israel, were themselves largely poor people. The ancient synagogue, especially for gatherings on *Shabbat*, was supposed to be a place which epitomized all of the great virtues of love, honor, and service unto God. The First Century Jewish philosopher Philo said,

---

[17] Reicke, 27.

"[I]n accordance with which custom, even to this day, the Jews hold philosophical discussions on the seventh day, disputing about their national philosophy, and devoting that day to the knowledge and consideration of the subjects of natural philosophy; for as for their houses of prayer in the different cities, what are they, but schools of wisdom, and courage, and temperance, and justice, and piety, and holiness, and every virtue, by which human and divine things are appreciated, and placed upon a proper footing?" (*Life of Moses* 2.216).[18]

Sadly, these sorts of positive traits were not always present in the gatherings of many among James' audience. May we, as Twenty-First Century Messianic Believers, see that they are present in our own fellowships and assemblies!

2:3 James warns his readers not to give preferential treatment to the rich person, saying, "Here's a good seat for you," while telling the poor person, "'You stand there' or 'Sit on the floor by my feet'" (NIV). The poor person, *ptōchos*, is actually *"one who crouches or cringes, a beggar"* (LS).[19] Not only is his poor state bad enough, but upon entering the assembly of Believers, this one is forced to remain in his crouched position—when presumably every effort should be made to attend to his physical needs and comfort. Donald W. Burdick explains, "'the poor man' is abruptly told to 'stand there,' perhaps in the back of the assembly or in some other out-of-the-way place. His other alternative is to 'sit on the floor.'...The contrast between the speaker who has a stool for his feet and the beggar who must sit on the floor heightens the discrimination."[20] Yeshua's words in Matthew 23:6-7 to the Pharisaical leaders might be considered: "They love the place of honor at banquets and the chief seats in the synagogues," whereas the poor are left off to the side.

Perhaps even more important to be considered might be how the verb *epiblepō*, rendered in v. 3 as "pay special attention," also is used in Luke 9:38: "Teacher, I beg You to look at [*epiblepō*] my son, for he is my only *boy*." Just as Yeshua the Messiah reached out with compassion to the demon possessed boy (Luke 9:39-45), who the Disciples themselves were powerless to help—surely those in James' audience could take notice of the poor and destitute among them, expelling some degree of effort. McKnight chooses to observe in his commentary,

"The messianic community gazes upon the rich man but, whether star-struck, envious, manipulative, or hoping to gain something, it chooses to break down its essential commitment to showing mercy to the poor. Instead of treating a person according to his or her God-given eikonic status, the community chooses to honor the wealthy man for what his ostentatious attire represents."[21]

The Messianic community can do this today in various other forms, not necessarily based on wealth, but instead on other kinds of prestige. Usually, but not always, showing

---

[18] *The Works of Philo: Complete and Unabridged*, 510.
[19] LS, 709.
[20] Burdick, in *EXP*, 12:178.
[21] McKnight, 187.

preference to a particular group or clique of people is based on their perceived positions of power and influence—while others, who are accomplishing more genuine work of the Kingdom, are widely shuffled away or ignored.

2:4 James rebukes those in his audience who receive those into their assembly with financial means and wealth and show them preferential treatment, versus poor people who are treated as though they are not there or unimportant. He asks them, "have you not made distinctions among yourselves, and become judges with evil motives?" The Phillips New Testament paraphrases v. 4 with, "doesn't that prove that you are making class distinctions in your mind, and setting yourselves up to assess a man's quality from wrong motives?" Inequity is something regularly condemned in the Tanach (Leviticus 19:15; Deuteronomy 16:19; 27:19, 25; Psalm 82:2; Malachi 2:9), and evil thoughts are regularly condemned in the Apostolic Scriptures (Matthew 15:19; Luke 2:35; 5:22; 9:47; 24:38; Romans 1:21; 14:1; 1 Corinthians 3:20; Philippians 2:14; 1 Timothy 2:8). While a worship service or some other fellowship gathering is most probably being targeted, it is not out of the realm of possibilities to think that the distinctions being criticized against could also involve the kinds of deliberations that the assembly of Believers would make, when presented with various disputes that needed resolution.

James' admonition to treat others equally, without discrimination for their physical appearance, social status, or economic benefit—remains true for us today every bit as much as it did in the First Century. *IVPBBC* validly remarks, "Biblical law, most Jewish law and traditional Greek philosophers had always rejected such distinctions as immoral."[22] James is not writing something that was unique only to the Jews of his time, nor is he writing something unique to us today. The laws which govern a country like the United States, in particular, are intended to guarantee that all will be treated equally in court, regardless of financial or social status. This is also true of most places in the West, which have been significantly influenced by a Biblical ethic. Fair and equal treatment in the assembly, where a distinct group which needs the help and service of the faith community—and is consequently ignored—is noticeably different, though, than expressing honor to those who genuinely deserve it, such as deferring to the elderly, or those who serve well in a position of political leadership. J. Alec Motyer provides us with some worthwhile thoughts that we need not overlook:

> "It is in this matter of 'looks' which must be stressed if we are to be faithful to James' teaching and at the same time keep within the balance of Scripture. The Bible is too courteous a book to allow us to lack proper respect for people to whom it is due. It does not reduce all to a common level in all things or refuse to take note of worldly distinctions; certainly it does not sanction rudeness or unconcern for what people are. It would not be showing *partiality*, for example, to offer the last remaining seat to an

---

[22] Craig S. Keener, *The IVP Bible Background Commentary: New Testament* (Downers Grove, IL: InterVarsity, 1993), 694.

elderly person and to invite a younger person arriving to simultaneously stand or to sit on the floor. The elderly command respect and considerate attention (Lv. 19:32). Or again, were Her Majesty the Queen or the President of a country to come to worship, we would consider it both right and indeed our privilege to stand when they entered and to have the best seat held in readiness. Again, we would be obeying Scripture (*e.g.* Pr. 24:21a; 1 Pet. 2:17). But it is one thing thus to acknowledge inherent dignity, whether of age or position; it is another thing altogether to be swayed by the mere chance that one possess worldly advantages such as money and the other does not.

"James' illustration is timeless. It speaks as loudly today as when he penned it. It is still not always easy to know how to accommodate a tramp in a worship-service and it is still easy to assume that wealth gives a commanding voice in church affairs. The sin of *partiality* is the sin of judging by accidentals and externals and, as James noted, it always bears down on the poor and disadvantaged."[23]

As Believers in Messiah Yeshua, how many of us have made a conscious effort to get along—and express some degree of honor and respect—toward others who are not exactly "like us"? Even I will admit, that in various contemporary situations and settings, I have not always honored the thrust of James 2:4.

5 Listen, my beloved brethren: did not God choose the poor of this world *to be* rich in faith and heirs of the kingdom which He promised to those who love Him? 6 But you have dishonored the poor man. Is it not the rich who oppress you and personally drag you into court?

2:5 James goes further in his rebuke to those who are favoring the wealthy in their midst, admonishing, "Listen, my dearly loved brothers and sisters. Didn't God choose the poor in this world to be rich in faith and heirs of the Kingdom that He promised to those who love Him?" (TLV). He says that God has chosen the poor to be rich and be heirs of His Kingdom, but that they have obviously been dishonored by not being cared for in the congregation (vs. 2-4, 15-16). A great deal of James' audience is thought to have been made up of agricultural workers, who earned their living by tending crops or processing them in some way (5:4). The vast majority of all the early Believers, be they Jewish or non-Jewish, were drawn from the poorer classes of First Century Mediterranean society.

Throughout the Holy Scriptures, we definitely see a concern to be demonstrated toward the poor, destitute, and lonely (Deuteronomy 10:18; Psalm 68:5; Proverbs 17:5; 14:31; Amos 2:6-7; Matthew 5:3; Luke 1:51-53; 6:20; cf. 1 Corinthians 1:26). The Prophets were especially direct in their condemnation of the rich, who oppressed the poor:

---

[23] Motyer, pp 81-82.

"Hear this word, you cows of Bashan who are on the mountain of Samaria, who oppress the poor, who crush the needy, who say to your husbands, 'Bring now, that we may drink!' The Lord GOD has sworn by His holiness, 'Behold, the days are coming upon you when they will take you away with meat hooks, and the last of you with fish hooks'" (Amos 4:1-2).

"They have treated father and mother lightly within you. The alien they have oppressed in your midst; the fatherless and the widow they have wronged in you" (Ezekiel 22:7).

"'Then I will draw near to you for judgment; and I will be a swift witness against the sorcerers and against the adulterers and against those who swear falsely, and against those who oppress the wage earner in his wages, the widow and the orphan, and those who turn aside the alien and do not fear Me,' says the LORD of hosts" (Malachi 3:5).

The Torah itself says that God "executes justice for the orphan and the widow, and shows His love for the alien by giving him food and clothing" (Deuteronomy 10:18). Psalm 68:5 repeats this, saying that the Lord is "A father of the fatherless and a judge for the widows." Yeshua was likewise concerned for the poor, saying, "Blessed *are* you *who are* poor, for yours is the kingdom of God" (Luke 6:20). Also not to be overlooked, is how Deuteronomy 7:7 communicates of God's selection of Israel, "The LORD did not set His love on you nor choose you because you were more in number than any of the peoples, for you were the fewest of all peoples."

In the very early, First Century community of faith, there was a definite urge to see that all of the Believers had what they needed for daily care. Acts 4:34 attests, "For there was not a needy person among them, for all who were owners of land or houses would sell them and bring the proceeds of the sales." Everyone who needed food, clothing, and shelter (should have) had it. Among some of James' targeted audience, however, these basic needs were not being met. The rich were being given preferential treatment to those who really needed to be cared for physically. Witherington is keen to note for us, though, how "James is not saying that poverty is the way of salvation or even salvation itself. He is rather warning about the dangers of the other extreme."[24] God choosing the poor of the world in v. 5 is an observation of how God takes special care of those who are without—and will especially reward them in the world to come.

2:6 James makes the further point, "But you have insulted the poor. Is it not the rich who are exploiting you? Are they not the ones who are dragging you into court?" (NIV). He makes the inquiry, asking his audience what would really be achieved in showing favoritism to rich people in the assembly. The verb of note in v. 6, *katadunesteuō*, means "to

---

[24] Witherington, 458.

exercise power over" (LS),[25] but is often rendered as "oppress" or "exploit." The verb *katadunesteuō* is used in the Septuagint, to represent oppression of the poor:

> "That sorely oppress the people of the land with injustice, and commit robbery; oppressing [*katadunesteuō*] the poor and needy, and not dealing justly with the stranger" (Ezekiel 22:29, LXE).

> "[A]nd oppress [*katadunesteuō*] not the widow, or the fatherless, or the stranger, or the poor; and let not one of you remember in his heart the injury of his brother" (Zechariah 7:10, LXE).

It has also been suggested that there might be some parallel between the rich dragging the poor into court, and the actions of Saul in persecuting many of the early Believers (Acts 9:1-2).

The intention of v. 6 is not to say that all rich people are of poor spiritual character, or that all poor people are of high spiritual character. The rich people in these assemblies were the same ones who would be the oppressive landowners, overseers, or merchants, with their main concern being their self-interest. McKnight points out, "Those using force against the poor messianists to prosecute are the *plousioi*, and this alone should give them pause about showing deference to preference to the rich."[26] The logic of trying to curry favor with the rich here, given their actions, is a bit confounding to James.

James' comments about the rich should not be viewed that he is condemning of all wealthy people. God desires to see that all come to the knowledge of salvation. Moo astutely comments, "James writes to a...community that is made up largely of poor people; and...for them it was evident on every side that God was choosing poor people to be saved. But to infer from James's positive assertion about poor people a negative verdict on rich people— God does not choose rich people to have faith—is unwarranted. Balance is perilously difficult to maintain on this issue."[27]

Money, like all Earthly things, is a tool. It can be used as a tool for good or a tool for evil. In far too many cases, it can be a tool for evil. Paul wrote Timothy, "For the love of money is a root of all sorts of evil, and some by longing for it have wandered away from the faith and pierced themselves with many griefs" (1 Timothy 6:10). Likewise, money can be used to further the Kingdom of God. *It all depends on how one uses it.* But being wealthy cannot be the goal of a person's life. Qohelet was forced to say, "He who loves money will not be satisfied with money, nor he who loves abundance *with its* income. This too is vanity" (Ecclesiastes 5:10). Being wealthy will not bring a person salvation or happiness. James was forced to observe that many of his readers were impressed by its appearance to cater to its demands,

---

[25] *LS*, 25.

[26] McKnight, 199.

[27] Moo, 107.

rather than equally serving all in the community of faith. James' audience too often forgot the Torah's admonitions to care for those who needed extra physical help.

7 Do they not blaspheme the fair name by which you have been called?

2:7 In v. 7 James observes, "Are they not the ones who blaspheme the honorable name by which you were called?" (ESV). The NIV renders this with, "Are they not the ones who are slandering the noble name of him to whom you belong?", although the verb *blasphēmeō* is what is actually employed. The rich who oppressed James' audience—were bringing some kind of disrepute, dishonor, slander, or ridicule upon them, hence, blasphemy—because of their dedicated faith in Yeshua. These were the same rich who were being given preferential treatment in the assembly. This problem is by no means something that was unique to the Jewish members of James' audience, but is something that is equally a First Century non-Jewish problem. It was, however—especially if these rich people regarded themselves as members of the faith community in some way—absolutely a travesty for James to conclude that **they were blasphemers of Lord.** Davids further explains,

"'The good name called upon you' is certainly the name of Jesus...The phrase 'to call a name upon one' is a septuagintalism, indicating possession or relationship, particularly relationship to God...Thus the blasphemy referred to indicates the reviling of the name of Jesus...By siding with the rich the [assembly] was siding with blasphemers!"[28]

James' audience is to be most aware of *to kalon onoma to epiklēthen ep' humas*, "that noble name by which you are called" (NKJV). Being called of the Lord into His salvation in Yeshua, reflecting it in the world, is quite serious (Romans 10:13; 1 Peter 4:14-16). Also to be considered is God's calling upon Israel, representing Him in the world (Deuteronomy 28:10), calling upon Him for national healing or deliverance (2 Chronicles 7:14), and how the nations are called by God's name into the final restoration of Israel's Kingdom (Amos 9:11-12)—something James himself acknowledged at the Jerusalem Council (Acts 15:15-18). Having the noble name of the Messiah invoked over the audience is something that incorporates many important concepts from the Tanach and Apostolic Scriptures, *and which is not limiting to Jews, Greeks, or Romans.* Ronald A. Ward especially observes, "The citation of Am. 9:12 in Acts 15:17, from the LXX, by James himself shows that he was of broader vision than some have supposed: Gentiles have civic rights in the [assembly] of Christ. Over them the name is invoked"[29] as well.

Why did these rich in v. 7 blaspheme? Was defaming the Lord Yeshua something simply in their nature? Whatever the specific negative motives, these rich were the product

---

[28] Davids, 113.
[29] Ronald A. Ward, "James," in D. Guthrie and J.A. Motyer, eds., *The New Bible Commentary Revised* (Grand Rapids: Eerdmans, 1970), 1227.

of a very poor spiritual condition. They thought that their wealth must have been sufficient for their security and salvation, and did not care too much about the needs of others.

8 If, however, you are fulfilling the royal law according to the Scripture, "YOU SHALL LOVE YOUR NEIGHBOR AS YOURSELF" [Leviticus 19:18]**, you are doing well.**

2:8 Even with James having just issued some firm admonitions to his audience about the problem of partiality (vs. 2-7), he gives an answer to their problems: "Supposing, however, you keep the royal law, as it is written, 'You shall love your neighbor as yourself'; if you do this, you will do well" (Kingdom New Testament). James makes light of "fulfilling the royal law," *nomon teleite basilikon*, which the CJB extrapolates as "truly attain[ing] the goal of Kingdom *Torah*." The emphasis here is how the Torah is to be kept in a mature and complete context for Believers. The foremost of all the commandments of Scripture is that God's people love Him and make Him the first priority in their lives. Out of that love for God will come a love for others. James partially quotes from Leviticus 19:18, "You shall not take vengeance, nor bear any grudge against the sons of your people, but you shall love your neighbor as yourself; I am the LORD." The Torah is fully brought to its goal when Messiah followers love other people—and not only love other people regardless of their status—but leave the judgment of other people to the Lord alone. The Leviticus 19:18 commandment has a very important place in the teachings of Yeshua (Matthew 22:39; Mark 12:31; Luke 10:27).

Various Christian interpreters have had to (significantly) struggle with what "the royal law" actually composes,[30] with some thinking that "law" in James 2:8 should only be regarded as a single commandment, perhaps as a so-called "law of Christ" widely, if not entirely, independent from the Mosaic Torah (often based on a mis-interpretation of Galatians 6:2).[31] Others see the commandment to love neighbor as summarizing the whole of the Torah itself. It is important that we review some perspectives. Richard Bauckham draws our attention to how very rarely in either the Greek Septuagint or Apostolic Scriptures does the term *nomos* represent a single piece of instruction, but rather the whole of the Torah. He favors v. 8 regarding a summation of the principle thrust of the Torah's code of conduct:

"Since in the LXX and NT 'law' *(nomos)* only very rarely refers to an individual commandment, it is unlikely that 'the royal law' (2:8) is the commandment to love the neighbor (Lev 19:18b) as one commandment among others (and 'royal' as sovereign over others). It must be understood as the commandment which summarizes the whole law...The law is 'royal' in that it pertains to the kingdom (2:5), and perhaps as interpreted by Jesus (with emphasis on the love commandment) in his preaching of the kingdom. James's point is that the law is a whole, summed up in Lev 19:18b, in which the prohibition of partiality is a necessary part. One cannot love one's neighbor while

---

[30] Cf. McKnight, pp 206-207.
[31] Witherington, pp 459-460.

dishonoring the poor. One cannot pick and choose which commandments to obey and be judged by."[32]

Davids also has to note how "the use of [*nomos*] instead of [*entolē*] makes it appear decisive that the whole law rather than a single command is intended."[33] While he does believe that the Torah or Moses' Teaching has been abolished for the post-resurrection era, noting 1:25, "the perfect law, the *law* of liberty," we should not find fault with the basic thrust of Moo: "the 'royal law' may well extend beyond the Mosaic law as fulfilled and reinterpreted by Jesus to include the teaching of Jesus."[34] McCartney might have the best approach, first asserting how "It is better to say that Lev. 19:18 gives expression to a controlling and central principle of God's ethical imperative for human conduct (cf. Gal. 5:14) and serves as a framework for understanding its parts."[35] He further observes, on the verb *teleō*:

> "[G]iven James's frequent use of the [*tele*-] stem (1:4 [2x], 17, 25; 2:8, 22; 3:2), its use here may be a deliberate emphasis of the comprehensive nature of Biblical ethics (2:10-11). For James, 'fulfilling' or carrying out the royal law is a piece with fulfilling or carrying through on faith by works in 2:22, where law is not set over against faith, but rather law and faith together are fulfilled or made complete by obedient action. Further, 2:8 connects with the fact that the law is a complete and perfect (...*teleios*) law (1:25), and it therefore does not admit of partial obedience (2:10), because all parts of the law come from one source (2:11)."[36]

Loving other people is one of the most important things that born again Believers should certainly be doing. It requires the redeemed in Yeshua, regardless of who they might be, to put aside any prejudice or preconceptions that they might have, serving the world at large so that others might be given a glimpse of God's Kingdom. *It is the essence of the Torah.* J. Ronald Blue validly indicates that it is called the "royal law" because "The law is royal or regal...because it is decreed by the King of kings, is fit for a king, and is considered the king of laws."[37] *TDNT* explains that the word *basilikos* "is fairly common in the NT...the reference is to law as it is given by the king, and thus having royal dignity, rather than to preeminent law."[38] To properly keep the command to love one's neighbor is to be a representative or ambassador of God's Kingdom in the world.

---

[32] Bauckham, in *ECB*, 1487.

[33] Davids, 114; cf. McCartney, 147.

[34] Moo, 112.

[35] McCartney, 147.

[36] Ibid.

[37] J. Ronald Blue," James," in John F. Walvoord and Roy B. Zuck, eds., *The Bible Knowledge Commentary: The New Testament* (Wheaton, IL: Victor Books, 1983), 825.

[38] K.L. Schmidt, "*basilikós*," in *TDNT*, 102.

For many of Yeshua's generation, loving one's neighbor was something that may not have always been something easy to do. First Century Israel was under Roman occupation, and the Jewish people, except for a brief period of independence following the Maccabean crisis of the Second Century B.C.E. with the Hasmoneans, had been dominated by foreign powers since the Babylonian dispersion. Loving others outside the community of Israel was admittedly something very difficult to do. Is this why Yeshua had to refer to this as a "new commandment" in John 13:34-35? "A new commandment I give to you, that you love one another, even as I have loved you, that you also love one another. By this all men will know that you are My disciples, if you have love for one another."

Yeshua does not refer to this as a "new commandment" in the sense that it was something brand new. It was likely, rather, something that had been forgotten by many of His generation. *CGEDNT* defines the word *kainos* as "*new; of new quality; unused; unknown, unheard of.*"[39] To many of Yeshua's generation, and sadly many today, the Scriptural admonition to love one's neighbor has become "an unused commandment." It is a reflection on our fallen human nature that we can only overcome with the Holy Spirit resident inside of us. Paul A. Cedar, reflecting from an evangelical Christian pastor's point of view, says, "Jesus understands that we cannot keep God's moral law. However, the problem was not with His law. In fact, His law is good. The problem is with us because we are too sinful to obey it (Rom. 8:1-4)."[40] How much more is this important for Messianic Believers who endeavor to keep *both* the moral and the outward aspects of the Torah? How much more do we have to ask for God's forgiveness when we fall, and not succumb to the temptations of the flesh which want us to do anything but love others?

In First Century Jewish thought, the Torah was thought of as being a royal road. This is based on Numbers 20:17, "Please let us pass through your land. We will not pass through field or through vineyard; we will not even drink water from a well. We will go along the king's highway, not turning to the right or left, until we pass through your territory." The Torah was to keep the traveler on the correct path, within defined boundaries during his Earthly sojourn. The philosopher Philo observed,

"[T]his royal road, which we have stated to be true and genuine philosophy, the law calls the word and reason of God; for it is written, 'Thou shalt not turn aside from the word which I command thee this day, to the right hand nor to the left,' So that it is shown most manifestly that the word of God is identical with the royal road, since Moses' words are not to depart either from the royal road, or from this word, as if the two were synonymous, but to proceed with an upright mind along the middle and level road, which leads one aright" (*The Posterity and Exile of Cain* 102).[41]

The Torah is likened unto a royal road, and the principal law which governs that road is that God's people love their neighbors. This is because as God's people travel the road of

---

[39] *CGEDNT*, 90.
[40] Cedar, 68.
[41] *The Works of Philo: Complete and Unabridged*, 142.

life, keeping the Torah's instructions, their testimony to other people should be indicated by how they love them. We have to treat them as Yeshua did, and we demonstrate ourselves to be citizens of God's Kingdom, reflecting His goodness, grace, and salvation to those in need.

Many well-meaning Christians think that loving God and one's neighbor is all that matters, and that various areas of outward conduct in other things are widely unimportant. These are often the ones who, unfortunately, look down upon Messianic Believers, be they Jewish or non-Jewish, who are convicted to keep the seventh-day Sabbath or *Shabbat*, the appointed times of Leviticus 23, and eat kosher. While loving God and one's neighbor are absolutely imperative, it does not stop there; in fact, that is where it begins. Our obedience to God comes as a natural outworking of the Spirit because we love Him. Martin is forced to conclude, "Though James is not limiting his thinking to the OT law with his use of 'supreme law,' neither is he advocating an abandoning of it."[42]

Nowhere in James' writing is he supposing that the outward observances of the Torah are nullified by the command to love others. On the contrary, James is trying to expand the depths of the Mosaic Torah in his words, to people who already were to know that they need to be loving others. From true love, fulfilling the "Kingdom Torah" as it were, people will not be prone to judge with evil motives (v. 4), and they will want to reach out to help those in need (v. 15). James is commenting on concepts that are by no means foreign to his predominantly Jewish audience, which would have been aware of the high regard for the Torah's morality that they should have been adhering to. The Talmud records the story of an outsider to Judaism who was told by Rabbi Hillel not to do hateful things to one's neighbor:

"There was another case of a gentile who came before Shammai. He said to him, 'Convert me on the stipulation that you teach me the entire Torah while I am standing on one foot.' He drove him off with the building cubit that he had in his hand. He came before Hillel: 'Convert me.' He said to him, "*What is hateful to you, to your fellow don't do.*" That's the entirety of the Torah; *everything else is elaboration. So go, study*"" (b.Shabbat 31a).[43]

According to this Jewish tradition, the Torah begins with loving one's neighbor. Every part of one's Torah obedience is to involve edifying other people, which as Believers **equates to us having a living and active testimony.** By loving others, we show them what God's Kingdom is all about, and our outward obedience to the Torah's commandments—especially via good works of mercy (vs. 13-14), is a part of that testimony. By others in the world seeing how God is able to bless us because of our obedience to Him, we will be able to share the message of salvation in Messiah Yeshua.

---

[42] Martin, 67.

[43] *The Babylonian Talmud: A Translation and Commentary.*

9 But if you show partiality, you are committing sin *and* are convicted by the law as transgressors. 10 For whoever keeps the whole law and yet stumbles in one *point*, he has become guilty of all.

2:9 James admonishes his audience, "But if you show favoritism, you are committing sin and are convicted by the *Torah* as transgressors" (TLV). Disobedience to God's Torah can come in some of the least likeliest of ways for various people, as showing partiality or favoritism toward sectors of people—which hence means that other people are not being issued a level of honor or respect in the assembly (vs. 2-3, 6)—is a certain violation of the command to love neighbor (v. 8). Love toward neighbor is to be impartial, as **all are to be loved**, not just those people of one's own choosing or preference. This can be, admittedly, very difficult for anyone to do, as human beings prefer to give attention to those whom they know will give them attention back. In the case of James' audience, preference was being shown toward the rich, at the expense of the poor.

2:10 The gravity of those who violate the commandment to love others (v. 8) is intensified by James, as he says, "For a person who keeps the whole *Torah*, yet stumbles at one point, has become guilty of breaking them all" (CJB). The NLT paraphrases his words, "the person who keeps all of the laws except one is as guilty as the person who has broken all of God's laws." Martin makes the keen observation, "it is this commandment in particular that transcends all others, and so to break it in essence casts one as intentionally rejecting the heart and soul of God's will, namely the love of one's neighbor."[44] Those who fail to love other people, no matter how much they may think they are keeping "all" of the Torah or Law of Moses, are found to not only be violators of such Instruction—but they may be said to quantitatively be contemptuous of it, because they have disregarded one of its most sacred principles. That the violation of a single commandment of the Torah, may be classified as a violation of the Torah's code as a whole (and likely a rejection of God Himself as well), is a sentiment detectable in Moses' Teaching itself, ancient Jewish literature, as well as by Yeshua the Messiah:

> "'Cursed is he who does not confirm the words of this law by doing them.' And all the people shall say, 'Amen'" (Deuteronomy 27:26).

> "[T]o transgress the law in matters either small or great is of equal seriousness, for in either case the law is equally despised" (4 Maccabees 5:20-21).

> "And who, some one perhaps, may say, ever escapes in-doors? Do not many do so? Or have not some people, avoiding the guilt of sacrilege, committed robberies in private houses, or though not beating their own fathers, have not they insulted the fathers of others? Now these men do escape from one class of offenses, but they run into others. But a man who is perfectly temperate, ought to avoid every description of offense,

---

[44] Martin, 69.

whether greater or less, and never to be detected in any sin whatever" (Philo *Allegorical Interpretation* 3.241).[45]

"One time R. Reuben spent the Sabbath in Tiberias, and a certain philosopher came across him. He said to him, 'What is most hateful in the world?' He said to him, 'This is one who denies the One who created it.' He said to him, 'How is it possible that [God] then said to [Moses], *Honor your father and your mother…, You shall not kill. You shall not commit adultery. You shall not steal. You shall not bear false witness against your neighbor. You shall not covet* (Ex. 20:12-17)?' [He said to him,] 'Lo, a person does not deny a matter of detail before he already has denied the main Principle, and a person does not turn to a matter of transgression unless he already has denied the One who gave a command concerning it'" (t.*Shevuot* 3:6).[46]

"Whoever then annuls one of the least of these commandments, and teaches others *to do* the same, shall be called least in the kingdom of heaven; but whoever keeps and teaches *them*, he shall be called great in the kingdom of heaven" (Matthew 5:19).

Keeping all of the Torah or Law of Moses, for James the Just, given the tenor of what he has been describing in his letter, pertains to being in observance of its extremely high, moral and ethical statutes such as the Ten Commandments (vs. 11-12). This is ultimately epitomized in how one follows and implements, *or fails to follow and implement*, the instruction to love neighbor (Leviticus 19:18). In McKnight's estimation,

"The person who does not love others, as the community has failed to love the poor (2:2-4), has broken the law of love from Leviticus. This infraction of the Law makes them not observant but *transgressors*. If one keeps the whole Law (2:10a) but breaks just one commandment (2:10b), one is assigned to the category of a transgressor who has, in effect, broken the whole (2:10c). Why? Because there are only two options: one is either observant or a transgressor."[47]

Many readers and examiners of the Epistle of James have been acclimated to think that this letter, in widely addressing a Jewish audience, perhaps only addressed First Century Jewish concerns, as v. 10 could be taken as only regarding Messianic Jewish observance of God's Torah. It is useful for us to keep in mind the sentiment of Isaiah 24:5: "The earth is also polluted by its inhabitants, for they transgressed laws, violated statutes, broke the everlasting covenant." The violation of God's *torot* is one which is universal to all of humanity, which means that it is every bit as much a problem for those of the nations as for Jewish people.[48] If those from the nations fail to love neighbor, or follow gross sins such as

---

[45] *The Works of Philo: Complete and Unabridged*, 78.
[46] Jacob Neusner, ed., *The Tosefta: Translated from the Hebrew With a New Introduction*, 2 vols. (Peabody, MA: Hendrickson, 2002), 2:1232.
[47] McKnight, 214.
[48] For a further review, consult the FAQ, "Isaiah 24:5."

idolatry or sexual immorality (Romans 1:22-32), it is as though they have violated all of the Torah or Law of Moses. **The only definite solution available, for such violation, is the sacrifice of Yeshua the Messiah at Golgotha** (Calvary) **for all human beings!**

Frequently, various Torah-positive Christian examiners have compared James' statement of v. 10, "For whoever keeps the whole law but fails in one point has become guilty of all of it" (RSV), as though God's Law may be compared to a broken sheet of glass. As Motyer observes,

"There is no way in which we can pick and choose between the commandments, because to break one is to break 'the law'....[T]he whole law of God is represented in every individual precept. Or, to put it another way, the law is not like a heap of stones but like a sheet of glass. We could take one stone from a heap and leave the heap itself still intact; but when we throw a brick through a window, it strikes only one place but it fragments the whole. The law of God is like the glass: a break at one point cannot be contained; the cracking and crazing spreads over the entire area."[49]

Obviously, there is specificity in the commandments of the Torah when one begins to classify them. Yet for the most part, all of the groups within Ancient Israel were expected to observe the same core series of commandments, and a daily observance of God's Law would be essentially the same for all (cf. Numbers 15:22-23; Deuteronomy 31:12).[50] One of the most critical aspects, of expressing fidelity to God's Torah, is heeding its instruction, regarding it as holy, authoritative, and the One who gave it as the Supreme Deity. If a command as rudimentary as loving neighbor can be broken, what is that to say about the rest of the commandments?

Motyer is a Christian examiner who recognizes the value of God's Law for those who intend to live a life like Jesus. He further states, "To take away a precept from the law is to damage the revelation of God which he has given us in his law. To say that one of the commands does not apply to me is to say that there is some aspect of the nature of God which does not matter, as far as I am concerned."[51] Obviously, there are commandments which do not apply to some people based on their station in life or gender/anatomy—but the point made is that willful omission of commandments, and/or remaining deliberately ignorant of Moses' Teaching, is tantamount to saying that God's holiness and righteousness cannot be learned by studying it. Surely, if born again Believers have been spiritually regenerated and have a new heart, then the Lord has written His commandments upon their hearts by His Spirit so that they might not only respect them, **but keep them** (Jeremiah 31:32-33; cf. Hebrews 8:10)!

Because we are human beings with fleshly limitations, it is going to be impossible for us to keep God's Torah perfectly. In the context of James' epistle, James is reflecting on the

---

[49] Motyer, 99.

[50] For a further discussion, consult the relevant sections of the *Messianic Torah Helper* by Messianic Apologetics.

[51] Motyer, 100.

fact that many of his readers have failed to follow the ethical guidelines of the Torah, and have demonstrated favoritism in dealing with diverse members of the assembly. As it relates to us as Messianic Believers today, who should be endeavoring to obey God—even though we should be striving to observe the Torah—we will still disobey it unintentionally. The Apostle Paul's steadfast word is, "all have sinned and fall short of the glory of God" (Romans 3:23). Thankfully, God has provided a way of salvation in Yeshua so we can be redeemed from the penalty of sin, eternal separation from Him.

Some contemporary Christians may choose to claim that since as human beings it is inevitable that we will falter, that we should not expel any effort as Believers to really keep God's Torah. *Is this an attitude of maturity?* Would not such a mentality merit a condition of least-ness in God's Kingdom (among other things)? As born again Believers who have the grace of God covering us, when we fall short, Messiah Yeshua's sacrifice is there to provide us with the assurance of our salvation, and that we have permanent forgiveness. Should we not be doing the best that we can, entreating the Lord every day to be guided by His Spirit and a course of obedience, rather than be (completely) ignoring the Instruction of God? If we do not strive for godly obedience, then we could find ourselves in the state of many people who think they will enter into Heaven because they are just "good people," and fooling themselves in the process.

There are many people in Western society, who believe in God and believe themselves to be "Christian," namely because they were raised in a cultural Christianity, who think they will enter into Heaven because they have done more good deeds than they have done bad deeds. Unfortunately, the person who has violated the smallest principle of the Torah has become a lawbreaker. This person is condemned by the Torah as a sinner. By Yeshua's sacrifice on the cross at Golgotha (Calvary), that sentence has been commuted. But we have to ask God to forgive us of our sin and we must repent. When we receive the new birth, we are enabled to obey the Father through the empowerment of His Holy Spirit, and the penalty of eternal punishment has been lifted.[52]

11 For He who said, "DO NOT COMMIT ADULTERY" [Exodus 20:14; Deuteronomy 5:18], **also said, "DO NOT COMMIT MURDER"** [Exodus 20:13; Deuteronomy 5:17]**. Now if you do not commit adultery, but do commit murder, you have become a transgressor of the law. 12 So speak and so act as those who are to be judged by *the* law of liberty. 13 For judgment *will be* merciless to one who has shown no mercy; mercy triumphs over judgment.**

2:11 James provides some further specification to what he means concerning those who might claim to keep the whole Torah, but then violates one of its commandments. Rather

---

[52] For a further discussion, consult the author's article "The Assurance of Our Salvation," appearing in his book *Introduction to Things Messianic*.

than focus on smaller ordinances or regulations of the Torah—which might be violated out of ignorance or unintentional human omission—statutes from the Ten Commandments themselves are instead highlighted. James states, "For the one who said, 'Do not commit adultery,' also said, 'Do not commit murder.' Now if you do not commit adultery but do commit murder, you have become a transgressor of the *Torah*" (TLV). James says that it is inconsistent for a person not to commit adultery, but to commit murder—hence meaning that if a person keeps one command of the Torah, but breaks another command, this person is still guilty in the eyes of God.

Readers are rightly led to consider the thought of Yeshua in His Sermon on the Mount, where He says that if a person intends to murder or commit adultery in the heart, or perform particular acts which could lead to these sins, then the person is already guilty of breaking the commandment:

"You have heard that the ancients were told, 'YOU SHALL NOT COMMIT MURDER' and 'Whoever commits murder shall be liable to the court.' But I say to you that everyone who is angry with his brother shall be guilty before the court; and whoever says to his brother, 'You good-for-nothing,' shall be guilty before the supreme court; and whoever says, 'You fool,' shall be guilty *enough to go* into the fiery hell...You have heard that it was said, 'YOU SHALL NOT COMMIT ADULTERY'; but I say to you that everyone who looks at a woman with lust for her has already committed adultery with her in his heart" (Matthew 5:21-23, 27-28).

Aside from the fact that the Torah prohibitions against murder and adultery, highlighted by James in v. 11, are not only quite serious but were engraved in stone upon the tablets of the Ten Commandments—might there be any additional reason as to why an avoidance of adultery, but a committal of murder, is highlighted here? As it specifically concerns the material James is communicating to his audience, there are references in Jeremiah, which associate murder with mistreatment of the poor, the very group of people that various members of James' audience have been accused of ignoring (vs. 5-6):

"[I]f you do not oppress the alien, the orphan, or the widow, and do not shed innocent blood in this place, nor walk after other gods to your own ruin" (Jeremiah 7:6).

"Thus says the LORD, 'Do justice and righteousness, and deliver the one who has been robbed from the power of *his* oppressor. Also do not mistreat *or* do violence to the stranger, the orphan, or the widow; and do not shed innocent blood in this place'" (Jeremiah 22:2).

Perhaps there were members of James' audience who prided themselves on being sexually chaste and virtuous. What would this mean if they dishonored the poor, not providing them with the essentials of life (v. 15)? Could it be regarded as a kind of murder? Because favoritism or showing partiality was a serious problem that James has to address, by failing to give the poor in the congregation required support, which would include seeing that they were properly fed, those violating the Torah would be, in essence, guilty of "murder via starvation."

2:12 Rather than see his audience overlooking and breaking some of the Torah's most significant directions for God's people, James' admonition is "So speak and so act as those who will be judged according to a *Torah* that gives freedom" (TLV). Many Christians have struggled with James' emphasis on Messiah followers being judged "by *the* law of liberty" (NASU), or "by the law that treats them as free" (Williams New Testament), because it is a very clear example of how positive a figure like James viewed God's Torah for born again Believers. A Reformer like John Calvin notably took "the law of liberty" to represent how sinners who are forgiven by God, have been remitted from the curse or condemnation of the Torah:

"The law of liberty...is equivalent to God's clemency, which frees us from the curse of the Law. So we must take this, and what follows, in the one context of being tolerant towards weakness. This line of argument flows very well: since none of us would stand in God's presence if we were not absolved and made free from the rigorous application of the Law, our actions should follow like a course, and not exclude God's generosity by over-severity; in the end, we all need the same."[53]

What James has previously referred to as *nomon basilikon*, "the royal law" (2:8), is further detailed to be *nomou eleutherias*, "the law of liberty" (2:12). Such a "law that gives freedom" (NIV) is widely considered to be the summation of the Torah to the high principle of loving one's neighbor: "Do not take revenge, nor bear a grudge against the children of your people. You shall love your fellow as [you love] yourself, I am the LORD" (Leviticus 19:18, Keter Crown Bible). This can be undoubtedly connected to Yeshua's imperatives "Blessed are the merciful, for they shall receive mercy" (Matthew 5:7), "And forgive us our debts, as we also have forgiven our debtors" (Matthew 6:12).[54]

Interpreters of the Epistle of James are divided as to whether or not there is really a major break intended between "the royal law" of love for God and neighbor, and the Torah of Moses. Is *nomon basilikon* something which is contrary to the Torah of Moses? Martin thinks, "The antitheses of the Sermon on the Mount in Matthew 5:21-48 make the same point, namely, that the new law of love sets a higher standard than Torah obedience can demand and produce."[55] But is the command to love one's neighbor, Leviticus 19:18, really totally "new" to the First Century—or simply something that needed to be reemphasized and would be viewed as "new" by many in Yeshua's and James' audiences?[56]

---

[53] Calvin, 281.

[54] Witherington, 462 also notes how "The theme of mercy is common in wisdom literature (Sirach 27.30-28.7)."

[55] Martin, 71.

[56] The term *kainos*, appearing in John 13:34, can "**pert. to being not previously present, unknown, strange, remarkable**" (BDAG, 496) or simply "*unknown, unheard of*" (CGEDNT, 90). Yeshua's reference to *entolēn*

The issue of the Torah needing to be obeyed by Messiah followers—emphasized by James as "the royal law" focused around the directive to love others—is something that makes various commentators feel a bit uncomfortable. Moo has to still conclude, though, "the law in question here is not the OT law as such, but the OT as reinterpreted and imposed by Christ on his followers."[57] No Bible reader can honestly disagree with the claim that the Messiah's interpretation and application of Moses' Teaching, as is principally seen in His Sermon on the Mount (Matthew chs. 5-7) and commented on by figures such as James, needs to be steadfastly remembered. Such an obedience with the Messiah's self-sacrificial example of service, and kindness to others as prime, is something that none of us should ever be found dismissing. McCartney's words are well taken here:

"[T]he law of the kingdom of God is complete, kingly, and liberating. The liberating law of the kingdom (i.e., Jesus's view of the law), by which believers are to reckon that they will be judged, is also the law into which the godly gaze (1:25) and remember to do....[T]o behave as those about to be judged by the law of freedom is to remember mercy and justice and thereby to proclaim liberty. God is merciful and just; therefore, Christians must be merciful and just."[58]

That all born again Believers should be committed to following "the law of liberty," whereby the ways of the Creator can be known and enacted to all human beings—the true thrust of Micah 6:8, "He has told you, O man, what is good; and what does the LORD require of you but to do justice, to love kindness, and to walk humbly with your God?"—**is paramount to a healthy and active faith in Messiah Yeshua.** James has stated earlier, "But one who looks intently at the perfect law, the *law* of liberty, and abides by it, not having become a forgetful hearer but an effectual doer, this man will be blessed in what he does" (1:25).

It cannot go overlooked how the RSV has rendered v. 12 with, "So speak and so act as those who are to be judged under the law of liberty." The clause in question is *dia nomou eleutherias*, with the preposition *dia*. When used with a genitive case noun (indicating possession), *dia* should be viewed as "*through, by means of, with; during, throughout*" (*CGEDNT*).[59] The NRSV correctly changed the rendering of *dia nomou eleutherias* to "by the law of liberty," following the KJV before it. The HCSB has the similar, "by the law of freedom." Even a significantly paraphrased version like The Message has, "by the Rule that sets us free."

---

kainēn or "a new commandment" could very easily relate to how *properly embodying* the Torah command to love had gone out of favor.

[57] Moo, *James*, 117.

[58] McCartney, pp 149, 150.

[59] *CGEDNT*, 41.

Why a version like the RSV[60] chose to render *dia nomou eleutherias*—which would be best translated as either "by *the* law of liberty" (NASU) or "through the law of liberty"—with "under the law of liberty," has to be because of theological reasons. A clause correctly rendered as "under [the] law of liberty" would be *hupo [ton] nomon tēs eleutherias*. One can only speculate that those who render *dia nomou eleutherias*, "through/by the law of liberty," as "under the law of liberty," want such a law of liberty to be viewed as independent from the Torah of Moses *and* to supplant and replace the rightful position of the Torah of Moses in the hearts and minds of born again Believers. Such people are thought to not be "under the Law *of Moses*," but instead "under {a separate} law of liberty." (It is the author's position that the correct view of "under the Law," in contrast to "under grace," actually regards its condemnation pronounced upon sinners.)[61] Yet what the Greek of James 2:12 says is that people are to be judged "through/by the law of liberty," which is correctly concluded to be the Torah of Moses as interpreted through the ministry and actions of Yeshua the Messiah, and early Messianic leaders like James the Just. Davids rightly confirms,

"'[T]he law of liberty,' which, as has already been observed (cf. 1:25), is nothing less than the law of Moses as interpreted (and to some extent altered) by Jesus and the early church, which took its cues from Jesus. This standard, which focuses on the example of Jesus and thus the command of love, should cause all to examine their lives and channel them into obedience to Jesus' commands (cf. Mt. 7:15-23; Lk. 6:43-45)."[62]

Yeshua the Messiah surely upheld the Torah principle of love for God and one's neighbor being primary, the same as various Rabbis like Hillel contemporary to His time (b.*Shabbat* 31a).[63] In fact, Yeshua requires that the righteousness of His followers exceed that of the scribes and Pharisees (Matthew 5:20), whose human standard was fairly high. Given how adherence to their strict regulations can be impossible for many of us, entry into God's Kingdom must be ultimately reliant upon His magnificent grace and mercy! Obedience to His Instruction, though, is still expected of the faithful who love Him and who want to please Him. Motyer's observations on what the royal law involves, and how obedience is expected of the redeemed, are quite excellent:

"First, because it is *the royal law*, the law that in a special sense belongs to the king, we would *wish* to obey it—simply because he would specially desire us to do so. Secondly, because it is a command of the law of God, we *must* obey it. To dismiss it is to dismiss the facet of the Glory of God which it represents; to leave it to others is to say that it is

---

[60] The ESV, which is part of the same translation family, follows the same rendering of James 2:12 as does the RSV: "So speak and so act as those who are to be judged under the law of liberty."

[61] Consult the author's article "What Does 'Under the Law' Really Mean?—A Further Study" (appearing in *The New Testament Validates Torah*). The following passages are addressed: Galatians 3:23; 4:4-5, 21; 5:18; 1 Corinthians 9:20-22; Romans 6:14-15; James 2:12; Romans 2:12; 3:19; 3:6; Hebrews 7:11; 9:22; Luke 2:27.

[62] Peter Davids, *New International Greek Testament Commentary: The Epistle of James* (Grand Rapids: Eerdmans, 1982), 118.

[63] "'*What is hateful to you, to your fellow don't do.*' That's the entirety of the Torah; *everything else is elaboration. So go, study*" (b.*Shabbat* 31a; *The Babylonian Talmud: A Translation and Commentary*).

immaterial whether this part of the Lord's likeness is seen in me. It comes to us as a revelation of God, and with his authority, therefore we must obey it. But, thirdly, it is part of *the law of liberty*, and therefore we can obey it."[64]

The freedom or liberty James talks about in v. 12 relates to the fact that born again Believers have experienced a remission from the penalties of condemnation, which originates from violating the Torah's commandments. *Those, who have liberty or freedom, have the forgiveness of sins accessible via the gospel.* Consequent obedience to God's commandments comes as an outworking of the love that the redeemed are to have for Him, concurrent with the supernatural compulsion to obey present in the New Covenant (Jeremiah 31:31-34; Ezekiel 36:25-27). As the Psalmist has said, "I will walk about in freedom, for I have sought out your precepts" (Psalm 119:45, NIV). When the redeemed in Yeshua keep the Torah through the empowerment of the Holy Spirit, they should indeed find themselves to be free and blessed people.

It is interesting that many Messianic people will quote Matthew 7:22-23, in reference to Yeshua telling those who performed miracles in His name, "DEPART FROM ME, YOU WHO PRACTICE LAWLESSNESS" (cf. Psalm 6:8), and apply it to many Christians. However, we have to keep in mind that "lawlessness" (*anomia*) entails much more than just failing to keep the seventh-day Sabbath, appointed times, or kosher dietary laws. It also applies every bit as much to our ethics, and whether or not we have hatred, adultery, theft, or covetousness in our hearts. Are there going to be some who say to Yeshua, "But didn't we keep the Sabbath and the feasts?" when they had an improper attitude toward others? **May it not be so!** If this indeed happens, then such people would be found committing lawlessness because they failed to have love for their fellow human beings, which James has stated is the quintessential proof of keeping God's Torah (v. 8). *People definitely transgress the Torah when they fail to love others...*

2:13 If a man or woman has been redeemed by Yeshua the Messiah, and can thusly be judged via the Torah/Law of liberty/freedom (v. 12)—then James understandably communicates, "judgment without mercy will be shown to anyone who has not been merciful. Mercy triumphs over judgment!" (NIV). Mercy (Heb. *racham*; Grk. *eleos*) doubtlessly involves a person having the right attitudes and approach toward other people, in the value that we place on one another, and in the case of James' audience, treating those in the assembly with a wide degree of equity. In James' specific situation, there would be those who discriminated against others in the assembly based on their appearance, and could very well be in danger of being judged by God without any mercy. Mercy is a Divine characteristic of the Lord that can only be properly exercised by those who have received it from Him, and have been spiritually regenerated. The importance of mercy is highlighted in the Tanach, Pseudepigrapha, Apocrypha, and the teaching of Yeshua:

---

[64] Motyer, pp 100-101.

"He will again have compassion on us; He will tread our iniquities under foot. Yes, You will cast all their sins into the depths of the sea. You will give truth to Jacob *and* unchanging love to Abraham, which You swore to our forefathers from the days of old" (Micah 7:19-20).

"Thus has the LORD of hosts said, 'Dispense true justice and practice kindness and compassion each to his brother; and do not oppress the widow or the orphan, the stranger or the poor; and do not devise evil in your hearts against one another'" (Zechariah 7:9-10).

"You also, my children, have compassion toward every person with mercy, in order that the Lord may be compassionate and merciful to you" (*Testament of Zebulun* 8:1).[65]

"He that takes vengeance will suffer vengeance from the Lord, and he will firmly establish his sins. Forgive your neighbor the wrong he has done, and then your sins will be pardoned when you pray. Does a man harbor anger against another, and yet seek for healing from the Lord? Does he have no mercy toward a man like himself, and yet pray for his own sins? If he himself, being flesh, maintains wrath, who will make expiation for his sins? Remember the end of your life, and cease from enmity, remember destruction and death, and be true to the commandments. Remember the commandments, and do not be angry with your neighbor; remember the covenant of the Most High, and overlook ignorance. Refrain from strife, and you will lessen sins; for a man given to anger will kindle strife, and a sinful man will disturb friends and inject enmity among those who are at peace" (Sirach 28:1-9).

"Blessed are the merciful, for they shall receive mercy" (Matthew 5:7).

Human beings, with a fallen sin nature, often have a serious challenge in restraining themselves from judging others, without a degree of fairness and temperance. Yet for those of us who claim to know Yeshua the Messiah as our Personal Savior, the requirement to act with mercy and kindness to others, *should* come as second nature. Even if this comes more easily for some, and more difficult for others, demonstrating grace to all we encounter is a character trait which is to be steadily inculcated into us as we mature in faith. This involves treating other people with respect, decency, and above all, love. James surely relied on his audience to understand these critical concepts, especially for the Jewish members of his audience who would have been exposed to the concept of "mercy" from a variety of potential, ancient sources.

One of the most critical parts of showing mercy to other people is forgiveness. Yeshua Himself said, "For if you forgive others for their transgressions, your heavenly Father will also forgive you. But if you do not forgive others, then your Father will not forgive your

[65] H.C. Kee, trans., "Testaments of the Twelve Patriarchs," in James H. Charlesworth, ed., *The Old Testament Pseudepigrapha*, Vol 1 (New York: Doubleday, 1983), 807.

transgressions" (Matthew 6:14-15). In some places, it can appear as though Yeshua made forgiving other people for wrongs done a prerequisite to be forgiven by the Father. Certainly, anyone who has been truly forgiven by God should be willing to forgive other people for wrongs done to them. This forgiveness is not only required once, but is continually required to be given of true followers of the Lord. As is further stated in Matthew 18:21-22

"Then Peter came and said to Him, 'Lord, how often shall my brother sin against me and I forgive him? Up to seven times?' Yeshua said to him, 'I do not say to you, up to seven times, but up to seventy times seven.'"

Out of a true forgiveness that we receive from God, is able to come His Divine mercy that we may show toward others when we are wronged. When matters come before us in life that require that we make judgments, evaluations, or various types of decisions, these must originate from a merciful and fair-minded spirit which considers the needs of others. When we exercise this mercy, God is able to bless us. Specifically referenced by James in v. 13 are those who have never shown mercy. Because true mercy is something that can only be produced by God's Holy Spirit, was James subtly admonishing his readers to see whether they truly have that salvation? It is probably fair to assess that much of James' audience had simply relapsed into old patterns of behavior, and that they were people who had truly been shown mercy and had demonstrated genuine mercy—the same as many of us today needing to be admonished to show mercy, when old, pre-salvation attitudes briefly try to influence us.

There may also be a warning issued in James' words for Messianic Believers today. How many people in the Messianic community today believe themselves to be Torah observant, but do not show a great amount of mercy, grace, love, or forbearance? How many demonstrate that they are harboring unforgiveness toward their Christian brothers and sisters who do not practice their faith exactly the same way? James' word for us as Messianics is that if you consider yourself a Torah observant Messianic Believer, you are to always show mercy and grace to other people, especially those other Believers who need to see our example of faith, and be properly led by a positive example which exudes God's mercy *par excellence*. The consequence of us not doing this could be a merciless judgment by God, finding ourselves judged by the full letter of the Law and its condemnation, indicating that someone may never have truly partaken of His mercy available in Messiah Yeshua.

14 What use is it, my brethren, if someone says he has faith but he has no works? Can that faith save him? 15 If a brother or sister is without clothing and in need of daily food, 16 and one of you says to them, "Go in peace, be warmed and be filled," and yet you do not give them what is necessary for *their* body, what use is that? 17 Even so faith, if it has no works, is dead, *being* by itself.

2:14-26 James 2:14-26 has been a very difficult section of this letter for many Christians to read, contemplate, and interpret throughout history, as it can be improperly approached from the perspective that human actions merit eternal salvation. Sometimes this has been caused by various lay readers only pulling out a verse, or clause or two, here or there—and not expelling a huge amount of consideration or attention for the issue(s) actually being discussed by James, *or* for that matter some more involved approaches to the topics of righteousness and justification, which might not involve a remission of sins at all. In 2:14-26, it is most important to be aware of how James posits the position of a person who purports to have faith, yet such a self-claimed faith is not one which has been followed by the proper works or actions. This particularly regarded the works and actions of kindness, mercy, and service toward those in need, rooted within the high ethical and moral imperatives of God's Torah.

2:14 James remarks how it is impossible to have a faith without works, stating, "What good is it, my brothers and sisters, if people claim to have faith but have no deeds? Can such faith save them?" (TNIV). While rendered as "What use is it" (NASU) or "What good is it" (NIV), *ophelos*, can also allow for a translation such as, "What does it profit" (RSV). It means "to heap up. Increase, profit, meaning furtherance, advantage" (*AMG*).[66] The NLT has a good paraphrase of this verse: "Dear brothers and sisters, what's the use of saying you have faith if you don't prove it by your actions? That kind of faith can't save anyone." V. 14 has been a cause of considerable confusion because James asks his audience how a faith without works can actually be demonstrated to have the value or capacity, of being able to save a person. Faith not evidenced by the appropriate works, actions, or deeds will not do anyone any good—because such a faith really does not have any substantial profit. **Faith without an incumbent supernatural impetus to perform actions reflective of the Holy God who saves sinners, is something with no real value.**

When James made these remarks, he was trying to instill in his readers a desire to obey God fully, and have them realize that they have a great responsibility as representatives of His Kingdom on Earth. Jewish tradition of the First Century held that the Patriarch Abraham's righteousness was demonstrated by his deeds, a sentiment which James' readers should have been familiar with. 1 Maccabees 2:51-52 attests, "Remember the deeds of the fathers, which they did in their generations; and receive great honor and an everlasting name. Was not Abraham found faithful when tested, and it was reckoned to him as

---

[66] Spiros Zodhiates, ed., *Complete Word Study Dictionary: New Testament* (Chattanooga: AMG Publishers, 1993), 1081.

righteousness?" As many of James' listeners were no doubt facing some trials, James was appealing to their common knowledge of Tanach Scripture, and the fact that the actions or works that Messiah followers perform in trials, are what cause Believers to mature. Such is the place where they are truly able to demonstrate their faith and put it into practice, where perhaps an intellectual ascent to the faith can naturally translate over into faithfulness to the will of God.

The challenge for many Christian theologians over the centuries has been what often appears to be, at least on the surface, an irreconcilable view of "works" from the writing of James the Just and the letters of the Apostle Paul. While James asked his readers if a faith without works has the power to save an individual, Paul widely considered human works or actions to be powerless to save an individual. Ephesians 2:8-9 states candidly, "For by grace you have been saved through faith; and that not of yourselves, *it is* the gift of God; not as a result of works, so that no one may boast." Here, human actions are targeted as **not** being the *source* or *cause* of eternal salvation, as eternal salvation is the free gift of God's grace. In James 2:14, the *quality* or *main value* of one's faith, which is to involve the appropriate works, is what is in view. This is not in contradiction with the Apostle Paul, for as Ephesians 2:10 following says, "For we are His workmanship, created in Messiah Yeshua for good works, which God prepared beforehand so that we would walk in them." Paul envisioned a Messiah faith for people that would involve Believers walking in good works.

It has, to be sure, been thought that while quantitatively James and Paul are not at all at odds with one another, that in their respective ministry services, they were having to address and confront some miscommunication that had occurred regarding their teachings. *James and Paul were not at odds, but others misconstrued their teachings.* It is hard to say if some of Paul's earlier letters like Galatians or 1&2 Thessalonians preceded the composition of the Epistle of James, but is it not difficult to assume that many in the audience of James were also familiar with or had heard some of Paul's teachings, and perhaps misunderstood them. Moo addresses some of this, observing,

"The readers of the letter, scattered by persecution into areas near Antioch, have become acquainted with a perverted form of the Pauline viewpoint, with the slogan 'faith alone justifies' as its hallmark. James writes, then, to counter this false view of the relationship between faith, works, and salvation. James and Paul, when properly interpreted in their own contexts, are not opposed to one another on this point. They give the appearance of a conflict because they are writing from very different vantage points in order to combat very different problems."[67]

It is valid to say, especially with what will follow in vs. 15-16, that the works which James is primarily looking to see manifest in the lives of Messiah followers, include acts of mercy, kindness, and love. They are essentially humanitarian deeds that contemporary Christians of all shapes and sizes believe are absolutely vital for Believers to demonstrate to

---

[67] Moo, 121.

others in our world. But it is inappropriate to say that other outward works of observance are also not implied in his statements as well. Our love to one another should be demonstrated in our attitudes toward one another, but likewise our proper attitude toward God should be demonstrated by how we obey Him in our weekly and seasonal routines, and how we identify ourselves as part of His collective people. James, the half-brother of Yeshua, continued to be quite Torah observant even until his death, as the historical record attests (see **Introduction**).

True faith is evidenced by a person's actions in the world, which demonstrate that such faith not only has great value, but is actually something that can change lives and how people reorient themselves to accomplishing the will of God, and not their own self-interest. These works are not to be forced as an act of the flesh—but should come naturally because of one's love for God and commitment to spiritual growth and continual perfection, such good works serving as a testimony to the world of one's salvation experience.

Yeshua says, "Let your light shine before men in such a way that they may see your good works, and glorify your Father who is in heaven" (Matthew 5:16). Ancient Israel was told, "So keep and do *them*, for that is your wisdom and your understanding in the sight of the peoples who will hear all these statutes and say, 'Surely this great nation is a wise and understanding people'" (Deuteronomy 4:6), as keeping the Torah's instruction was to be a testimony to the heathen nations around them. *This is why God wants all of us to have works.* A true faith or belief in God will be demonstrated by our works as part of the whole salvation experience. Salvation is not just being saved from eternal punishment, but encompasses a transformation of our hearts and minds that will enable us to have the good works that He desires of us. **A faith not demonstrated by outward actions is not a faith at all.**

2:15-16 James provides some specific examples of works in vs. 15-16, which God expects His people to have. He opens by stating, "If a brother or sister is without clothing and in need of daily food" (v. 15), with some versions rendering *gumnos* as either "ill-clad" (RSV) or "naked" (NRSV). Whether some purposeful exaggeration is intended or not, the point made is that there are not just people in the world at large—but within the faith community itself—who lack the life essentials of food and clothing. The works or deeds required by people of faith, are most especially going to involve seeing that such life essentials are provided to those who do not have them.

Yeshua talks about those who require physical care, by saying, "For I was hungry, and you gave Me *something* to eat; I was thirsty, and you gave Me *something* to drink; I was a stranger, and you invited Me in" (Matthew 25:35). The Apostle John observed, "We know love by this, that He laid down His life for us; and we ought to lay down our lives for the brethren. But whoever has the world's goods, and sees his brother in need and closes his heart against him, how does the love of God abide in him? Little children, let us not love with word or with tongue, but in deed and truth" (1 John 3:16-18). The Apostle Paul also spoke of "faith working through love" (Galatians 5:6) and "your work of faith and labor of love and steadfastness of hope in our Lord Yeshua the Messiah" (1 Thessalonians 1:3), which would all involve the necessary acts of mercy needed for one's fellow brothers and sisters in the faith.

Upon noticing the condition of the needy brother or sister, James observes how "one of you [may say] to them, 'Go in peace, be warmed and be filled'" (v. 16a), or "say "Shalom! Keep warm and eat hearty!" (CJB)—but then fail to offer any real help in any way. Somehow, a greeting of "peace" to a person, without any effort expelled to provide those who are without, with what they need, is considered to be an insufficient "work" demonstrated by those claiming faith.

James' reference to "peace" (Heb. shalom; Grk. eirēnē) is actually quite serious. In the Hebrew Tanach, "'Peace'...means much more than mere absence of war. Rather, the root meaning of the verb shālēm better expresses the true concept of shālôm. Completeness, wholeness, harmony, fulfillment, are closer to the meaning. Implicit in shālôm is the idea of unimpaired relationships with others and fulfillment in one's undertakings" (TWOT).[68] To wish God's "peace" upon a person should be taken that you wish somebody all of these great things. Presumably, a mature man or woman of God should be able to offer God's peace in some tangible form, to those who lack it. While this involves demonstrating a kind and graceful demeanor, it might also very much involve providing resources so that people can eat, be clothed, and have a place to live. To express so-called "peace" to a person, and then deny others in need by not demonstrating proper action, is tantamount to mockery of God.[69]

Unfortunately, for many in James' audience, wishing "peace" upon those who were in desperate need of physical help, reveals a somewhat shallow or selective faith on their part. James rebuked those who had a defective faith which was devoid of outward deeds—which really should have come as second nature to those following a Torah ethic, and were committed to the teachings of Yeshua the Messiah. James asks, "without giving them the things needed for the body, what good is that?" (v. 16b, ESV), and he will use this statement as a remark to chastise his audience for dead faith (v. 17). The thought in view is that if one cannot see to provide the basic physical essentials to a fellow brother or sister in the faith, but yet wish them peace, how on Earth can other commandments of God be kept properly? How can the God of Creation, who desires that all people be reconciled to Himself via His Son, at all be represented properly?

2:17 James has just highlighted the poor and needy, who require clothing and food, and how it is absurd to simply wish them "peace," but then proceed to do nothing about seeing such peace enacted within their lives. James is clear, "faith by itself, if it has no works, is dead" (RSV). The Phillips New Testament has, "a bare faith without a corresponding life is...quite dead." For James' audience, those who failed to offer the necessary care for others without, were regarded as having a lifeless faith, perhaps not reflective of people who had

---

[68] G. Lloyd Carr, "shālôm," in TWOT, 2:931.
[69] McCartney, 157.

been spiritually regenerated by the good news of Yeshua (v. 14). As Davids summarizes, "The so-called faith which fails to produce works...is simply not 'saving faith.'"[70]

Yet while in the case of James' ancient circumstances, the works or deeds of physical service toward fellow members of the Body of Messiah were lacking—what kinds of actions might be lacking by Believers today, who claim to express some kind of fidelity to the Holy Scriptures? Many of today's Messianic people have approached James 2:17 from the perspective that contemporary Christians who fail to observe the seventh-day Sabbath/*Shabbat*, appointed times of Leviticus 23, or eat a kosher diet, may not be saved. (Keep in mind that only our Eternal God ultimately knows who, and who is not, "saved.") While it is absolutely true that there are Christian persons who want nothing to do with God's Torah or their Hebraic Roots, there are also sincere evangelical Christians who are very much accomplishing the works of kindness and service emphasized by James (v. 15). These are the people—who if they can be shown a Torah observance by Messianics that exudes the grace and kindness of God at an excelsior level—may be convinced that a Messianic perspective is worthy of consideration. Alas, demonstrating such a mature faith, and being cautious to control our speech and attitudes (1:19-21; 3:2-11; 4:8), has not always been the easiest thing to do for our current Messianic generation.

18 But someone may *well* say, "You have faith and I have works; show me your faith without the works, and I will show you my faith by my works."

2:18 James posits the position of one who may be regarded as an imaginary, or hypothetical opponent, which serves the purpose of not having to be embarrassingly specific with any one person or sub-group among his audience, which has erred. He summarizes, "supposing someone says, 'Well: you have faith, and I have works.' All right; show me your faith—but without doing any works; and then I will show you *my* faith, and I'll do it by my works!" (Kingdom New Testament). The crux of what James is trying to communicate, is how a true faith which has changed people, has to be demonstrated via works. The verb *deiknumi* can mean "**to exhibit someth. that can be apprehended by one or more of the senses, *point out, show, make known*,**" or "**to prove or make clear by evidence or reasoning, *explain, prove***" (BDAG).[71] It is impossible, in James' estimation, to demonstrate a faith without works/deeds/actions.

James places an emphasis on *ek tōn ergōn mou tēn pistin*, "out of my works my faith" (YLT). Contrary to popular belief among many contemporary Christians, this is not in contradiction with the Apostle Paul, who definitely spoke of *pistis di' agapēs energoumenē*, "faith working through love" (Galatians 5:6). There is no doubting that among the many

---

[70] Davids, 122.

[71] *BDAG*, pp 214, 215.

"works" that James would have expected his audience to steadfastly adhere to, would have included those distinct virtues, or fruit of the Spirit classified by Paul (Galatians 5:22-23).[72]

19 You believe that God is one. You do well; the demons also believe, and shudder. 20 But are you willing to recognize, you foolish fellow, that faith without works is useless?

2:19 James is quite serious about the faith of his audience being followed by appropriate works. To really hammer hard this point, he informs them, "You believe that God is one; you do well. Even the demons believe -- and shudder" (RSV). The statement "God is one" (*eis estin ho Theos*) is taken directly from the *Shema* of Deuteronomy 6:4: "Hear, O Israel! The LORD is our God, the LORD is one!"; *Shema Yisrael, ADONAI Eloheinu, ADONAI echad*. The *Shema*, for both ancient Judaism and modern Judaism, remains something repeated multiple times, every day, in traditional prayers (and is also present in many traditional liturgies of many Christian sects). And, the *Shema* definitely served as a part of the Messianic understanding of God in the Apostolic Scriptures (i.e., 1 Corinthians 8:4-6). Aside from the different dynamics regarding the *Shema* and the co-existence of the Father and Son in the Godhead, the *Shema* is principally a declaration on the supremacy of the God of Israel in the lives of His people. Those who declare that He is the God of Creation, are bidden to Him exclusively.[73]

James observes on the fact that the forces of Satan also believe in this same God, and they shudder. Demons can recognize who God is, and they acknowledge His existence, likely having a far more tangible understanding of His supernatural reality than most mortals do. But simply because demons may acknowledge God, it can do nothing for them, except instill a high level of fear into them, as their eternal damnation is secure. Davids comments to this regard, on how "the NT knows of the monotheism of demons (Mk. 1:24; 5:7; Acts 16:17; 19:15) and their fear before Christ, whom they recognize (Mk. 1:23, 24; 5:7). The point is that their knowledge of who God is does not save them; in fact, it is this very knowledge of which makes them shudder...A faith which cannot go beyond this level is worse than useless."[74]

Are those who have a defective faith, and may believe that only a mental ascent of God, and then a selective obedience to Him is all that is necessary—not that much better off than the demons? Moo indicates, "James might be implying, as demons, knowing something of the true God, yet lacking true faith, shudder in fear of judgment, so also ought people whose

---

[72] "But the fruit of the Spirit is love, joy, peace, patience, kindness, goodness, faithfulness, gentleness, self-control; against such things there is no law" (Galatians 5:22-23).

[73] Consult the author's article "What Does the Shema Really Mean?", appearing in *Confronting Yeshua's Divinity and Messiahship*.

[74] Davids, 126.

verbal profession is not followed up with actions."[75] An acknowledgment of God's existence and primacy is not enough; James' point is that the demons know that God is primary, but that is certainly not going to provide them with salvation as eternally condemned creatures. Those who are committed to believing in the *Shema,* and who believe that Yeshua is the Messiah who provides eternal salvation to redeemed human beings, then have a duty to take such faith and demonstrate appropriate deeds.

To James the Just, a Believer cannot just say that he or she acknowledges the existence of God, go through a few religious motions, but then fail to act in the key works which should be present in all Believers. If a mental recognition of God is sufficient, then demons can apparently be saved—**which they obviously cannot.** James' argument is, admittedly, somewhat extreme, but it proves a valid point. If all that is required for salvation is a recognition that Yeshua died and rose again, then demons who likewise recognize this fact can be saved and redeemed from their fate. *This is why a human being's faith has to be more.* A man or woman's faith has to be evidenced in a transformation of heart and mind, which will enable the individual to carry out the good works that the Heavenly Father expects from each one of His children.

2:20 James speaks to his audience, inquiring, "Do you want to be shown, you senseless person, that faith apart from works is barren?" (NRSV). Those claiming to have faith in God, but do not have any kind of associated actions with such faith, only have something to be regarded as "useless" (NASU) or "lifeless" (Kingdom New Testament).

While the term **"faith"** has been frequently used in our examination of the Epistle of James, what are some of the main things our author is actually referring to? What are the main, underlying Hebrew and Greek terms used in the Bible to describe **"faith,"** needing a review? First consider this sufficient definition of **"faith"** from the *Pocket Dictionary of Theological Terms:*

"A biblical word that refers both to intellectual belief and to relational trust or commitment. The biblical authors generally do not make a distinction between faith as belief and faith as trust, but tend to see true faith as consisting of both what is believed (e.g., that God exists, that Jesus is Lord) and the personal commitment to a person that is trustworthy, reliable and able to save (that is, trust in the person of Christ as the way to salvation)."[76]

The Hebrew verb *aman* and derivative forms are used in the Tanach or Old Testament to describe concepts such as "faith," "belief," "trust," "faithfulness," and "firmness." As *TWOT* summarizes, "This very important concept in biblical doctrine gives clear evidence of the biblical meaning of 'faith' in contradistinction to the many popular concepts of the term. At the heart of the meaning of the root is the idea of certainty. And this is borne out by the

---

[75] Moo, 131.

[76] Stanley J. Grenz, David Guretzki, and Cherith Fee Nordling, *Pocket Dictionary of Theological Terms* (Downers Grove, IL: InterVarsity, 1999), 50.

NT definition of faith found in Heb 11:1."[77] Notably, the term *Amein* or "Amen" is derived from *aman*, roughly meaning "so be it." When we end our prayers with "Amen," we consent to God that we have complete trust, faithfulness, and assurance in Him.

The related Greek term for faith via the LXX, and which is employed in the Apostolic Scriptures, is *pistis*, and its related verb form is *pisteuō. TDNT* indicates that "Formally in the NT, as in Greek usage, *pisteúō* denotes reliance, trust, and belief."[78]

Having faith in God means that a human individual should put his or her complete trust and belief in Him. A critical part of having faith in God is having an internal assurance that when one obeys God, the Lord will honor a person for such obedience, being present through the challenges of life. Regardless of what anyone in the world may think or say of the actions required of a follower of God, faith looks beyond whatever problems may arise from one's obedience, because a person knows that God is truly there.

While possessing faith, trust, or belief in God definitely does involve a level of intellectual assent—to say that it ends there, is entirely **not** the point of James' message. For James, "faith divorced from deeds is barren" (NEB), which The Amplified Bible has for v. 20, with it being "inactive and ineffective and worthless." The term *argos* means "generally, *inactive, slothful, idle, lazy*" (LS),[79] and can involve being "*free from labor, at leisure,*" or "*lazy, shunning the labor which one ought to perform*" (Thayer).[80] A quality of faith which is *argos*, as James has previously stated, has no capacity to genuinely save people (v. 14). A quality of faith, which not only acknowledges God's existence (as the demons likewise do, v. 19), but has good works accompanying it (Ephesians 2:10), is one which shows that a man or woman truly has the word implanted within them (1:21).

If any of us truly has faith in God, then we will be able to act upon that faith, having the proper actions in the world. While we may not always have the same gifts, talents, and skills—we are to still act upon our trust and belief in the Lord, obeying Him, and testifying of Him as transformed people. Today's Messianic Believers widely claim to be Torah observant—and so the responsibility upon us is most enormous. *We verbally express a commitment to follow the Law of God.* How useful and beneficial is our testimony of faith, and the actions we demonstrate? What are the actions which we need to be demonstrating, which might be overlooked at present? How might such actions involve our attitudes and treatment of other people, rather than just today's Messianics going through some sort of motions of keeping *Shabbat*, the appointed times, or eating kosher?

---

[77] Jack B. Scott, "*aman*," in *TWOT*, 1:51.

As Hebrews 11:1 states, "Now faith is the assurance of *things* hoped for, the conviction of things not seen."

[78] R. Bultmann, "to believe, trust," in *TDNT*, 853.

[79] *LS*, 114.

[80] *Thayer*, 72.

21 Was not Abraham our father justified by works when he offered up Isaac his son on the altar? 22 You see that faith was working with his works, and as a result of the works, faith was perfected; 23 and the Scripture was fulfilled which says, "AND ABRAHAM BELIEVED GOD, AND IT WAS RECKONED TO HIM AS RIGHTEOUSNESS" [Genesis 15:6]**, and he was called the friend of God.**

2:21 Proceeding to explain how faith without works is worthless or barren (v. 20), James asks a complicated question: "Was not Abraham our father justified by works when he offered up Isaac his son on the altar?" Many have taken James' statement that Abraham was "justified by works," *ex ergōn edikaiōthē*, as not only a declaration of Abraham being declared free and forgiven of sin, but that Abraham received eternal salvation as a result of his human actions. Not only would such a conclusion sit in flat contradiction to other Biblical passages, such as Ephesians 2:8-9,[81] which steadfastly declare that human action cannot merit a person eternal salvation—**but it would most especially fail to consider the different dynamics and components of justification/righteousness.** While such contours of justification/righteousness do widely elude the lay reader of James, they do not elude those who are familar with discussions present in Biblical Studies. There has been much discussion within the past three decades or so (mid-to-late 1980s-present) regarding the different dynamics and components of justification/righteousness (Heb. *tzedaqah*; Grk. *dikaiosunē*). McKnight offers a fair summary of what has transpired, and various components of debates occurring in our time:

> "To be called 'righteous' is to be described, in general, as one who conforms to a standard. But life is not lived simply in the general; we live in particular worlds. So, to be called 'righteous' *in the Bible* means that one's behavior and life conform to the Torah, the standard of God (Gen 38:26). To be called 'righteous' *in Judaism* means that one's behavior and life conform to the Torah as interpreted by one's authorities—e.g., the Teacher of Righteousness at Qumran or Hillel or Shammai. To be called 'righteous' *in the messianic community of James* means that one's behavior and life conform to the Torah as interpreted by Jesus (Luke 18:14) and the leaders of that messianic community, most especially James (1:26-27; 2:8-13; etc.). To be called 'righteous' *in the world of Paul* means to be conformed to the standard of God by union with Christ (Gal 3:11-12; Rom 2:13; 3:23-26; 4:5)."[82]

There is certainly more that can be considered regarding contemporary theological debates per what justification/righteousness involves in Scripture—particularly in various places of the Apostolic Scriptures. Elements and components of how the Torah and Tanach,

---

[81] "For by grace you have been saved through faith; and that not of yourselves, *it is* the gift of God; not as a result of works, so that no one may boast" (Ephesians 2:8-9).

[82] McKnight, 246.

Ibid., 251 himself draws the conclusion that "Justification by works...is not by 'works of the law' so much as it is by 'works of mercy' as the way to interpret genuine Torah observance."

Second Temple Judaism, James, and Paul all describe justification/righteousness might be seen to overlap one another, requiring targeted investigation of various passages. The main point to be emphasized is that it is far too simple, and most inappropriate, to just assume that justification/righteousness can *only involve* a being declared free and forgiven from sins. Justification/righteousness can involve being identified as a member of God's own, in particular by demonstrating behavior and actions reflective of God. So, when James the Just says that the Patriarch Abraham was "justified by works," can this be more akin to, *Abraham demonstrated himself as being one of God's people/His own by his actions*? Noting the verb *dikaioō*, often rendered as "justify" or "declare righteous," McCartney lists five possible definitions that need not escape a reader's notice:

1. To *give justice* to someone; to correct a wrong
2. To *declare* someone righteous (generally) or in the right (on a specific issue); to render a verdict of "innocent"; to vindicate or acquit (and thus the opposite of condemn)
3. To *prove* or *demonstrate* that someone is righteous or in the right
4. To *clear a debt* obligation, either by forgiveness or by the debt being paid off
5. To *cause* someone to behave righteously[83]

Many examiners of v. 21, and noting how people have at times inappropriately concluded that James thinks that Abraham was granted eternal salvation via his works/actions/deeds, have opted to approach justification/righteousness from the third definition listed above. That Abraham was "proved righteous" (TLV), or "considered righteous" (NIV), is to be taken as a demonstration of Abraham having the appropriate character and actions incumbent of those who are a part of God's people. Davids succinctly says, "the [*edikaiōthē*] refers not to a forensic act in which a sinner is declared acquitted...but to a declaration by God that a person is righteous, *ṣaddîq*."[84] While there should be no doubting that there are indeed many places in the Scriptures where justification/righteousness involves being declared innocent and forgiven of sins, **James 2:21 is not one of those places.**

Abraham demonstrated the proper action incumbent upon those who express belief in God, and was regarded as being one of God's own, His friend (v. 23). In 1 Maccabees 2:52, it is stated, "Was not Abraham found faithful when tested, and it was reckoned to him as righteousness?" Here, being just/righteous, identified by the noun *dikaiosunē*, is directly associated with being faithful, identified by the adjective *pistos*. Abraham was obviously not granted eternal salvation via his offering up of Isaac (Genesis 22:9-10), but he did demonstrate himself to be in the proper standing, in his relationship with the Lord.

---

[83] McCartney, pp 162-163.
[84] Davids, 127.

2:22 Was the Patriarch Abraham at all "saved" by his works? This is not the perspective of James the Just, who has just referenced the offering up of Isaac as a sacrifice. James states how "faith was working with his works, and as a result of the works, faith was perfected." Some translations appear to be at a bit of a conundrum with how to render *hē pistis sunērgei tois ergois*, as the verb *sunergeō* means "**to engage in cooperative endeavor, work together with, assist, help**" (BDAG).[85] This clause may appear as "his faith and his actions were working together" (NIV); "faith was active together with his works" (HCSB); "faith was at work in his actions" (NEB); "faith was cooperating along with his works" (Kingdom New Testament).

Even with a variance of English renderings present for v. 22, when we take into consideration a small selection from different Bible versions, it is obvious *that faith and works go together*. A genuine faith in God is to work together, cooperate with, help, or assist a follower of God in his or her life encounters with Him. A quality of faith which has the capacity to genuinely save a person, produces good deeds. One of the most significant deeds ever performed in the Bible is Abraham offering up his son Isaac as a sacrifice—because not only was Abraham planning to kill the child of promise given to him by the Lord, but Abraham would have had to have the confidence of knowing that the Lord's promises would have been fulfilled regardless. As Hebrews 11:17 explains, "By faith Abraham, when he was tested, offered up Isaac, and he who had received the promises was offering up his only begotten *son*."

The intention of James in v. 22 is to communicate how actions resultant from faith, see that "faith [is] made complete" (NIV); "brought to completion" (NRSV); or "perfected" (NASU). When a person obeys the Lord via tangible actions—as in the case of Abraham offering up Isaac for sacrifice—his or her confidence and belief in Him, is to mature. Doubtlessly with Abraham, when God acknowledged his obedience and provided the ram for the sacrifice instead of Isaac (Genesis 22:11-19), Abraham's trust in God was significantly deepened and was greatly enhanced. While Abraham was not "saved" by this action, this action was a significant exercise in spiritual perfection.

2:23 Resultant from Abraham's action of offering up Isaac, James asserts, "and the Scripture was fulfilled that says, 'Abraham believed God, and it was counted to him as righteousness'—and he was called a friend of God" (ESV). Here, James quotes from Genesis 15:6, "Then he believed in the LORD; and He reckoned it to him as righteousness," as Genesis 15:6 is one of the main Torah passages which is often provided as a key support for the traditional Protestant doctrine of justification by faith. Here in v. 23, the dynamic of *dikaiosunē* in view is stated: **Abraham "was called the friend of God," meaning that he was in covenant relationship with Him.** James' specific perspective here, regarding Genesis 15:6, concerns the Patriarch Abraham being a member of God's own, and reflecting

---

[85] *BDAG*, 969.

behavior that demonstrates oneself a member of God's own. That Abraham was a friend of God, is a concept directly taken from the Tanach (Isaiah 41:8; 2 Chronicles 20:7).

There are conflicts between examiners, who are at a bit of a loss, as to what to do with Genesis 15:6 being quoted by James, here in v. 23, and with what Paul says in Galatians 3:6, where he too quotes from Genesis 15:6: "Abraham BELIEVED GOD, AND IT WAS RECKONED TO HIM AS RIGHTEOUSNESS." While there are debates regarding how both the Epistle of James and the Epistle to the Galatians (and to a lesser extent, the Epistle to the Romans) should be interpreted, there is a growing acceptance in New Testament Studies that there are specific places within the letter to the Galatians where the justification/righteousness in view does involve membership within God's covenant people via the Judaizers/Influencers' insistence upon proselyte circumcision for covenant inclusion, and not a being remitted from sins; one of Paul's main points in Galatians is that belief in the Messiah reckons a person as a part of God's people.[86] At the same time, one's status within God's people as justification/righteousness, can widely be predicated upon being forgiven of sins by trust in Him and in the Messiah He has sent. So, might Genesis 15:6 be a kind of *nexus passage*, if you will, where all of the main meanings of justification/righteousness come together? If so, this can definitely ease much of the tension that some readers may have between James and Paul. It would allow for Genesis 15:6 to be applied in some different ways, although ways more related than not.

Considering the different dynamics and components of justification/righteousness (*tzedaqah, dikaiosunē*), will be necessary, as Messianic Biblical Studies improves, as will our understanding of the diverse range of passages employing this terminology.[87]

24 You see that a man is justified by works and not by faith alone.

2:24 What is James saying in v. 24? *Horate hoti ex ergōn dikaioutai anthrōpos kai ouk pisteōs monon*, "You see that a person is justified by works and not by faith alone" (ESV). Some have taken James' comments, "You see that a man is proved righteous by works and not by faith alone" (TLV), and have come to the conclusion that human or mortal actions can actually merit eternal salvation for a person. Yet, this cannot be a position sustained from the wider cotext of vs. 10-25, where the godly actions incumbent upon those who claim the Creator God as their own are in view. Such works or deeds are important evidence of an active and living faith, and that men and women who claim the One True God are in a covenant relationship with Him.

The debate, however, as to whether or not James the Just actually promoted a salvation message where human actions could merit eternal salvation (and would be in conflict with

---

[86] This is explored within the author's commentary *Galatians for the Practical Messianic*.

[87] Hopefully in the future, the author will be able to write a detailed theological analysis of the doctrine of salvation.

the sentiments expressed in Romans 4:1-9), or whether some other dynamics regarding justification/righteousness are in view in v. 24, has at least gone back to the early Protestant Reformation. Calvin actually had some useful perspectives to consider in his commentary on the Epistle of James, in the Sixteenth Century:

"So when the sophists set James against Paul, they are deceived by the double term 'justification'. When Paul says we are justified by faith, he means precisely that we have won a verdict of righteousness in the sight of God. James has quite another intention, that the man who professes himself to be faithful should demonstrate the truth of his fidelity by works. James did not mean to teach us where the confidence of our salvation should rest—which is the very point on which Paul does insist. So let us avoid the false reasoning which has trapped the sophists, by taking note of the double meaning: to Paul, the word denotes our free imputation of righteousness before the judgment seat of God, to James, the demonstration of righteousness from its effects, in the sight of men; which we may deduce from the preceding words, *Shew me thy faith, etc.* In this latter sense, we may admit that without controversy that man is justified by works, just as you might say a man is enriched by the purchase of a large and costly estate, since his wealth, which beforehand he kept out of sight in a strong-box, has become well known."[88]

Some have read James' statement, "You see that a man is proved righteous by works and not by faith alone" (TLV), as a correction issued to various Pauline teachings—or far more likely, a correction to those who have misunderstood various Pauline teachings. More contemporary examiners over the past two to three decades, with the kind of specification to detail as elucidated by Calvin above—and with some desire to read Scripture holistically—have been fairer, in various degrees, to distinguish between the different vantage points of James the Just and the Apostle Paul.[89] Martin asserts, "Whereas Paul's audience is in danger of relying on 'works' for salvation, James' readers are excusing themselves from good works, thereby showing a faith that is dead."[90] N.T. Wright more elaborately talks about how, "a person is justified by works and not by faith alone" (Kingdom New Testament), involves,

"It wasn't a bare acknowledgement of God, but rather an active friendship (verse 23, referring to passages like Isaiah 41.8). That friendship, embodied in the '**covenant**' which

---

[88] Calvin, pp 285-286.

[89] Bauckham, in *ECB*, 1488 is one who I think, wrongly, has concluded that "James...is entirely oblivious to the question of Gentile believers in Christ," and concludes that "works" in the Pauline letters and in the Epistle of James are largely different, with one pertaining to so-called "boundary markers" of Jewish exclusivity (Paul), and the other with acts of grace and kindness (James). Cf. McKnight, 228 in part/partially.

For a further exploration of the different aspects and contours regarding "works" in the Apostolic Scriptures, consult the author's article "What are 'Works of the Law'?" in his book *The New Testament Validates Torah*.

[90] Martin, 95.

God established in Genesis 15.7-20 and reaffirmed in 22.15-18, is the basis for what James, like Paul, calls '**justification**', God's declaration that a person is a member of the covenant, is 'in the right', is part of God's forgiven family."[91]

With Wright's comments in mind, and even though he offers the traditional rendering of "justified" in both his commentary and Kingdom New Testament publications, "**vindicated**" might be a valid alternative English offering for v. 24, for what is intended via the verb *dikaioō*. Thusly, when the different vantage points of James and Paul are considered, as well as the different dynamics of justification/righteousness, what we see presented in v. 24 is that external evidence of a true internal heart change oriented toward God, with people demonstrating that they are truly His, is what is to be shown toward the world.

James the Just's epistle does not contradict the letters of the Apostle Paul, which tend to emphasize that people are saved by grace through faith. In James' epistle, he contrasts a mental ascent of faith without good, appropriate works, which are required actions of those who are serving God—to Paul's writings which largely emphasize a living faith, where one has to continually rely upon God for His redemption and forgiveness, as human works/actions/deeds do not merit any person eternal salvation. One early Messianic leader confronted an immature faith without good works (James), and another early Messianic leader confronted a salvation believed to be produced by human/mortal works (Paul). To this end, it is useful for each of us to consider the observations of John Wesley, who said in the Eighteenth Century, that "there is no contradiction between the apostles: because (1) they do not speak of the same faith: St. Paul speaking of *living* faith; St. James here, of *dead* faith. (2) they do not speak of the same works: St. Paul speaking of works antecedent to faith; St. James, of works subsequent to it."[92]

Messianic Believers today need to take important note of what James is truly saying in v. 24. It is a fact that a faith which is not manifested via good works, *is no faith at all.* People who do not demonstrate their faith via their works are in a sorry state indeed. They have not allowed salvation to encompass every part of their being, including a regeneration of the will to do what is pleasing to God. On a similar note, however, James would not communicate to today's Messianic people that by keeping the Sabbath, the Biblical festivals, and eating kosher—that they will hence, "be saved." A person's faith and works go together, and one can outwardly "obey God," while at the same time be internally demonstrating a low state of morality, ethics, and respect toward other people (outside *or* inside the Body of Messiah). A born again Believer's obedience to the Father **must permeate every aspect of his or her being,** and affect both physical actions *and* internal heart attitude.

---

[91] Wright, 19.

[92] John Wesley, *Explanatory Notes Upon the New Testament*, reprint (Peterborough, UK: Epworth Press, 2000), 863.

Excursus: Will Torah-Keeping Merit a Person a "Righteous" Status?

adapted from the author's book *The New Testament Validates Torah*

"Many people think the Law was given so that by keeping it we will become righteous."

The idea that observing the Torah will merit righteousness for people is based on Deuteronomy 6:25, where the Ancient Israelites declare, **"It will be righteousness for us if we are careful to observe all this commandment before the LORD our God, just as He commanded us."** The Hebrew word for righteousness in the Tanach is *tzedaqah*.[93] *HALOT* offers a variety of definitions for it, including: "loyalty to the community, in conduct, **honesty**," "**justice**, of the human judge and of the king; it includes the elimination of anything breaking the peace and the preservation of good order," "**justness** of the divine judge," "justness, meaning **community loyalty**," "**justness, justice**, meaning God's loyalty to the community," "**entitlement, just cause...deeds of justice**, deeds of loyalty to the community, or covenant."[94] *Tzedaqah* is derived from the word *tzedeq*, which "refers to an ethical, moral standard and of course in the OT that standard is the nature and will of God" (*TWOT*).[95]

The underlying terms for righteousness and justification in the Bible (the Hebrew root *tzqd* and Greek root *dik-*) have a wider array of application than do their equivalent English terms today. To be "righteous/justified" can relate to one's identity as God's people, or being made a part of God's people, as much as it can mean being forgiven of sin, or demonstrating proper and virtuous behavior.[96]

The *Keil & Delitzch Commentary on the Old Testament* states for Deuteronomy 6:25, "our righteousness will consist in the observance of the law; we shall be regarded and treated by God as righteous, if we are diligent in the observance of the law."[97] If righteousness or *tzedaqah* is to be taken from the perspective of a right and cleared standing before God, then this surely presents one obvious problem: **Where in the history of the Bible have God's people ever perfectly obeyed Him?** Where has the keeping of the commandments resulted in His people being considered righteous, blameless, perfect, and without any error before Him? If we were all righteous because we followed the Torah, then we would really not need a Savior for eternal redemption (Galatians 3:21b).

The perspective that Torah-keeping will bring salvation seems to be represented in the NJPS translation of Deuteronomy 6:25: "It will be therefore to our merit before the LORD our God to observe faithfully this whole Instruction." In his commentary on

---

[93] Its main Greek equivalent in the Septuagint and Apostolic Scriptures is *dikaiosunē*.

[94] *HALOT*, 2:1006.

[95] Harold G. Stigers, "tzadeq," in *TWOT*, 2:752.

[96] Cf. Philip F. Esler, *Conflict and Identity in Romans: The Social Setting of Paul's Letter* (Minneapolis: Augsberg Fortress, 2003), pp 163-168.

[97] E-Sword 8.0.8: Keil & Delitzsch Commentary on the Old Testament. MS Windows 9x. Franklin, TN: Equipping Ministries Foundation, 2008.

Deuteronomy, Jewish scholar Jeffrey H. Tigay argues for this verse, "That is, 'it will be to our credit,' implying that one accumulates credit for meritorious good deeds."[98] As his corroborating evidence, he references statements witnessed in both the Tosefta and the Mishnah, some early Rabbinic literature from the Second Century C.E. t.*Peah* 1:2 says, "Doing good...creates a principal [for the world-to-come] and bears interest...[in this world],"[99] followed by m.*Peah* 1:1, which more fully attests:

"These are the things the benefit of which a person enjoys in this world, while the principal remains for him in the world to come: [deeds in] honor of father and mother, [performance of] righteous deeds, and [acts which] bring peace between a man and his fellow. But the study of Torah is as important as all of them together."[100]

None of us can argue against that honoring one's parents, accomplishing holy deeds reflective of God's own righteousness, and trying to facilitate peace among one's neighbors are things that we should all be doing. The question is whether the performance of these various works can result in human beings having a right standing before God. Yeshua said quite directly, "For I say to you that unless your righteousness surpasses *that* of the scribes and Pharisees, you will not enter the kingdom of heaven" (Matthew 5:20). The scribes and Pharisees often had such high and elite standards of what was considered "righteousness," that the Lord says common human righteousness must exceed *their standards* in order to enter into the Kingdom. For us today, this would mean that without Yeshua, we basically need to keep all of the extra-Biblical laws of Orthodox Judaism perfectly to be saved. But this is impossible in our human condition. We might be able to learn from Rabbinic commentary in order to be more effective in holy conduct, but our sinful inclinations will often get the better of us no matter how hard we really try.

Various Christian Old Testament theologians, who generally have a rather positive outlook on the Law of Moses, tend to propose another perspective on Deuteronomy 6:25. Rather than arguing that Torah-keeping will merit people righteousness before God, Christopher J.H. Wright instead indicates how this verse "is virtually the OT 'gospel' in a nutshell. The crucial point here, however, is that this definitive statement of Israel's salvation history is given as the answer to a fundamental question about *the law*...The basis of the law lies in the history of redemption (vv. 21-23); the reason for keeping the law is to enjoy the blessings of redemption (v. 24); the fruit of obeying the law is the righteousness that is the goal of redemption (v. 25)."[101] Wright is entirely correct in emphasizing the positive, educational nature of the Torah, particularly in terms of how successive generations of the Ancient Israelites would learn of God's deliverance by the Exodus. Deuteronomy 6:21 instructs, "then you shall say to your son, 'We were slaves to Pharaoh in Egypt, and the LORD brought us from Egypt with a mighty hand.'" A proper response to God's intervening and saving action should be

[98] Jeffrey H. Tigay, *JPS Torah Commentary: Deuteronomy* (Philadelphia: Jewish Publication Society, 1996), 83.
[99] Roger Brooks, trans., "Peah," in Jacob Neusner, ed., *The Tosefta: Translated from the Hebrew With a New Introduction*, 2 vols. (Peabody, MA: Hendrickson, 2002), 1:47.
[100] Roger Brooks, trans., "Peah," in Neusner, *Mishnah*, 15.
[101] Christopher Wright, *New International Biblical Commentary: Deuteronomy* (Peabody, MA: Hendrickson, 1996), 104.

obedience to Him. The history of Ancient Israel, especially in texts like 1&2 Kings, sadly reveals that this was frequently not the case. Furthermore, the history of humanity in general is one of disobedience and rebellion toward the Creator (i.e., Romans 1).

The question of whether or not Deuteronomy 6:25 lays forth the hypothesis that if the Ancient Israelites were able to keep the Torah, they would be "righteous" or "justified," is a legitimate one, because of how the verse is constructed. What is communicated is *u'tzedaqah ti'heyeh-lanu ki-nishmor l'asot et-kol-ha'mitzvah ha'zot*, "And it shall be counted as our righteousness, when we take care to fulfill all this commandment..." (Keter Crown Bible). The result of whatever *tzedaqah* is to be considered here, however worthwhile it may be, originates from the action of people. However, one can certainly debate whether such *tzedaqah*/righteousness/justification is an individual vindication of sin before Him, or a corporate demonstration of being of His own covenant people.

Can any kind of righteousness/justification result from human obedience to God's commandments? Deuteronomy 6:25 seems to present the possibility that at least an excellent obedience of God's commandments could somehow result in *tzedaqah* status. Once again, though, we are most soberly reminded of how fallen human nature is often prone **to do exactly the opposite** of what God expects. The Psalmist affirms, "They have all turned aside, together they have become corrupt; there is no one who does good, not even one" (Psalm 14:3; cf. 53:3b). Paul reaffirms, "THERE IS NONE RIGHTEOUS, NOT EVEN ONE" (Romans 3:10). The kind of obedience, that would merit *tzedaqah* status, is frequently unattainable for human beings with a fallen sin nature.

As high and as holy as God's Torah is, and as much as His people should seek obedience to it and compliance with it, so much of the consternation we experience in life is over what happens in our relationship with Him *when we are caught breaking the Law*. Even in a Messianic community that emphasizes God's grace and mercy as super-abounding to be there to cover some of the most problematic of sins (cf. Romans 5:20), so much of our time is spent worrying over matters like having to fill up our gas tanks on *Shabbat* when we forget to do so, or even going to the drug store to buy aspirin or antacid. Sins where we can all clearly be found in the wrong are in violating those commandments and principles where harm to a neighbor's person or his/her character will be found, where we are guilty of elevating our own self-worth and we cheapen the value of other people in our own estimation—perhaps even thinking that God approves of our attitudes.

Only Yeshua the Messiah, who expressly stated He came to "fulfill all righteousness" (Matthew 3:15)—which was definitely manifested in His fulfilling the Torah (Matthew 5:17)—**perfectly kept Moses' Teaching.** He was the One sacrificed for the transgressions of all people. Our common inability to keep the thrust of Deuteronomy 6:25 **is what should precisely drive us to Him as our Divine Savior.** People have all failed to obey the Torah and its commandments. *We have all fallen short of God's standard.* With all thankfulness and gratitude, though, the sacrifice of Yeshua has been provided so we do not have to have the condemnation of the Law come crashing down upon us! We can each be redeemed from the Torah's penalties via the power of the gospel, and then be supernaturally empowered by the Holy Spirit within us to let the Lord write His commandments on our hearts just as He has promised (Jeremiah 31:31-34; Ezekiel 36:25-27).

What this means is that the *real righteousness* Messiah followers must be reaching out for is none other than that which is granted to them from Yeshua's very work on their behalf at Golgotha (Calvary). As a direct result of being saved by God's grace through faith (Ephesians 2:8-9), the Apostle Paul says "For we are His workmanship, created in Messiah Yeshua for good works, which God prepared beforehand so that we would walk in them" (Ephesians 2:10). Yeshua Himself bids His disciples, "Let your light shine before men in such a way that they may see your good works, and glorify your Father who is in heaven" (Matthew 5:16). Good works of obedience to the Torah are to surely come as a result of the redemption we experience by faith, and demonstrate that we are truly God's own (James 2:17-18, 22). But, such good works will be *natural evidence* of the Holy Spirit inside of redeemed people, will be tempered by His grace, and will not be rigidly forced.[102]

25 In the same way, was not Rahab the harlot also justified by works when she received the messengers and sent them out by another way? 26 For just as the body without *the* spirit is dead, so also faith without works is dead.

2:25 James refers to another example of one who was regarded as "justified" via works: "In the same way, wasn't Rahab the prostitute justified by works when she gave shelter to the spies and sent them off by another road?" (Kingdom New Testament). Similar to what has just been asserted about Abraham (vs. 21, 23b), Rahab was "considered righteous" (NIV) or "proved righteous" (TLV), *edikaiōthē*. Rahab being "justified by works," *ex ergōn*, though, does not constitute her receiving eternal salvation for actions performed; the specific issue is how she demonstrated herself as faithful to Israel's God, and was counted among the company of His own, **as a non-Israelite,** by helping the Israelite spies. As Joshua 2:8-10 records,

"Now before they lay down, she came up to them on the roof, and said to the men, 'I know that the LORD has given you the land, and that the terror of you has fallen on us, and that all the inhabitants of the land have melted away before you. For we have heard how the LORD dried up the water of the Red Sea before you when you came out of Egypt, and what you did to the two kings of the Amorites who were beyond the Jordan, to Sihon and Og, whom you utterly destroyed.'"

Rahab helped the Israelite spies to hide in the city of Jericho. This is why the author of Hebrews would be able to write, "By faith Rahab the harlot did not perish along with those who were disobedient, after she had welcomed the spies in peace" (Hebrews 11:31).

---

[102] For a further discussion, consult the FAQ, "Deuteronomy 6:25."

Do not overlook how Joshua 2:1 states that the spies went into a *beit-ishah*, literally "a house of a woman," but understood to be "the house of a prostitute" (NIV, NRSV).[103] A Jewish tradition in the Talmud states that after Jericho was defeated that Rahab became Joshua's wife:

"R. Judah says: Huldah the prophetess was also a descendent of Rahab the prostitute. Here it says 'Son of Tikvah' (*ben tiqvah*), and there it says 'the line (*tiqvat*) of the red thread' (Jos. 2:18). *He said to him: Old Eye [playing on his name, Eina Saba]; and some say 'Black Pot' [suggesting that he was accustomed to study, as a blackened pot is well used]! From me and from you [together] the matter is finalized, for she converted, and Joshua married her*" (b.Megillah 14b).[104]

In spite of Rahab being a for-hire prostitute, because of her acts of courage by extending support to the Israelites, she is afforded great acclaim in Jewish and Christian tradition. Josephus stated that the "spies acknowledged that they owed her thanks for what she had done already, and withal swore to requite her kindness, not only in words, but in deeds" (*Antiquities of the Jews* 5.13).[105] The Second Century letter of First Clement to the Corinthians attests that Rahab was the ideal model of hospitality and rewarded by God for it:

"On account of her faith and hospitality, Rahab the harlot was saved. For when spies were sent by Joshua, the son of Nun, to Jericho, the king of the country ascertained that they were come to spy out their land, and sent men to seize them, in order that, when taken, they might be put to death. But the hospitable Rahab receiving them, concealed them on the roof of her house under some stalks of flax" (*1 Clement* 12).[106]

Certainly not also to be overlooked is how Rahab is actually listed on the genealogy chart of Messiah Yeshua in Matthew 1:5. By her deeds of faithfulness in helping the Ancient Israelites, she was definitely regarded as justified, and counted among the company of God. Helping the Israelites in their defeat of Jericho was doubtlessly important, as it was one of the first significant campaigns in the Conquest of the Promised Land.

2:26 James uses the examples of Abraham offering up Isaac (vs. 21-23) and Rahab helping the Israelite spies (v. 25), to make the point, "For as the body apart from the spirit is dead, so faith apart from works is dead" (RSV). One's internal belief in the existence of God, or even the natural goodness or grace of God—cannot be separated from the required actions of belief. The works or deeds of God's people, are to serve as the external evidence of their faith and belief in God. By their acting upon the Lord's instructions and His promises, His own are able to demonstrate via their works that they truly possess not only a sincere and saving faith—**but a living faith!** *Such obedience comes naturally out of love for Him, and is not to be forced or coerced,* as though human actions can actually merit eternal salvation.

---

[103] This is reflected in the LXX rendering of *beit ishah* as *oikian gunaikos pornēs*, literally the "house of a woman/female prostitute."

[104] *The Babylonian Talmud: A Translation and Commentary.*

[105] *The Works of Josephus: Complete and Unabridged*, 127.

[106] *The Ante-Nicene Fathers.* Libronix Digital Library System 1.0d: Church History Collection.

Much of the Messianic community today would do well to know what James meant, when he largely spoke about a Believer's works. While outward works of obedience, which would include those Torah observant elements which make us distinctively "Messianic" are by no means excluded—*our "works" do not solely consist of these things either.* For James' audience, the necessary works of a Messiah follower largely included the ethics and morality of the Torah that were being forgotten, as the poor were being dishonored (vs. 1-5) and not being cared for (vs. 15-20). For today's generation of Believers, it is largely reversed with many people having forgotten to obey God outwardly. There exists a delicate balance of our obedience to the Heavenly Father, both inwardly and outwardly. A man or woman, truly maturing in faith, will allow the Spirit of God to permeate all aspects of their being, as Believers should be transformed in what they think, what they say, and what they do.

JAMES 3
COMMENTARY

1 Let not many *of you* become teachers, my brethren, knowing that as such we will incur a stricter judgment.

3:1 James the Just's message in ch. 3 widely pertains to proper speech and control of the tongue (vs. 2-12), as well as a discussion of godly versus evil wisdom (vs. 13-18). James' words on these matters are notably preceded by a key admonition: "Not many of you should become teachers, my brothers and sisters, for you know that we who teach will be judged with greater strictness" (NRSV). While this is a directive which would have been most important for the First Century Believers, it has had a significant impact on teachers and leaders within the Body of Messiah ever since—but it is something, most unfortunately, which the contemporary Messianic movement has not heeded enough.

There is no doubting the importance of good teachers for the First Century Body of Messiah (Acts 13:1; Romans 12:7; 1 Corinthians 12:28). At the same time, though, Yeshua criticized various Pharisaical leaders for being enthralled with their teaching positions and apparent prestige (Matthew 23:6-8). While no human teacher or spiritual leader is at all faultless, the need for teachers to not only hold themselves—but be held to by others—to a very high standard, is most imperative. People should not simply desire to be a teacher within the Body of Messiah, but approach such a position with a great deal of fear, sobriety, caution, and by making sure that a set of prerequisites have been met, along with a time of adequate preparation.

V. 1a says *Mē polloi didaskaloi ginesthe*, "Many teachers become not" (YLT). Donald W. Burdick observes, "The Greek construction (*mē* with the present imperative *ginesthe*) probably suggests that it had been a common practice for many of the readers to seek to become teachers. So James warns that they should stop becoming teachers in such large numbers. No doubt many who were not qualified by natural ability or spiritual gift were coveting the prestige of teaching."[1] It has been speculated on the type of unqualified or false teachers possibly in view, ranging from those promoting blatant heresy to proto-Gnostic ideas,[2] but these suggestions only remain suggestions. What is particularized in the verses

---

[1] Burdick, in *EXP*, 12:186.
[2] Martin, 108.

following is the necessity for those in the Body of Messiah to have edifying speech—which is most especially required of teachers.

Teachers are admonished by James, "we shall receive the greater condemnation" (KJV), with James actually placing himself among those who can be evaluated harshly by God. It might be important to note that *krima* can mean both "*sentence, condemnation*" and "*a decision, judgment*" (LS),[3] so a "judgment" upon a teacher does not necessarily have to be negative. Godly teachers who have faithfully served the Lord will be judged approvingly by Him, perhaps per the thought of Luke 12:48, "From everyone who has been given much, much will be required." Alas, though, far too many of the admonitions encountered regarding teachers in the Bible, concern false teachers. The Apostle Peter warns, "But false prophets also arose among the people, just as there will also be false teachers among you, who will secretly introduce destructive heresies, even denying the Master who bought them, bringing swift destruction upon themselves" (2 Peter 2:1).

The main reason why teachers will be held accountable, so strictly by God, is how teachers within the faith community *influence others*. They not only influence others' opinions and beliefs concerning Holy Scripture, but the spirituality, attitudes, and actions of those who hear them. James had to say, "Not many of you should presume to be teachers" (NIV), because being raised up as a teacher requires both a Divine vocational calling from God, a steady temperament, as well as proper training and skills. Among many in James' audience, individuals were rising up as teachers who had no qualifications to do so. Douglas J. Moo remarks that this "Particularly would have been the case in a society where few people could read and where people in the lower classes had fewer opportunities for advancement in status...Too many were seeking the status of teacher without the necessary moral (and perhaps also intellectual) qualifications."[4] The point to be made, albeit somewhat difficult for a few to acknowledge, is how the role of teacher within the Body of Messiah is hardly one that can be democratized.

Obviously in the centuries since James issued his word about not many becoming teachers, there have been various religious institutions and denominations which have forbidden those who are not exceptionally learned from becoming teachers. They have literally required those who would teach people to have such weighty degrees, and go through such rigorous academic learning—that many potential servants of the Lord have found it too overbearing and excruciating to even consider being a teacher. At the same time, though, the opposite extreme—which has been manifest in sectors such as the charismatic Christianity of the past half century or so—is that pastors and teachers within the assembly might not be required to have any formal training or education in teaching the Bible. Whoever "feels" like he or she can be a teacher, can be a teacher. *Balance and fair-mindedness is tenuously needed on this.*

---

[3] *LS*, 450.
[4] Moo, 149.

Whether it was ancient Jewish Rabbis being trained, or various pastors and teachers today going through some reasonable degree of academic learning—one of the main purposes of being formally prepared as a teacher, is to make sure that various key issues and debates have been reasoned through before entering into a position of leadership. There is nothing worse than for a teacher to have a great deal of internal stress, anxiety, or even anger—which is then spewed onto unsuspecting people in submission. For my own self and my seminary experiences, there was one particular professor (Robert G. Tuttle)[5] who told our class, *"Gentlemen, get it out of your system now!"* His purpose for saying this was that no one should be publicly reasoning from the pulpit on an entire host of foundational doctrinal issues, and in the process potentially lead people astray and/or get them mad. As Yeshua said in Matthew 12:36-37, "But I tell you that every careless word that people speak, they shall give an accounting for it in the day of judgment. For by your words you will be justified, and by your words you will be condemned." Careless words can often be spoken, when potential teachers are thrust into leadership positions a bit too prematurely.

While there is a responsibility on teachers to be careful with what they say—and there are teachers with weighty credentials *and* teachers with no credentials, who are both guilty of error—there is also a responsibility on people who listen to a teacher, to be careful and discerning. The following thoughts of N.T. Wright should be well taken:

> "...James says that teachers will be judged with greater strictness. One hint in the wrong direction, and someone else's life—perhaps a full classroom of other lives—can be sent down a wrong path. Now there are, of course, different kinds of wrong paths. Many people will realize something is amiss and find their way back. But in other cases the damage will be done.
>
> "How much more is this the case in the church! One sermon pushing a line, pouring scorn on a cherished doctrine or advocating something that's not quite right, and a whole churchful of people may be set off in the wrong direction. One word out of place in a pastoral conversation, and the listener, at a vulnerable and impressionable moment, can be encouraged to make a false move. Teachers, beware! is the lesson here. Perhaps that's why many vocational advisors tell prospective ministerial candidates that if they can find anything else to do, they should do it."[6]

Both the denominations of the Jewish Synagogue and Christian Church, because of their long establishment, have procedures to ordain rabbis and pastors, and to make sure that those teaching people are generally prepared enough to do so. Many of the same procedures are present in today's Messianic Judaism, although they may not be as strictly followed. Within the more independent Messianic or Hebrew/Hebraic Roots movement, though, a wide number of the teachers and leaders, one is likely to encounter, would not

---

[5] Among his various books include, *The Story of Evangelism: A History of the Witness to the Gospel* (Nashville: Abingdon, 2006).

[6] Wright, pp 20-21.

meet the minimum requirements for ordination in either the modern Synagogue or Church. While it is very true that God is not at all limited to only use people with a formal, post-graduate religious education to teach His Word—the need to have more formally trained leaders in the contemporary Messianic movement is going to increase, especially given the more complicated issues of the Twenty-First Century. Many of the serious errors, that have plagued the independent Messianic movement, have been precisely caused by teachers and leaders with no formal religious studies training. This will obviously need to change...

In any new move of God, the willing servants and vessels which are available will be used by Him to accomplish His tasks. This need not always involve people from among the well educated, but the position of a teacher is unique, and it does demand excellence. In James' immediate First Century context, there were people who were untrained, or perhaps worse, illiterate, seeking the position of teacher. As James himself demonstrates throughout his letter—especially here in ch. 3—he was well read not only in matters of spirituality, but also in both Jewish tradition *and* Greco-Roman philosophy, giving him the ability to adequately communicate to a broad audience. Any Bible teacher today, in whatever part of the world, should be able to do the same, *and* be familiar with an audience's unique cultural needs.

Messianic Bible teachers today often advocate things which are unpopular in the larger theological spectrum of beliefs. This can widely relate to the Torah and why it is still to be followed today. James' admonition about teachers in v. 1 is especially poignant for the developing Messianic movement. **Each of you has the responsibility to always examine what Messianic Bible teachers are advocating.** Because ours is a still-developing movement, always be sure to: (1) question the motives of the teacher, making sure that the teacher is trying to help people grow and mature spiritually, and (2) make sure that what is being taught can be supported both by Scripture and well-supported evidence from Biblical lexicons, dictionaries, encyclopedias, and other reputable sources.

God in His sovereignty will raise up the proper leaders with sound character, who will help the Messianic community move forward in the future. Likewise, any teacher who leads others astray, or at the very least gets them to doubt who Yeshua is, will be judged severely. The Messiah tells us, "It would be better for him if a millstone were hung around his neck and he were thrown into the sea, than that he would cause one of these little ones to stumble" (Luke 17:2). An important Rabbinical tradition, transcribed later in the Mishnah, which James' audience may have been familiar with, further says, "Sages, watch what you say, Lest you become liable to the punishment of exile, and go into exile to a place of bad water, and disciples who follow you drink [bad water] and die, and the name of heaven be thereby profaned'" (m.*Avot* 1:11).[7]

James' instruction about teachers is directly connected to control of the tongue and speech (vs. 2ff), and whether or not one's speech is edifying or destructive. While teachers

---

[7] Neusner, *Mishnah*, 674.

can be some of the greatest offenders at times, of those who do not speak the way they ought—teachers alone are not the only ones who are to control what they say with the tongue.

> **2 For we all stumble in many *ways*. If anyone does not stumble in what he says, he is a perfect man, able to bridle the whole body as well. 3 Now if we put the bits into the horses' mouths so that they will obey us, we direct their entire body as well.**

3:2 James observes, "we all make many mistakes, and if any one makes no mistakes in what he says he is a perfect man, able to bridle the whole body also" (RSV). While teachers are immediately in view (v. 1) and should not be excluded from among those who need to control their speech, people in general are also being described. James has previously said, after all, "everyone must be quick to hear, slow to speak *and* slow to anger." Immediately to be asked is a sentiment seen in the Apocrypha, "Who has not sinned with his tongue?" (Sirach 19:16, NRSV). As Luke T. Johnson summarizes, there is a rich trove of material across the ages, which admonishes people to control their speech:

"From the sages of ancient Egypt, through the biblical books of Proverbs and Sirach [in the Apocrypha], to the essays of Plutarch and Seneca [in classical materials], there is a consensus that silence is better than speech, that hearing, not speaking, is the pathway to wisdom, that speech when necessary should be brief, that above all speech should be under control and never the expression of rage or envy. The mark of the wise person was above all control of speech (see Sir 5:13)."[8]

Some of the most important statements regarding control of the tongue or speech, which should add insights to our examination of James' letter and our own spirituality, are seen in the Books of Proverbs and Sirach, the Mishnah, the Dead Sea Scrolls, and the teaching of Yeshua:

"The one who guards his mouth preserves his life; the one who opens wide his lips comes to ruin" (Proverbs 13:3).

"A soothing tongue is a tree of life, but perversion in it crushes the spirit" (Proverbs 15:4).

"Death and life are in the power of the tongue, and those who love it will eat its fruit" (Proverbs 18:21).

"Glory and dishonor come from speaking, and a man's tongue is his downfall" (Sirach 5:13).

---

[8] Johnson, in *NIB*, 12:203.

"Slander has shaken many, and scattered them from nation to nation, and destroyed strong cities, and overturned the houses of great men. Slander has driven away courageous women, and deprived them of the fruit of their toil. Whoever pays heed to slander will not find rest, nor will he settle down in peace. The blow of a whip raises a welt, but a blow of the tongue crushes the bones. Many have fallen by the edge of the sword, but not so many as have fallen because of the tongue. Happy is the man who is protected from it, who has not been exposed to its anger, who has not borne its yoke, and has not been bound with its fetters; for its yoke is a yoke of iron, and its fetters are fetters of bronze; its death is an evil death, and Hades is preferable to it. It will not be master over the godly, and they will not be burned in its flame. Those who forsake the Lord will fall into its power; it will burn among them and will not be put out. It will be sent out against them like a lion; like a leopard it will mangle them" (Sirach 28:14-23).

"See that you fence in your property with thorns, lock up your silver and gold, make balances and scales for your words, and make a door and a bolt for your mouth" (Sirach 28:24-25).

"A sage does not speak before someone greater than he in wisdom" (m.*Avot* 5:7).[9]

"And now, O discerning one, listen to me, and devote your heart [...] speak knowledge to your innermost part and [...] meditate [...] with righteous humility utter [your] words. Do [no]t give [...Do not] turn aside the words of your companion, let he [gi]ve you [...] answer in accordance to what you hear, as a merchant which brings out the [...] with him [...Do not] utter a complaint before you hear their words [...] exceedingly. First, hear their explanation, and then answer [...] patiently bring them out. Answer correctly in the midst of princes and do not [...] with your lips. Be very careful of causing offense with your tongue [...] lest you be entrapped by your lips [and ens]nared together with [your...] ... [...] from me and [...]" (4Q525).[10]

"And He was saying, 'That which proceeds out of the man, that is what defiles the man. For from within, out of the heart of men, proceed the evil thoughts, fornications, thefts, murders, adulteries, deeds of coveting *and* wickedness, *as well as* deceit, sensuality, envy, slander, pride *and* foolishness. All these evil things proceed from within and defile the man'" (Mark 7:20-23).

"You have heard that the ancients were told, 'YOU SHALL NOT COMMIT MURDER [Exodus 20:13; Deuteronomy 5:17]' and 'Whoever commits murder shall be liable to the court.' But I say to you that everyone who is angry with his brother shall be guilty before the court; and whoever says to his brother, 'You good-for-nothing,' shall be guilty before

---

[9] Neusner, *Mishnah*, 686.
[10] Wise, Abegg, and Cook, 425.

the supreme court; and whoever says, 'You fool,' shall be guilty *enough to go* into the fiery hell" (Matthew 5:21-22).

"You brood of vipers, how can you, being evil, speak what is good? For the mouth speaks out of that which fills the heart" (Matthew 12:34).

While we cannot know for certain what James may have been thinking as he originally communicated, "For we all stumble in many ways. If someone does not stumble in speech, he is a perfect man, able to bridle the whole body as well" (TLV)—that James placed a high priority on control of the tongue cannot be denied. That there was a strong emphasis seen in the above quotations, on watching what one says, being quick not to speak, being wise with speech, and recognizing that what people say is what is in their hearts—only intensifies the need for Messiah followers to seek maturity in this area. James wants each of his listeners to be a *teleios anēr*. This involved not only the Jewish members of his original audience, but likely various Greeks and Romans as well. Richard Bauckham comments,

"The tongue is portrayed now as the key element in attaining 'perfection'...This is intelligible if we supply the close relationship in Jewish thought between the heart (or mind) and the tongue (e.g., Ps 15:2-3; Sir 27:4-7; 4Q525 2 ii 1; Matt 12:34). The evil of the heart becomes manifest in speech. This also helps to explain the images of the tongue as the bit by which the whole horse is guided and the rudder by which the whole ship is directed (3:3-5). These images had a long history in Greek literature, in which they were mostly used to portray the mind's control of the body. James can use them of the tongue because the thoughts and intention (v. 4....) of the heart are expressed by the tongue. Therefore anyone who can control the tongue (cf. 1:26) can also control the whole body (3:2)."[11]

Much sin can occur as a result of using the tongue improperly. In more than a few cases, it is better for a person to remain silent than to speak at all. Proverbs 10:19 admonishes, "When there are many words, transgression is unavoidable, but he who restrains his lips is wise." Teachers need to be careful with what they say, especially because they impact others and their opinions about God and other people. People in general also need to be careful with what they say, not only so that negative opinions about others are not unleashed and wreak havoc, but also so that misinformation regarding a topic or issue is not passed along. Talking simply for the sake of talking, where there is unrestrained banter occurring, is not at all a productive or useful exercise according to the Scriptures. A viewpoint encountered in the Mishnah is, "whoever talks too much causes sin" (m.*Avot* 1:17).[12]

A person, who is able to control the tongue, should then be able to control the rest of his or her being as well: "able to keep his whole body in check" (NIV). Burdick validly observes, "Since the person resides in the body and uses the body as his instrument, James

---

[11] Bauckham, in *ECB*, 1488.
[12] Neusner, *Mishnah*, 674.

seems to use 'body' to refer to the whole man. In reality, he is not referring to the tongue of flesh but to the intelligent, communicating mind that uses the tongue as its instrument. So the mind corrupts the whole person."[13] This is because, as Yeshua says in Luke 6:45, "The good man out of the good treasure of his heart brings forth what is good; and the evil *man* out of the evil *treasure* brings forth what is evil; for his mouth speaks from that which fills his heart." A Talmudic tradition notes how the tongue is often directly associated with evil and slander:

"From the specific case we turn to the general principle that gossip and slander are evil. This is richly illustrated in the following composite. Said R. Yohanan in the name of R. Yosé b. Zimra, *'What is the meaning of the following verse of Scripture:* "What shall be given to you and what more shall be done for you, you lying tongue" (Psa. 120: 3). Said the Holy One, blessed be he, to the tongue, "All the parts of the human body stand upright, but you recline. All the parts of the human body are outside, but you are inside. Not only so, but I have set up as protection for you two walls, one of bone [the teeth] and one of flesh [the cheeks]. What shall be given to you and what more shall be done for you, you lying tongue!"' Said R. Yohanan in the name of R. Yosé b. Zimra, 'Whoever repeats slander is as if he denied the very principle [of God's rule], as it is said, "Who has said, Our tongue will we make mighty, our lips are with us, who is lord over us" (Psa. 12: 5)'" (b.*Arachin* 15b).[14]

J.A. Motyer's general observations on controlling the tongue should also be noticed:

"Sin remains our universal experience and it takes all sorts of forms. Among them, as every self-aware believer will admit, sins of speech are prominent—the hasty word, the untruthful statement, the sly suggestion, harmful gossip, innuendo, impurity. Indeed, not to sin in speech would demand perfection, and we would be unrealistic not to see James' thoughts going back as he voices this thought to a thirty-year experience, within his own home, of one who 'committed no sin; no guile was found on his lips' (1 Pet. 2:22). Yet James' purpose in this section of his letter is not to warn us to be on our guard against the hasty or impure or lying tongue—or whatever our weakness may be—but to make the positive point that control of the tongue leads to a master-control of ourselves and of our lives."[15]

Scot McKnight directs his conclusions on v. 2, more in the direction of James' words about controlling the tongue pertaining to teachers. Surprisingly from a Christian interpreter, he has more of an appreciation for the role that the Torah plays in proper speech, than many teachers and leaders across the broad Messianic movement tend to have:

"[W]hen James speaks of a 'perfect' teacher in 3:2, his concern is more focused than on just Torah observance. This person is a fully developed follower of Jesus' own teachings of the Torah as the Torah of loving God and loving others. The perfect teacher is one whose

---

[13] Burdick, in *EXP*, 12:187.
[14] *The Babylonian Talmud: A Translation and Commentary.*
[15] Motyer, pp 119-120.

love shapes how he or she teaches and speaks of others. Indeed, the term speaks of maturity and completeness or, even better, of having arrived at the destined goal designed by God."[16]

Learning how to control the tongue, and with it our entire selves, is indeed an art and a science that can only be mastered by men and women who are born again and filled up with the Holy Spirit!

3:3 James compares the human tongue to a bit that would be placed within a horse's mouth, in order to control the horse while riding: "When we put bits into the mouths of horses to make them obey us, we can turn the whole animal" (NIV). This was obviously a common enough element of either Jewish or Greek or Roman life, with horses as one of the main forms of transportation, and with the point made that a rather small object can direct a rather large creature.

A mature Believer allows the Holy Spirit to bridle him or her, and what is always said in the context of Biblical teachings needs to be from the leading of the Spirit. Such will be evidenced by a person's demeanor not being offensive, condescending, or condemning. This is because a person's tongue or speech can have great effect, either for the better or the worse. Job 33:2-3 says, "Behold now, I open my mouth, my tongue in my mouth speaks. My words are *from* the uprightness of my heart, and my lips speak knowledge sincerely." The Psalmist declares, "The mouth of the righteous utters wisdom, and his tongue speaks justice" (Psalm 37:30).

While it is most natural for readers to take "the whole body" (*holon to sōma*) as being a reference to individual people, some have thought that the reference to "body" by James is not a reference to an individual human being, but rather to the Body of Messiah. This is a possible factor that should not be disregarded. Ralph P. Martin is reflective of this view, stating, "James' intention is to show that the tongue is the means by which a body of great size...namely, the church [or, the assembly/*ekklēsia*]—is controlled by a separate part of a much smaller size, namely, the teachers who are decisively influential out of proportion to their number, as they control...the direction of the whole body."[17] If this is the case, than what a teacher says not only will direct his or her own person, but also the lives of many other people. Regardless of whether or not James specifically intended to refer to the Body of Messiah in v. 3, a teacher who speaks to an assembly does have influence over others, and needs to be highly cautious of what is said. And, individual people in general, if they speak rather loudly about a particular issue, can have an inappropriate influence over many, many others within a local faith community.

These admonitions from James have remained true to Bible teachers and religious leaders since he composed them in the First Century. However, we in the Messianic community need to take them very seriously. As a still-developing and rather small movement, there are teachers who do not exemplify the qualities of which James speaks.

[16] McKnight, 275.
[17] Martin, 110.

Rather than being careful with what they say, especially in an effort not to unnecessarily offend, there are teachers who specifically *do their best to offend*, and will not hesitate to speak condemning words about our Christian brothers and sisters who have yet to even hear about the existence of the Messianic movement, much less about their Hebraic Roots or a restoration of Torah to the Body of Messiah.[18] We all need to consider what James has to say seriously, and speak words of edification, true wisdom, and above all have our speech be bridled by the Holy Spirit. In some instances, as it has already been observed, it is likely better for us to remain quiet than say anything at all.

4 Look at the ships also, though they are so great and are driven by strong winds, are still directed by a very small rudder wherever the inclination of the pilot desires. 5 So also the tongue is a small part of the body, and *yet* it boasts of great things. See how great a forest is set aflame by such a small fire! 6 And the tongue is a fire, the *very* world of iniquity; the tongue is set among our members as that which defiles the entire body, and sets on fire the course of *our* life, and is set on fire by hell.

3:4 Having just compared the human tongue to a bit in a horse's mouth (v. 3), James further observes, "Or take ships as an example. Although they are so large and are driven by strong winds, they are steered by a very small rudder wherever the pilot wants to go" (NIV). While ships driven by wind power with a rudder were a common part of First Century Mediterranean society, v. 4 is a particular, key area of James' letter, that serves to strongly support the idea that his audience was mixed and included some Greeks and Romans, and was not exclusively Jewish.

There is a huge bevy of possible classical references that concern the image of a ship or helmsman.[19] A poignant example to consider, per what James says in v. 4, includes the following thought from Plutarch. Plutarch compares out of control words to a ship that has been carried away with no definite course:

"The Poet, in fact, says that 'words' are 'winged': neither when you let go from your hands a winged thing is it easy to get back again, nor when a word is let slip from the mouth is it possible to arrest and control it, but it is borne away *Circling on swift wings*, and is scattered abroad from one to another. So when a ship has been caught by a wind, they try to check it, deadening its speed with cables and anchors, but if a story runs out of harbour, so to speak, there is no roadstead or anchorage for it, but, carried away with a great noise and reverberation, it dashes upon the man who uttered it and

---

[18] Consult the relevant sections of *Hebraic Roots: An Introductory Study* by William Mark Huey and this author, as well as the author's book *Introduction to Things Messianic*.

[19] Cf. Davids, 139.

submerges him in some great and terrible danger. *With but a little torch one might set fire to Ida's rock; and tell one man a tale, soon all the town will know*" (On Talkativeness 10).[20]

At times, such a classical sentiment, possibly present in this letter, has been used by some examiners to think that the Epistle of James is a much, much later piece, incorporating thoughts expressed in customary Greek materials. Yet, even though holding a two-stage composition of the letter, Peter Davids informs us,

"It would require no great knowledge of Hellenistic literature to be aware of such proverbs wherever one lived. Second, since horses and boats were the sum total of what men steered in those days, the linkage of the two was so natural from common observation that there is no need for any given author to depend on a traditional usage...One recognizes that the author of James knows his Greek well, so he undoubtedly had read some Greek literature. Also the usage of traditional material is not unknown to him."[21]

If anything, likely classical connections, to what is expressed in v. 4, should be used to support a broader audience for the Epistle of James, than what is commonly asserted. As Moo observes, "So widespread were the images of horse, ship, and fire in the literature [of the day] that they must have been common sources for illustrations in the everyday world of James's environment. And, indeed, all three were so common that they would have been natural sources for illustrations."[22] His main conclusion, weighing in the wider themes of the letter, and encountering something classical such as the appeal to a ship with its rudder, is that "The picture of James that emerges is of a reasonably well-educated Jew who knows his OT thoroughly and who is well acquainted with Hellenistic-Jewish culture, language, and literature."[23] The Jewish philosopher Philo compared and contrasted disciplined and undisciplined minds to a charioteer and a shipmaster, which might be said to parallel the thought of vs. 3-4:

"And the mind is better than the outward senses. As, therefore, when the charioteer has his horses under command and guides the animals with the rein, the chariot is guided wherever he pleases; but if they become restive, and get the better of the charioteer, he is often dragged out of his road, and sometimes it even happens that the beasts themselves are borne by the impetuosity of their course into a pit, and everything is carried away in a ruinous manner. And, as a ship holds on her right course when the pilot has the helm in his hand and steers her, and she is obedient to her rudder, but the vessel is upset when some contrary wind descends upon the waves and the whole sea is occupied by billows; so when the mind, which is the charioteer or pilot of the soul, retains the mastery over the entire animal, as a ruler does over a city,

---

[20] Plutarch: *Moralia: On Talkativeness*, Loeb Classical Library edition (1939). Accessible online at: <http://penelope.uchicago.edu/Thayer/E/Roman/Texts/Plutarch/Moralia/De_garrulitate*.html>.

[21] Ibid., pp 139-140.

[22] Moo, 154.

[23] Ibid., 148.

the life of the man proceeds rightly. But when the outward sense, which is devoid of reason, obtains the supremacy, then a terrible confusion overtakes the man, as might happen if a household of slaves were to conspire and to set upon their master. For then, if one must tell the truth, the mind is set fire to and burnt, the outward senses handling the flame and placing the objects of their operation beneath, as fuel" (*Allegorical Interpretation* 3.223-224).[24]

The need for Messiah followers to control their tongue and speech is true whether one originally encountering James' letter would have been Jewish, Greek, or Roman. A small part of the human body has a seemingly unbalanced influence on the whole person—which means that how it is used must be carefully monitored and controlled, lest a man or woman veer dangerously off course.

3:5 How significant is the tongue to the human being? James describes, "the tongue is a small member, yet it boasts of great things" (a, ESV). The tongue is *mikron melos*, "a small part," although it is able to make *megala auchei*, extrapolated as either "it makes great boasts" (NIV) or "it boasts of great exploits" (NRSV). That a small organ such as the tongue can make outlandish and arrogant claims, is something recognized by the Psalmist:

"They speak falsehood to one another; with flattering lips and with a double heart they speak. May the LORD cut off all flattering lips, the tongue that speaks great things; who have said, 'With our tongue we will prevail; our lips are our own; who is lord over us?' 'Because of the devastation of the afflicted, because of the groaning of the needy, now I will arise,' says the LORD; 'I will set him in the safety for which he longs'" (Psalm 12:2-5).

James' further thought on the tongue is, "Consider what a great forest is set on fire by a small spark" (b, NIV), or "What an immense stack of timber can be set ablaze by the tiniest spark!" (NEB). The point made is that the human tongue is like the ignition of a fire, which can then cause a significant disaster. Martin is forced to conclude, "With the setting of a hillside covered with dry brush or wood, such an environment is literally a tinderbox just waiting to explode at the slightest spark."[25] The description of the tongue, or speech to a fire, is one which is found in the Books of Proverbs and Sirach, as well as in the Pseudepigrapha:

"A worthless man digs up evil, while his words are like scorching fire" (Proverbs 16:27).

"For lack of wood the fire goes out, and where there is no whisperer, contention quiets down. *Like* charcoal to hot embers and wood to fire, so is a contentious man to kindle strife" (Proverbs 26:20-21).

---

[24] *The Works of Philo: Complete and Unabridged*, 76.
[25] Martin, 113.

"In proportion to the fuel for the fire, so will be the burning, and in proportion to the obstinacy of strife will be the burning; in proportion to the strength of the man will be his anger, and in proportion to his wealth he will heighten his wrath" (Sirach 28:10).

"Lord, save my soul from the criminal and wicked man, from the criminal and slandering tongue that speaks lies and deceit. The words of the wicked man's tongue (are) twisted so many ways; (they are) as a fire among a people which scorches its beauty. His visit fills homes with a false tongue, cuts down trees of joy, inflaming criminals; by slander he incites homes to fighting" (Psalms of Solomon 12:2-3).[26]

Concurrent with the above thoughts about the tongue are the words of Isaiah 9:18: "For wickedness burns like a fire; it consumes briars and thorns; it even sets the thickets of the forest aflame and they roll upward in a column of smoke."

The tongue, immature and/or wicked speech, or an undisciplined mind or thought life that manifests itself in evil talk—is something that can have an influence the same as a forest fire getting started. It should not escape our notice, though, that given James' likely location in the vicinity of Jerusalem in composing his letter, that some of the local geography might play a role in his example of a fire. McKnight indicates, "It might...be observed that forests are uncommon in the Land of Israel, and this leads some to suggest that hylē, 'forest,' might have its more common meaning 'wood,' suggesting brush fires instead of the conflagulation of a forest."[27] He references Isaiah 10:17: "And the light of Israel will become a fire and his Holy One a flame, and it will burn and devour his thorns and his briars in a single day."

It does have to be noticed that the majority of instances which take place within the Body of Messiah, regarding the tongue as a fire—are more likely to manifest themselves in proverbial "brush fires," than in major "forest fires." Most of what any of us encounter regarding improper speech, malicious gossip, rumors, and hearsay, will involve highly localized situations.

Bringing together the thoughts expressed by James in vs. 3-5, Dan G. McCartney issues the following, important admonition:

"One's speech does not direct one's literal body, although it does direct the course of one's life, and a loose tongue can send shock waves into the future for its owner as well as for those around the owner. The point of the ship illustration, like that of the horse and also the forest fire, is that the tongue's effectual power is grossly out of proportion to its size. Huge ships and the harsh winds that drive them are ruled, as it were, by a tiny rudder."[28]

The human tongue is a very small part of the body, and the boasting that almost always tends to originate from it is of a negative or derogatory context. In far too many cases, this

---

[26] R.B. Wright, "Psalms of Solomon," in James H. Charlesworth, ed., The Old Testament Pseudepigrapha, Vol 2 (New York: Doubleday, 1985), 662.

[27] McKnight, 280.

[28] McCartney, 184.

involves elevating self above others. A proper Bible teacher or spiritual leader cannot do this, as he or she must serve the Body of Messiah faithfully with edifying words of support. People in general are to make sure to embody Paul's word of Ephesians 4:29, "Let no evil talk come out of your mouths, but only such as is good for edifying, as fits the occasion, that it may impart grace to those who hear" (RSV). How we learn to do this as an emerging Messianic movement is going to become increasingly difficult in the future. Once again, we have to sadly observe how a small verse of a letter like James is being overlooked at best, but ignored at worst, by far too many of us.

3:6 James the Just's most damning evaluation of the human tongue is seen in v. 6: "And the tongue is a fire. The tongue is a world of evil placed among our body parts. It pollutes the whole body and sets on fire the course of life—and is set on fire by Gehenna" (TLV). The tongue is labeled as *ho kosmos tēs adikias*, "the world of the unrighteousness" (YLT). As John Calvin astutely noted, "A tiny part of our anatomy has all the evil of the world within its touch."[29] That the human tongue is directly associated with being a dangerous fire, and associated with the power of Hell, cannot and should not go unnoticed by readers of James' letter.

Proverbs 18:21 says, "Death and life are in the power of the tongue, and those who love it will eat its fruit." As previously referenced, Proverbs 16:27 issues the most condemning word, "A scoundrel plots evil, and his speech is like a scorching fire" (NIV). The Hebrew *ish belia'al* is widely rendered as "scoundrel" or "worthless man" (RSV/NASU). *TWOT* describes how "The concepts of Belial became a proper name for the prince of evil, Satan, in the pseudepigraphical literature...and II Cor 6:15 and II Thes 2:3."[30]

Is anyone speaking evil or speaking things not edifying to one's fellow brothers and sisters, effectively a servant of Satan? In His Sermon on the Mount, Yeshua said, "But I tell you that everyone who is angry with his brother shall be subject to judgment. And whoever says to his brother, '*Raca*' shall be subject to the council; and whoever says, 'You fool!' shall be subject to fiery Gehenna" (Matthew 5:22, TLV). A further word from the Lord is, "You are of *your* father the devil, and you want to do the desires of your father. He was a murderer from the beginning, and does not stand in the truth because there is no truth in him. Whenever he speaks a lie, he speaks from his own *nature*, for he is a liar and the father of lies" (John 8:44). Those not speaking the truth of God are speaking lies and serve the father of lies, the Devil himself.[31]

To an interpreter like Davids, "the tongue represents the evil world itself among the parts of the body....the tongue does not stop there, for it sets fire to the whole course of life, as anyone who has seen a plot develop into action or an argument turn into a fight will testify."[32] Motyer is more to the point, saying, "The first feature of the tongue was that it is

[29] Calvin, 290.
[30] Walter C. Kaiser, "bᵉlîyaʻal," in *TWOT*, 1:111.
[31] Also to be considered can be Romans 3:13-14; with its appeals to Psalm 5:9; 140:3; 10:7.
[32] Davids, pp 142, 143.

anti-god (the world); the final feature is that it is pro-Satan."[33] A human tongue which is not bridled by the power of God's Spirit and the example of Yeshua the Messiah to guide it, is most probably going to be (actively) accomplishing the Adversary's objectives.

James says that an uncontrolled tongue "defiles the entire body" or is "staining the whole body" (ESV). It also "sets on fire the cycle of nature" (NRSV). He employs the Greek phrase, *ton trochon tēs geneseōs*, which can be literally translated as "the cycle of genesis," with the Moffat New Testament having "the round circle of existence." This expression likely originates from classicism, as would be seen in a work such as Plato's *Timaeus*, where Timeaus tells Socrates about the Creator making the universe as a series of circles: "he established a single spherical universe in circular motion, alone but because of its existence needing no company other than itself, and satisfied to be its own acquaintance and friend. His creation, then, for all these reasons, was a blessed god" (4.46-50).[34] Martin concludes, though, that "By the time of James...the expression had probably become popularized and was used in a nontechnical way."[35] In the later literature of the Talmud, for example, one sees "*A Tannaite statement of the household of R. Ishmael:* 'What goes around comes around'" (b.Shabbat 151b).[36] Within the period of the broad First Century, the Roman Virgil, writing his *Aeneid*, employed similar terminology when talking about "time's wheel": "All these others whom you see, when they have rolled the wheel for a thousand years, are called out by God" (6.748-749).[37]

James uses the terminology "the wheel of nature" (Kingdom New Testament) to describe the common cycle of human life. The fact that the Greek and Roman authors employed similar terms, which steadily worked their way into Jewish discussion as well, only universalizes James' overall message. As an eloquent communicator, James may be making use of terms with which his broad audience would have been familiar.

James says that the tongue is a fire which has actually been "set on fire by hell" itself, or "it is set on fire by *Gei-Hinnom* itself" (CJB). *Gehenna* is the Greek transliteration of the Hebrew *Gey-Hinnom* or the Valley of Hinnom on the southern side of Jerusalem. It appears in the Tanach as a place where there was a cult that forced children to pass through fire in the worship of Molech (1 Kings 23:10; 2 Chronicles 28:3; 33:6; Jeremiah 7:31; 32:35). "In the first century B.C., this name came to be used in a metaphorical sense, to denote the place of fiery torment believed to be reserved for the wicked either immediately after death or ultimately after the Last Judgment" (IDB).[38] Yeshua uses the term Gehenna numerous times in the Gospels describing the place of eternal punishment for sinners.[39] Whether one views

---

[33] Motyer, 123.

[34] Plato: *Timaeus and Critias*, trans. Desmond Lee (London: Penguin Books, 1977), 46.

[35] Martin, 115; cf. Davids, 143.

[36] *The Babylonian Talmud: A Translation and Commentary*.

[37] Virgil: *The Aeneid*, trans. David West (London: Penguin Classics, 1990), pp 135-136.

[38] T.H. Gaster, "Gehenna," in *IDB*, 2:361.

[39] Matthew 5:22, 29, 30; 10:28; 18:9; 23:15, 33; Mark 9:43, 45, 47; Luke 12:5.

Gehenna as the final place of judgment for condemned sinners, a place which epitomizes evil and Satan (and which was originally intended for them), or some combination of the two—those who are unable to control their tongues are directly associated with a place opposite of the Kingdom of Heaven![40]

> 7 **For every species of beasts and birds, of reptiles and creatures of the sea, is tamed and has been tamed by the human race.** 8 **But no one can tame the tongue; it is a restless evil** *and* **full of deadly poison.**

3:7 The need ,for people to know how serious it is to control the tongue, is exemplified by James' assertion, "For every species of beast and bird, of reptile and sea creature, can be tamed and has been tamed by the human species" (NRSV). Humankind, man and woman, was made in the image of God and given dominion over Planet Earth and the animal kingdom (Genesis 1:28). Even though people are to be regarded as having this authority over such creatures, there is little human control over the tongue or speech. The verb *damazō* means, "**to reduce from an uncontrolled to a controlled state,** *subdue, tame, control*" (*BDAG*).[41]

Whether James is referring to every single animal species in the First Century being tamed by people is uncertain, but he is certainly referring to the ability of people to tame animals. This is because human beings, made in the image of God, have the ability to reason, think, and act on much more than instincts for basic survival and reproduction. However, improper usage of the tongue can and will reduce people to their baser instincts, and can cause their behavior to be little better than the animals.

Cain was admonished all the way back in Genesis 4:7 to master sin: "And if you do not do well, sin is crouching at the door; and its desire is for you, but you must master it." The Hebrew verb *mashal* appears in the Qal stem (simple action, active voice), and means "to **rule**," perhaps pertaining to a "ruler, the one in authority" (*HALOT*).[42] Human beings in their own strength actually have some capacity to "conquer it" (ATS), mastering sin to an extent—and the struggle to not be able to control one's tongue or speech is reflected in religious and philosophical literature all during the ages, from many cultures. Ancient Judaism, in particular, considered the evil tongue to be a grave sin, and this sentiment is certainly reflected in James' epistle. The Talmud makes some interesting observations about the tongue:

> "R. Hama bar Hanina said, 'What is the meaning of the verse of Scripture, "Death and life are in the hands of the tongue" (Pro. 18:21)? 'Now does the tongue have a hand?

---

[40] For some further, useful discussion, consult the author's publication *Why Hell Must Be Eternal*.
[41] *BDAG*, 211.
[42] *HALOT*, 1:647.

Rather it is to indicate to you that just as the hand can commit murder, so the tongue can commit murder. If you wish then to reason that just as the hand can commit murder only in the case of one who is nearby, also the tongue can commit murder only in the case of one who is nearby, [to prevent one's reaching that false conclusion,] Scripture states, "Their tongue is a sharpened arrow" (Jer. 9: 7). [It can commit murder even from a distance like an arrow.] If you wish then to reason that just as the arrow can reach only what is forty or fifty cubits away, so the tongue can reach only for forty or fifty cubits, [to prevent one's reaching that false conclusion,] Scripture states, "They have set their mouth against the heaven and their tongue walks through the earth" (Psa. 73: 9).' [Pursuing the analysis of the cited verse], since it is written, 'They have set their mouth against the heaven,' why did the author find it necessary to say as well, 'Their tongue is a sharpened arrow'? In this latter part of the verse, we are informed that [the tongue] kills like an arrow. *And since it is written, 'Their tongue is a sharpened arrow,' why was it necessary to state, 'Death and life are in the hands of the tongue' (Pro. 18:21)? It is in accord with what Raba said. For Raba said, 'Whoever wants life will find it in his tongue, whoever wants death will find it in his tongue'"* (b.Arachin 15b).[43]

If those who do not recognize Yeshua the Messiah as Redeemer have some human ability to control their speech and attitudes—**how much more should born again Believers in Him have the supernatural compulsion to control themselves!?**

3:8 James says "no single human is able to tame the tongue. It is an irrepressible evil, full of deadly poison" (Kingdom New Testament). The tongue is an *akatastaton kakon*, "a restless evil" (NASU), "an unruly evil" (KJV), or "a plague of disorder" (Moffat New Testament). The adjective *akatastatos*, while most often rendered as "restless," can also mean "*unstable, unsettled*" (LS).[44] No matter how it is rendered, though, the tongue "is an evil always liable to break out, and the poison it spreads is deadly" (Phillips New Testament).

The fact that the tongue is "full of deadly poison" is not a new concept for a figure like James to describe. King David attests in Psalm 140:1-3, "Rescue me, O LORD, from evil men; preserve me from violent men who devise evil things in *their* hearts; they continually stir up wars. They sharpen their tongues as a serpent; poison of a viper is under their lips. Selah." David also would say, "I will guard my ways that I may not sin with my tongue; I will guard my mouth as with a muzzle while the wicked are in my presence" (Psalm 39:1). In early Christian writing, we see the view expressed, "For slander is evil and an unsteady demon. It never abides in peace, but always remains in discord. Keep yourself from it, and you will always be at peace with all" (Hermas *Mandate* 2.3).[45]

The spiritual instability inside of a person can be most definitely wielded by an evil tongue. This is especially poignant of those who might be in a position of spiritual authority,

---

[43] *The Babylonian Talmud: A Translation and Commentary.*

[44] LS, 26.

[45] BibleWorks 8.0: Ante-Nicene Fathers. MS Windows Vista/7 Release. Norfolk: BibleWorks, LLC, 2009-2010. DVD-ROM.

as one who does not know how to control his or her speech—and is not as mature as should be desired—can infect others with his or her instability. Unregenerate people, no matter how hard they try and no matter how hard human beings have tried to philosophize about the tongue, speech, or their thoughts—ultimately cannot control them. **Yeshua the Messiah**, or Jesus Christ, **is the only answer.** As born again Believers, when it relates to what we say with our tongues, or however we conduct ourselves, we have to be able to master the temptations of the Adversary. God has given us His Holy Spirit to convict us and control us when we go off course. Thankfully, with the power of the Holy Spirit, we have the advantage over non-Believers. But, we all must make the conscious, free will decision to choose the right way over the wrong way. We have to be conscious of what we say and realize that the tongue is an animal that needs to remain tamed. All too frequently, even the best of us still have progress to make in this area.

9 With it we bless *our* Lord and Father, and with it we curse men, who have been made in the likeness of God;

3:9 James says that "With [the tongue] we bless ADONAI and Father, and with it we curse people, who are made in the image of God" (TLV). The human tongue is an element which can bless and praise the Creator God, and with that same human tongue, people can find themselves cursing and damning their fellow human beings, who compose the pinnacle of God's Creation. *To curse others is to effectively curse God...*

The famed word of Yeshua from His Sermon on the Mount, which is most worthy of repeating, is where He says, "You have heard that the ancients were told, 'YOU SHALL NOT COMMIT MURDER' [Exodus 20:13; Deuteronomy 5:17] and 'Whoever commits murder shall be liable to the court.' But I say to you that everyone who is angry with his brother shall be guilty before the court; and whoever shall say to his brother, 'Raca,' shall be guilty before the supreme court; and whoever shall say, 'You fool,' shall be guilty *enough to go* into the fiery hell" (Matthew 5:21-22, NASB). Transliterated into the Greek text as *rhaka*, BDAG defines this word as "**a term of abuse/put-down relating to lack of intelligence, numskull, fool**," but indicates that it is "fr. the Aramaic [*reiqa*] or [*reiqah*] 'empty one.'"[46] It is entirely possible that this was a First Century curse word employed by many in the Jewish community, and the Messiah specifically used it to make an important point to His listeners.

The mouth is supposed to be a venue where the people of God bring forth words of edification, encouragement, and above all praise for God. Yeshua admonished, "bless those who curse you, pray for those who mistreat you" (Luke 6:28). Concurrent with this, Paul told the Romans, "Bless those who persecute you; bless and do not curse" (Romans 12:14). Cursing someone—**a practice, which most lamentably, every single man or woman has committed at some point in their lives**—may be regarded as tantamount to murder.

---

[46] *BDAG*, 903.

Genesis 9:6 informs us, "Whoever sheds man's blood, by man his blood shall be shed, for in the image of God He made man." Because human beings are made in God's image, those who curse other human beings show that they have no regard for the Creator who made man and woman. Various members of James' audience may have found themselves in dire straights, either through persecution, bad treatment via poverty, teachers who were not edifying them, or some combination thereof. The rich, who James has condemned, could have been keen to curse the poor among them as some kind of "rabble." Regardless of what specifically was going on, James appeals to how important it is to speak life and not death.

Martin makes the highly useful observation of how "one cannot praise God in worship along with a murderous disposition and then stand before God and the church body as claiming to fulfill the law (2:8, 12)."[47] One of the most common phrases used in Ancient Judaism, and Judaism today, is the expression "Blessed are You O Lord our God." This statement begins a noticeable number of liturgical prayers in the *siddur*. The custom of using this blessing, and close derivatives, goes all the way back to Second Temple times, and remains the same for no matter how large a crowd is present to cant it. The Mishnah indicates,

"The same [rule applies for] ten and for ten thousand. For one hundred he says, 'Let us bless the Lord our God.' For one hundred and himself he says, 'Bless.' For one thousand he says, 'Let us bless the Lord our God, God of Israel.' For one thousand and himself he says, 'Bless.' For ten thousand he says, 'Let us bless the Lord our God, God of Israel, God of the Hosts who sits upon the Cherubim, for the food we have eaten.' For ten thousand and himself he says, 'Bless'" (m.*Berachot* 7:3).[48]

This quotation details how the congregation of people and leader would bless the Lord in corporate worship. It is thusly imperative for anyone who claims to be faithful to Israel's God to do the same in private worship, prayer, and in their dealings and interactions with other people. Each of us has the capacity to either say "God bless you" **or** "Damn you." We have a definite need and requirement to say the former—rather than the latter—and realize that if we curse others we are cursing God's prize, human creation(s). When we can speak words of blessing and edification, we not only reflect God's good character to others, but we will find ourselves in true obedience to His Instruction. As Johnson aptly concludes,

"[James'] religious framework is that of Torah. He evaluates speech in relational—that is, covenantal—terms. Human speech and action must be normed by the speech and action of God, who has chosen to become involved with humans. Human behavior, therefore, is judged not only on its capacity to perfect or to flaw an individual's character, but above all on the way it manifests right or wrong relationships."[49]

---

[47] Martin, 119.

[48] Tzvee Zahavy and Alan J. Avery-Peck, trans., in Neusner, *Mishnah*,11.

[49] Johnson, in *NIB*, 12:204.

Excursus: Human Beings Made in God's Image

adapted from the *Messianic Torah Helper* by Messianic Apologetics

One of the most significant issues that is avoided by most Messianics today appears in the very first Torah portion, *Bereisheet* (Genesis 1:1-6:8). Considering the fact that we encounter this issue every single year, and thousands of pages of thoughts, commentary, and theological analysis of this issue are seen in both the Jewish and Christian scholastic traditions—the fact that most Messianics do not deal with it is a sign that we are not at all where we need to be. The Biblical assertion that human beings are made in the image of God (Lat. *imago Dei*) is significant not only as it concerns human origins, but also as it concerns the composition and value of the human person. The ramifications of what it means to understand human beings made in God's image concern not only the uniqueness of the human race in His Creation, but also affect the mission and outlook of the *ekklēsia* in today's world as Believers should desire to see other people the way that He sees them.

As the Creation activities of God begin to draw to a close, He says something very important in Genesis 1:26-27, "'Let Us make man in Our image, according to Our likeness; and let them rule over the fish of the sea and over the birds of the sky and over the cattle and over all the earth, and over every creeping thing that creeps on the earth.' God created man in His own image, in the image of God He created him; male and female He created them." *Elohim*—actually speaking to Himself—says "Let us make humankind in our image, according to our likeness" (NRSV), *b'tzalmenu k'demutenu*. The human being possessing these qualities would be able to have dominion over God's Creation. Being made in God's image not only concerned the human male, but *also* the human female.

This assertion of Genesis 1:26-27 would have run completely contrary to Ancient Near Eastern concepts of rulership. Victor P. Hamilton writes, "It is well known that in both Egyptian and Mesopotamian society the king, or some high-ranking official, might be called 'the image of God.' Such a designation, however, was not applied to the canal digger or to the mason who worked on a ziggurat...In God's eyes all of mankind is royal. All of humanity is related to God, not just the king."[50] Both the male and female were originally created by God and intended to rule over God's Creation as His viceroy. In the words of Nahum M. Sarna,

"A human being is the pinnacle of Creation. This unique status is communicated in a variety of ways, not least by the simple fact that humankind is last in a manifestly ascending, gradual order. The creation of human life is an exception to the rule of creation by divine fiat...Human beings are to enjoy a unique relationship to God, who communicates with them alone and who shares with them the custody and administration of the world."[51]

---

[50] Victor P. Hamilton, *New International Commentary on the Old Testament: The Book of Genesis, Chapters 1-17* (Grand Rapids: Eerdmans, 1990), 135.

[51] Nahum M. Sarna, *JPS Torah Commentary: Genesis* (Philadelphia: Jewish Publication Society, 1989), 11.

In this schema, at least before the Fall, man was intended to be second *only to God* in Creation—a status which is restored to him to eternity. However, because of the Fall and the introduction of sin, the image of God on man has been marred.

I actually encountered one Messianic teacher who actually took up the subject of human beings made in God's image. This individual advocated that it was only Adam, the first human being, who was created in God's image.[52] Because of Adam and Eve's fall from grace, it was said, human beings are no longer made in God's image. Genesis 5:3 was supplied as a proof text: "When Adam had lived one hundred and thirty years, he became the father of *a son* in his own likeness, according to his image, and named him Seth." The Hebrew text says *v'yoled b'demuto k'tzalemo*, "and begot a son in his own likeness, after his image; and named him Shet [*v'yiqra et-shemo Sheit*]" (Jerusalem Bible-Koren). According to this, Seth was made after the image and likeness of Adam, as opposed to the image and likeness of God. And this is where the argument stopped.

But the Book of Genesis itself does not stop there. Genesis 9:6 further says, "Whoever sheds man's blood, by man his blood shall be shed, for in the image of God He made man." Mortals who are killed by sinful mortals are still considered by God to be made in His image. The difference is, of course, unlike Adam who was originally created without a sin nature, is that every human born since Adam has inherited that sin nature (cf. Romans 5:12). In that context *alone* are all human beings made "in Adam's image." A human being still possesses the unique Divine imprint of his or her Creator.

James, half-brother of Yeshua, says that the tongue can curse other people, all of whom "have been made in the likeness of God" (James 3:9). He uses the Greek word *homoiōsis*, "a making like" (Vine).[53] This is the same word used in the Greek LXX to translate *tzelem* in Genesis 1:26, and UBSHNT renders *homoiōsin Theou* as *tzelem Elohim*, indeed indicating that human beings—even after the Fall in the Garden of Eden—have been made in "the image of God." James expects his audience to show due respect for other human beings through what they say, regardless of whether or not they are saved and of the community of faith. John Wesley commented, "Indeed we have now lost this likeness; yet there remains from thence an indelible nobleness, which we ought to reverence both in ourselves and others."[54] While people are not as perfect as Adam was prior to the Fall, they still have enough of God's image within them as fallen humans to show others proper respect and character. We have enough of God's image within us that we should be drawn to things of God rather than things of Satan—and for those regenerated by the power of the Holy Spirit via the gospel of Yeshua the Messiah, that image should indeed have been restored.

Understanding what it means for a person to be made in the *tzelem Elohim* is significant. Christopher J.H. Wright asserts, "this forms the basis of radical equality of all human beings, regardless of gender, ethnicity, religion or any form of social,

---

[52] Cf. Monte Judah. "The Leaven of the Pharisees" <u>Yavoh: He is coming!</u> Vol. 9 No. 9, September 2003.

[53] *Vine*, 372.

[54] John Wesley, *Explanatory Notes Upon the New Testament*, reprint (Peterborough, UK: Epworth Press, 2000), 864.

economic, or political status."[55] He goes on to conclude, "Anything that denies other human beings their dignity or fails to show respect, interest and informed understanding for all that they hold precious is actually a failure of love."[56] If one is to truly demonstrate God's commanded love (seen in both the Tanach and Apostolic Scriptures) to His human creatures, then one must recognize that there is a strong value placed on them as made in His image. To stretch the meaning of Genesis 9:6, "Whoever sheds the blood of man, by man shall his blood be shed; for God made man in his own image" (RSV), by not demonstrating Yeshua's love to others—could it be considered tantamount to murder?

The human being is of extremely high value, especially in comparison to the rest of Creation. Being made in God's image (Genesis 1:26) obviously means that human beings possess unique qualities that those of the animal kingdom do not possess. In the Creation account, Genesis 2:7 says "the LORD God formed man of dust from the ground, and breathed into his nostrils the breath of life; and man became a living being." One part of the human being, his/her body, is clearly of this Earth. Yet it is significant that nowhere in the creation of the animals is it said that the animals had *nishmat chayim* breathed into them. The *Keil & Delitzch Commentary on the Old Testament* makes the important point, "the vital principle in man is different from that in the animal...The beasts [only] arose at the creative word of God."[57]

The *nishmat chayim* breathed into man indicates that people do possess a uniqueness specifically endowed by their Creator, a part made not of this Earth. The Hebrew language has no specific word for "mind" or "consciousness," but it is safe to say that this *neshamah* or specific "breath" from God, would help constitute it. In fact, when Adam ate the forbidden fruit, the Apostle Paul only makes the point that "death spread to all men" (Romans 5:12), *eis pantas anthrōpous* or "to all humans." **Human death is by no means the same as animal death.** To equate animal death and human death as being the same is to disregard the uniqueness of the human race in God's Creation, and the Divine imprint He has placed upon all men and women. Throughout history, human culture has demonstrated a number of unique qualities, bearing witness to God's imprint, including:

1. awareness of a moral code "written" or impressed with a conscience
2. concerns about death and about life after death
3. propensity to worship and desire to communicate with a higher being
4. consciousness of self
5. drive to discover and capacity to recognize truth and absolutes[58]

---

[55] Christopher J.H. Wright, *The Mission of God: Unlocking the Bible's Grand Narrative* (Downers Grove, IL: InterVarsity, 2006), 423.

[56] Ibid., pp 423-424.

[57] E-Sword 7.6.1: Keil & Delitzsch Commentary on the Old Testament. MS Windows 9x. Franklin, TN: Equipping Ministries Foundation, 2005.

[58] This list of five character traits is copied from Hugh Ross, *The Genesis Question: Scientific Advances and the Accuracy of Genesis*, second expanded edition (Colorado Springs: NavPress, 2001), 55.

Indeed, it is only the human race among all of God's Creation which possesses intelligence, a capacity to reason, and verbal speech—making it different when compared to the animals.

Psalm 8 picks up on the theme of man made in God's image, and specifically on the fact that God made man to rule over His Creation (Psalm 8:6-8). But the Psalmist's assertion is a very important one that cannot be overlooked: "You have made him a little lower than God" (Psalm 8:5a) or "You made him a little lower than the heavenly beings" (NIV). The Hebrew clause of interest is *m'at m'Elohim*, "lower than God," rendered in the Greek LXX as *brachu...par angelous*, "a little less than angels" (LXE), due to the ambiguous nature of *Elohim*.[59] Regardless, though, the lot of humanity is not cast with the animal kingdom **but instead** with the Heavenly host; the Psalmist **did not say** that man was made "a little higher than the animals." The debate that the Messianic movement has from time to time, about the intermediate state between the death of a person and resurrection would, in fact, be easily solved if we could understand what it means to be made in God's image with human beings possessing qualities different than the rest of Creation.[60]

The day-to-day aspects of understanding what it means for human beings to be made in God's image are quite severe for where sectors of the Messianic movement stand right now. Every person on Earth today has value in the eyes of the Creator, and it is the responsibility of those who have placed their trust in Yeshua to see value in other people. In today's Messianic community, we often see a great deal of vehemence and hatred released against fellow brothers and sisters in the Christian Church, and even the Jewish Synagogue, much less those of other religions. I have sat in Messianic worship services where people have prayed that the Israeli army roll their tanks over "the cursed bones of their Muslim enemies," but then have seen Israeli military being interviewed on television, testifying to the ethical dilemmas they face in defending their country. For some reason or another, rather than seeing value in Muslims as human beings made in God's image, various persons in our faith community have thought that it is appropriate to treat them as animals—even though our Heavenly Father *does not*. The Lord is every bit as concerned for their salvation and redemption as we should be!

There are undoubtedly any number of reasons why the image of God, a critical issue in the Torah, is avoided every year in the annual cycle. Have we adequately dealt with the questions of a person's composition? Do we really think that a human being is unique compared to the animals, or is no different than a dog or cat? Do we realize that each of us has a connection to the Heavenly dimension? Do we understand the responsibility for each of us to demonstrate love and respect toward others, because all

---

Among Hugh Ross' other notable works include: *A Matter of Days: Resolving a Creation Controversy* (Colorado Springs: NavPress, 2004); *Why the Universe Is the Way It Is* (Grand Rapids: Baker Books, 2008).

[59] The author of Hebrews applies Psalm 8:4-6 to Yeshua the Messiah and His Incarnation (Hebrews 2:6-10), whose ministry and service for the world restores redeemed humanity as second only to God in Creation. Consult the author's commentary *Hebrews for the Practical Messianic*.

[60] Consult the author's publication *To Be Absent From the Body*.

of humanity bears the Divine imprint? This is an issue that simply cannot be avoided any more. What will it mean for the redeemed to rule and reign with the Lord throughout eternity?

10 from the same mouth come *both* blessing and cursing. My brethren, these things ought not to be this way.

3:10 Continuing from v. 9, James makes the observation, "Out of the same mouth come praise and cursing. My brothers, this should not be" (NIV). Born again Believers, who should be changed by the power of God via His Son Yeshua, and following the example of the Messiah, should not be double-mouthed, as it were—as a double-mouthed person tends to be a major, outward manifestation of being doubled-minded (1:8). As Bauckham asserts, "It is the double-minded who bless God and curse God's human image. The inconsistency reveals duplicity."[61] There are some useful associated expressions of this found in the Apocrypha and Pseudepigrapha:

"Do not winnow with every wind, nor follow every path: the double-tongued sinner does that" (Sirach 5:9).

"Do not be called a slanderer, and do not lie in ambush with your tongue; for shame comes to the thief, and severe condemnation to the double-tongued" (Sirach 5:14).

"[A]nd do not become an enemy instead of a friend; for a bad name incurs shame and reproach: so fares the double-tongued sinner" (Sirach 6:1).

"The good set of mind does not talk from both sides of its mouth: praises and curses, abuse and honor, calm and strife, hypocrisy and truth, poverty and wealth, but it has one disposition, uncontaminated and pure, toward all men. There is no duplicity in its perception or its hearing. Whatever it does, or speaks, or perceives, it knows that the Lord is watching over its life" (*Testament of Benjamin* 6:5-6).[62]

When James says that from the same human mouth, both blessing and cursing can originate, there are various Jewish philosophical sentiments present which he could have been drawing from (and many more than just those referenced above), emphasizing the double-mindedness of those who are caught damning other people. Yeshua Himself said, in His famed word, always worth repeating, "*It is* not what enters into the mouth *that* defiles the man, but what proceeds out of the mouth, this defiles the man...But the things that proceed out of the mouth come from the heart, and those defile the man. For out of the heart

---

[61] Bauckham, in *ECB*, pp 1488-1489.
[62] Kee, "Testaments of the Twelve Patriarchs," in *The Old Testament Pseudepigrapha*, Vol 1, 827.

come evil thoughts, murders, adulteries, fornications, thefts, false witness, slanders. These are the things which defile the man..." (Matthew 15:11, 17-20). When curses upon a person come out of someone's mouth—they come directly from the heart. Moo astutely thinks that "James...views what comes out of the mouth as a barometer of spirituality."[63] Those who are mature can control what they say—particularly what they say in public—and are conscious of making sure that the need to be blessing both God and other people, neutralizes the temptation to curse.

Today in our Messianic faith community, what are we to do with those various teachers and individuals who tend to spend more time condemning and cursing others, especially Christians who are not Torah observant as they are? Should we not be encouraging change on the part of those Christians by blessing them and testifying to them of the blessings of Torah obedience? *Should we not be blessing Torah-friendly Christians, who are ethical and moral, already keeping a fair amount of God's Law, via words of encouragement and commendation?* Which is more becoming of the example of Messiah Yeshua? We each need to be careful of what we say and what comes out of our mouths. What we say needs to bring blessings as opposed to condemnation.

Have you ever heard a person be told, "Do you kiss your mother with that mouth?" after hearing that person use some foul language? James is essentially saying the same thing in v. 10. How can any of us praise God with our mouths on the one hand, but curse our fellow human beings on the other? And do be aware, that now with our electronic age, one does not have to actually physically speak a negative word of cursing; it can now be typed for all the world to see on a Facebook profile page, or in the comments on someone's blog. This provides a documented record for many others to access, reference, and perhaps (rightly) use against a person at a future (ill-opportune) time.

11 Does a fountain send out from the same opening *both* fresh and bitter *water*? 12 Can a fig tree, my brethren, produce olives, or a vine produce figs? Nor *can* salt water produce fresh.

3:11-12 Having just stated that a human mouth can issue both blessing and curses, James asks some pertinent questions, "A spring doesn't pour out fresh and bitter water from the same opening, does it? My brothers and sisters, these things should not be. A spring doesn't pour out fresh and bitter water from the same opening, does it?" (v. 11, TLV). In nature, a spring of water is either going to "pour out fresh water [or] brackish" water (Moffat New Testament). Similarly, a tree producing some kind of fruit, is going to produce one species of fruit, and not multiple species. The purpose of James' observation here, as stated by Martin, is how "The spring was made to produce one type of water; likewise the tongue was created to bring forth only one type of speech—namely, a 'good' speech (of

---

[63] Moo, 164.

blessing)."[64] There is a definite necessity to implore God, so that He can direct a man or woman to use the mouth as He originally intended it to be used.

The analogy that James makes between human speech and water is especially important, as he was likely alluding to the geography around the dry Middle East where water is scarce. Moo indicates, "Many a village owed its origins to the discovery of a spring, and depended on its reliable production of potable water for its continuing existence."[65] This is interesting, because just as a village often relied on a reliable source of fresh water, so does a congregation or fellowship of Believers rely on edifying and instructive teaching from a sound pastor-teacher. Communities of Believers rely on leaders who do not have bitter words. Communities of Believers are internally supported and edified by people who do not have bitter words as well. "Bitter" is used in the Tanach and Apocrypha to describe improper speech, which comes forth out of a person who is unstable and not serving the Lord:

"For the lips of an adulteress drip honey and smoother than oil is her speech; but in the end she is bitter as wormwood, sharp as a two-edged sword" (Proverbs 5:4).

"It is a miserable life to go from house to house, and where you are a stranger you may not open your mouth; you will play the host and provide drink without being thanked, and besides this you will hear bitter words" (Sirach 29:24-25).

Interestingly enough, Epictetus said something quite similar to what is encountered in James 3:11-12:

"So strong and unconquerable a thing is human nature! For how can a vine be moved to behave, not like a vine, but like an olive tree? Or an olive tree, not like an olive tree, but like a vine? It is impossible. It is inconceivable. Neither, therefore, is it possible for a human being entirely to lose human affections. And even those who have their male organs cut off cannot cut off their desires as men" (*Discourses* 2.20.28-29).[66]

James' words in vs. 11-12 are, most importantly, quite close to those of Yeshua. The Lord said, "You will know them by their fruits. Grapes are not gathered from thorn *bushes* nor figs from thistles, are they?" (Matthew 7:16). Also key is where Yeshua asserts, "For there is no good tree which produces bad fruit, nor, on the other hand, a bad tree which produces good fruit" (Luke 6:43).

Proper teaching and instruction is to yield mature Believers. Likewise, bad teaching and instruction yields, at the very least, immature Believers—or worse yet, those who spew spiritual venom. Only a regenerated heart can produce proper speech. The Messianic community today, which is still maturing in many areas, would learn much from James'

---

[64] Martin, 121.
[65] Ibid., 165.
[66] Epictetus: *The Discourses*, ed. Christopher Gill (London: Everyman, 1995), pp 127-128.

words about bitter water. We cannot be spewing bitter water by the words we say, but need to be gushing forth the living water of Yeshua. The Messiah admonished how, "He who believes in Me, as the Scripture said, 'From his innermost being will flow rivers of living water'" (John 7:38).

13 Who among you is wise and understanding? Let him show by his good behavior his deeds in the gentleness of wisdom. 14 But if you have bitter jealousy and selfish ambition in your heart, do not be arrogant and so lie against the truth.

3:13 James asks his audience, "Who is wise and understanding among you? By his good conduct let him show his works in the meekness of wisdom" (ESV). *Sophos*, used for "wise," was a term used by Ancient Judaism to describe a proper teacher. *TDNT* details, "Preexistent wisdom is the law. The good things that wisdom confers are fruits of teaching the law. Compared to earthly wisdom, the treasure of the law is inestimable, but even in earthly wisdom the rabbis are sometimes said to surpass the wise of this world."[67] Considering James' background as one who kept the Torah, an allusion to a Torah-based wisdom is certainly what is being talked about here. Could we at all paraphrase James' statements in v. 13 as, "Which of you has the wisdom and understanding that comes from diligent study and obedience to the Torah?"

It is important to understand that Hebraic wisdom is a practical, hands-on wisdom, which helps people in their daily lives and in concrete situations. Burdick observes how, "James does not have in mind the Greek concept of speculative wisdom but the Hebrew idea of practical wisdom that enables one to live a life of godliness."[68] For James' immediate audience, this meant that those who needed wisdom, especially teachers, needed to impact others with the ability to help the community of faith, and demonstrate a sound morality to others around them.

In the Messianic community today, Bible teachers and leaders must demonstrate the same things. It is absolutely true that there is a difference between knowledge and wisdom. One must have the spiritual ability, which comes from a sound relationship with God, to properly apply the information in Scripture to human life. Hebraic wisdom is a practical wisdom that impacts how people relate to one another, the world around us, and above all to our Creator. Hellenistic wisdom, in contrast, can widely be that which is theoretical or speculative, and frequently has little or no relevance to actual life situations. Ironically, there are Messianic Bible teachers who, while criticizing Hellenism and believe themselves to be espousing Hebraic wisdom, may actually be promoting things that are quite

---

[67] U. Wilckens, "wisdom," in *TDNT*, 1061.
[68] Burdick, in *EXP*, 12:190.

Hellenistic and have no relevance whatsoever to daily spiritual living. More than anything else, what they tend to promote are the vain speculations of their human imagination.[69]

True Biblical wisdom, as James puts it, will be shown by "works...done with gentleness born of wisdom" (NRSV), or "works by good conduct with wisdom's gentleness" (HCSB). A person will be led by good conduct if he or she is led by the wisdom rooted within God's Torah.[70] James is not emphasizing anything that should be new for his audience, and consequently is also something recognized in Jewish and early Christian traditions, which emphasize the importance of deeds or good works coming as a result of wisdom:

> "Anyone whose deeds are more than his wisdom—his wisdom will endure. And anyone whose wisdom is more than his deeds—his wisdom will not endure" (m.Avot 3:9b).[71]

> "If there is no learning of Torah, there is no proper conduct. If there is no proper conduct, there is no learning in Torah" (m.Avot 3:17a-b).[72]

> "Let the wise man display his wisdom, not by [mere] words, but through good deeds" (1 Clement 38).[73]

Demonstrating wisdom through good works is a continual theme throughout James' epistle. Take important note of the qualification here to properly do this; God's people must have "deeds done in the humility that comes from wisdom" (NIV). It is not just enough to have good works; good works must be performed in the proper manner. As Yeshua says in Matthew 5:3, "Blessed are the poor in spirit, for theirs is the kingdom of heaven." Messiah followers have to be gentle, kind, and considerate in their conduct—specifically in the actions that might distinguish them as specifically being "Torah observant."

3:14 Human nature is such that inappropriate and negative emotions and tendencies will often dominate relations between people, and relations between people and God. James states, "But if you have bitter envy and selfish ambition in your hearts, do not be boastful and false to the truth" (NRSV).

Unfortunately, many who consider themselves to have wisdom, especially teachers, possess a great deal of "jealousy and selfish ambition." Both of the Greek words for these terms need to be mentioned. Rendered as "jealousy" or "envy" (NIV/NRSV), zēlos means, **"intense negative feelings over another's achievements or success, jealousy, envy"** (BDAG),[74] and it is from zēlos where the term "zealot" is derived. It is interesting to briefly

---

[69] Consult the relevant sections of the author's compiled work *Confronting Critical Issues*.
[70] Cf. Martin, 129.
[71] Neusner, 680.
[72] Ibid., 681.
[73] *The Ante-Nicene Fathers*. <u>Libronix Digital Library System 1.0d: Church History Collection</u>.
[74] BDAG, 427.

think that James could have been targeting these words to any Zealots who might be encountering his message. James' admonition to them would be to be very careful with their devotion to Israel, as good works must be demonstrated in the proper spirit. The Zealots believed in a radical and bloody overthrow of the Roman authorities in Judea, and were often not concerned about their morality or treatment of Greeks and Romans. Even if there were no Zealots among James' audience, the Body of Messiah had no place for unbridled, human zealotry.

The second term, *eritheia*, while often rendered "selfish ambition," specifically relates to "*a courting distinction, a desire to put one's self forward, a partisan and factitious spirit which does not disdain low arts; partisanship, factitiousness*" (Thayer).[75] This selfish ambition or "self-seeking" (NKJV) is not only that which is concerned with one's own self and own self-interests, but also causes factions and divisions to build up in the community of faith.

Sadly, religious history has shown the examples of this time and time again, where a movement will be centered around a particular teacher or figure who is more concerned about espousing self-serving motives than with helping people in their relationship with the Lord. The Messianic movement today is not immune to this problem, either. There are teachers in the Messianic community who are more concerned about promoting themselves than helping people grow in their relationship with God. Specifically as Paul warned to one of his ancient audiences, "They eagerly seek you, not commendably, but they wish to shut you out so that you will seek them" (Galatians 4:17). These were the ones who secluded themselves so as to be perceived as great by the masses, who in turn would more enthusiastically seek them. This is especially true of some Messianic teachers in Israel today, who, simply because they live in Israel can be perceived as having "greater spiritual insight" than those living outside of Israel. These teachers may be promoting error, and it is often not questioned by those outside of Israel, regardless of the fact that such teachings may wreak havoc on those outside of where they live, and cause factions and divisions among brothers and sisters.

James says that those who are zealous only for themselves are the source of "insurrection and every evil matter" (v. 16, YLT). If in the case of Bible teachers, a teacher does not demonstrate a sincere desire to help people, and instead is only interested in self-promotion and various cardinal teachings, then problems can arise. James tells those in his audience who may be doing this not to deceive themselves. He asserts, "do not be arrogant and so lie against the truth." The verb *pseudomai* means "to lie," but specifically "to deceive by lies" (Vine).[76] James warns those who may cause these problems not only not to lie to themselves, but he warns his readers to be careful of those who deceive. Born again Believers are to use discernment and look out and beware for those who are self-consumed and self-absorbed who bring division to the community of faith, and are not operating in

[75] *Thayer*, 249.
[76] *Vine*, 367.

godly wisdom. Biblical wisdom, as is summarized in Proverbs, enables God's people to fear Him, be discerning, and operate in true righteousness:

> "The fear of the LORD is the beginning of knowledge; fools despise wisdom and instruction" (Proverbs 1:7).

> "He stores up sound wisdom for the upright; *He is* a shield to those who walk in integrity, guarding the paths of justice, and He preserves the way of His godly ones. Then you will discern righteousness and justice and equity *and* every good course" (Proverbs 2:7-9).

15 This wisdom is not that which comes down from above, but is earthly, natural, demonic. 16 For where jealousy and selfish ambition exist, there is disorder and every evil thing.

3:15 James actually makes the claim, having previously warned about "bitter jealousy and selfish ambition" (v. 14), that such negative qualities may be regarded as of "wisdom." Yet, James by no means applauds such wisdom, as he instead says, "This wisdom is not such as comes down from above, but is earthly, unspiritual, devilish" (RSV). James does not just think that this so-called wisdom originates from limited mortals, but actually employs *daimoniōdēs*, **"originating from the lower spirit-world, *infernal*, *demonic*"** (BDAG).[77] *This is the ultimate origin of "wisdom" which serves human self-interest.* It does not come from a strong relationship with the Heavenly Father and a humble spirit, but from thinking along worldly lines and from operating via a methodology little differently than that of Satan. Thankfully, though, James himself had previously admonished, "But if any of you lacks wisdom, let him ask of God, who gives to all generously and without reproach, and it will be given to him" (1:5).

3:16 The presence of demonic wisdom within a community of Messiah followers is most devastating according to James: "For wherever you find jealousy and rivalry you also find disharmony and all other kinds of evil" (Phillips New Testament). Those who operate in demonic wisdom—as opposed to godly wisdom—create a stir of problems in their wake. There will "be confusion (unrest, disharmony, rebellion) and all sorts of evil and vile practices" (Amplified Bible).

Akatastasia means *"disorder; insurrection...maltreatment by mob violence"* (CGEDNT).[78] If such individuals exhibiting these character traits are present, believing themselves to be something by affecting others spiritually, they are in actuality not helping people at all. They are, in fact, causing even more problems and even more damage. The Apostle Paul would say, "God is not *a God* of confusion but of peace, as in all the [assemblies] of the

---

[77] *BDAG*, 210.
[78] *CGEDNT*, 6.

saints" (1 Corinthians 14:33). While the human condition demands that peace will not always be present because of mortal limitations, peace is something nevertheless to be sought. Bible teachers must bring a stabilizing influence to the community, not something that creates havoc. Men and women within the assembly likewise are to use their speech and their demeanor, to see that potential discord is halted, lest the enemy have his way, and the mission of God is thwarted.

17 But the wisdom from above is first pure, then peaceable, gentle, reasonable, full of mercy and good fruits, unwavering, without hypocrisy. 18 And the seed whose fruit is righteousness is sown in peace by those who make peace.

3:17 While demonic wisdom is an evil to be steadfastly avoided (vs. 15-16), there is a godly wisdom from Heaven, which James highly commends to his audience: "The wisdom that comes from above is first pure, then peace loving, gentle, approachable, full of merciful thoughts and kindly actions, straightforward, with no hint of hypocrisy" (Phillips New Testament). These qualities are elaborated upon significantly in Yeshua's teaching from His Sermon on the Mount (Matthew 5-7), and the fruit of the Spirit that Paul lists in Galatians 5:22-23. Also to be considered could be some of the sentiments expressed in Wisdom 7:22-30 in the Apocrypha.[79]

The wisdom which decisively originates from God is that in which all Believers should be operating. Of all the qualities listed, perhaps the most important ones are "mercy and good fruits," *eleous kai karpōn agathōn*. True servants of God exemplify purity of spirit, peace, gentleness, obedience, and they have mercy and positive spiritual fruit evident in their lives. They do not waver or give into the pressures of the enemy, and they are without hypocrisy with a track record of faithfulness to the Lord. Those who are true servants of God have true righteousness, and are not only spiritually mature themselves, but are eager to rectify any mistakes that they might make.

These qualities, as should be expected, describe the character of God that should be present within us who have been born again. Godly wisdom is "considerate" (NIV) and takes

[79] "[F]or wisdom, the fashioner of all things, taught me. For in her there is a spirit that is intelligent, holy, unique, manifold, subtle, mobile, clear, unpolluted, distinct, invulnerable, loving the good, keen, irresistible, beneficent, humane, steadfast, sure, free from anxiety, all-powerful, overseeing all, and penetrating through all spirits that are intelligent and pure and most subtle. For wisdom is more mobile than any motion; because of her pureness she pervades and penetrates all things. For she is a breath of the power of God, and a pure emanation of the glory of the Almighty; therefore nothing defiled gains entrance into her. For she is a reflection of eternal light, a spotless mirror of the working of God, and an image of his goodness. Though she is but one, she can do all things, and while remaining in herself, she renews all things; in every generation she passes into holy souls and makes them friends of God, and prophets; for God loves nothing so much as the man who lives with wisdom. For she is more beautiful than the sun, and excels every constellation of the stars. Compared with the light she is found to be superior, for it is succeeded by the night, but against wisdom evil does not prevail" (Wisdom 7:22-30).

into view the needs of other people, which any good spiritual leader or Bible teacher should be doing. Burdick explains that God "is gentle and kind, although in reality he has every reason to be stern and punitive toward men in their sin."[80] It is only God in His mercy that enables Him to withhold judgment upon humanity, granting people ample opportunity to repent. When we emulate the character of our Heavenly Father, as His representatives on Earth we need to likewise withhold any punitive judgment toward others, exercising a wisdom that is truly Divine and not carnal.

3:18 How does a true, Heavenly wisdom manifest itself, according to James? "And **the fruit of righteousness** is sown in peace by those who make peace" (Kingdom New Testament). Here, James speaks of the *karpos...dikaiosunēs*. Previously, the Prophet Isaiah exclaimed of *ma'aseih ha'tzedaqah*: "And **the work of righteousness** will be peace, and the service of righteousness, quietness and confidence forever" (Isaiah 32:17). While a figure like James the Just would absolutely expect the peace enacted among brothers and sisters in the Lord to involve a cessation of conflict, the fuller meaning of *shalom* is most useful to remember here (see previous discussion for **2:16**). The DSS also include a useful thought, albeit fragmented, regarding wisdom:

"[...he who] seeks wisdom, [will find] wisdom...and nothing will] be hidden from him [...] he will lack nothing [...] in truth [...] from all who seek wisdom [...] reading and discipline [...] you will inherit them [...] great [honor] you shall give [...] honor" (4Q213).[81]

Yeshua Himself said, "Blessed are the peacemakers, for they will be called children of God" (Matthew 5:9, NRSV). James himself may be said to have been a peacemaker, given the important role that he played at the Jerusalem Council (Acts 15:13ff) and at Paul's return visit to Jerusalem (Acts 21:18ff). Rather than bow into the demands of the rigid, hyper-conservative Pharisees, who wanted the new, non-Jewish Believers to be circumcised as proselytes and keep the Torah to be saved (Acts 15:1, 5), James instead offered the non-disputable alternative, asserting that Tanach prophecy was in the process of fulfillment.[82]

Yeshua the Messiah says that each one of us will be known by our fruits (Matthew 7:17). The godly wisdom that the Lord wants to impart to each of us as His servants is to be used in the world, not just remain in our heads. It is a practical wisdom that is able to help others and give them the proper counsel, advice, comfort, and sometimes rebuke when they need it.

When we consider the instruction of v. 18, "Now the fruit of righteousness is sown in shalom by those who make shalom" (HNV), are we as Messianic Believers at all consciously trying to create and facilitate an environment of peace? *We live in interesting times as a Messianic movement that is still growing and maturing.* We all have the responsibility to see that the Messianic Bible teachers and leaders we submit to, have the godly wisdom that James describes, and that they are concerned for the spiritual well being of others. Those

---

[80] Burdick, in *EXP*, 12:191.
[81] Wise, Abegg, and Cook, 258.
[82] Consult the author's commentary *Acts 15 for the Practical Messianic*.

operating in godly wisdom are to be those who do not cause unnecessary problems, and are kind, considerate, and loving toward others. They do not cause factions and rivalry, but are concerned about the people who they serve. As our faith community matures, God will see to it that men and women of proper character rise up to serve the Body, as opposed to some who have arisen and have demonstrated nothing more than a "wisdom"—which at best, originates in their limited, human brains.

JAMES 4
COMMENTARY

1 What is the source of quarrels and conflicts among you? Is not the source your pleasures that wage war in your members? 2 You lust and do not have; *so* you commit murder. You are envious and cannot obtain; *so* you fight and quarrel. You do not have because you do not ask. 3 You ask and do not receive, because you ask with wrong motives, so that you may spend *it* on your pleasures.

4:1 While everything James the Just has communicated to his audience thusfar in his letter is extremely important, the contents of ch. 4 are noticeably more intense and severe. As he asks in v. 1, "What causes wars, and what causes fightings among you? Is it not your passions that are at war in your members?" (RSV). In the view of Ben Witherington III, "In terms of rhetorical strategy, James followed the protocol that one might expect when dealing with a difficult subject: one saves for last the most difficult and troubling of the subjects one must persuade the audience about. This rhetorical tactic is called insinuatio, and it is a regular practice when addressing an audience that one does not know personally or that the author does not already have a close relationship with."[1]

When reading that the various problems are *en humin* or "among you," we cannot overlook how "you" is in the plural. Are the problems mentioned by James speaking of an internal, personal conflict that people have within themselves, thus the plural "you" is to his audience or readers generally? Or, is the plural "you" to be taken as an internal congregational conflict among James' intended audience? In 1 Corinthians 12:14, "For the body is not one member, but many," Paul speaks of the Corinthian assembly and the different people in it, then being a component of a greater Body of Messiah. It might be best for v. 1, for readers to simply acknowledge that problems which erupt from the hearts and minds of individual people, then negatively affect the members of assemblies and fellowships of Believers as a whole, causing factions to manifest and for sinful activities to be displayed.

While commonly rendered as something like "quarrels and conflicts" (NASU) or "fights and quarrels" (NIV), *polemoi kai...machai*, it cannot go overlooked how James actually employs terminology that is used in the context of military battles. The term

---

[1] Witherington, 505.

polemos means *"battle, fight, war"* (LS),[2] and *machē* means *"battle, fight, combat"* (LS).[3] Ronald A. Ward notes, "'War' implies continued hostility; 'battle' the occasional outburst. There may possibly be a further distinction. 'To battle' is used in Greek for a violent verbal dispute and for 'making a scene.'"[4] While there is discussion as to whether or not James had a literal or metaphorical intention by using such battle language, **that whatever was going on was most problematic cannot be disputed.** A possible sort-of scene of what might have been going on, is paralleled in Josephus' record of when Ismael was appointed as high priest by Agrippa:

"And now arose a sedition between the high priests and the principal men of the multitude of Jerusalem; each of whom got them a company of the boldest sort of men...and when they struggled together, they did it by casting reproachful words against one another, and by throwing stones also" (*Antiquities of the Jews* 20.180).[5]

If you can just picture what James' audience may have been going through: violent disputes, whether over teachings, doctrines, attitudes, or some combination thereof, where slanderous speech and insults were being thrown at people—and perhaps even some degree of physical violence—James wanted it all stopped immediately.

Paul communicates in 2 Corinthians 10:3-5, "For though we walk in the flesh, we do not war according to the flesh, for the weapons of our warfare are not of the flesh, but divinely powerful for the destruction of fortresses. *We are* destroying speculations and every lofty thing raised up against the knowledge of God, and *we are* taking every thought captive to the obedience of Messiah." Paul appeals to military imagery, which is that God's people are in a spiritual war against the forces of darkness. He notes that Believers' spiritual weapons of warfare "are powerful through God for the demolition of strongholds" (HCSB). One can see that while many of the quarrels and fights within the Body of Messiah are emotional (2 Timothy 2:23; Titus 3:9), that at the same time Believers are engaged in a real spiritual war with the forces of darkness (1 Peter 2:11), which at times will certainly manifest itself, at least in the threat of physical harm (2 Corinthians 7:5).

J.A. Motyer takes James' word of v. 1 to represent figurative battles taking place, but still advises how "we must not allow metaphor to take away from the force of his words and the horror that they are intended to strike."[6] Certainly, that there were violent activities being committed in the hearts of presumed Messiah followers, can be assumed. The cause of such conflicts occurring are the "pleasures" or "passions" (RSV) present in people, widely focused on self-pleasure and self-absorbsion. The term *hēdonē*, "marks a non-Christian orientation to life. It belongs to the sphere that is ruled by ungodly forces"

---

[2] *LS*, 653.
[3] Ibid., 489.
[4] Ward, in *NBCR*, 1231.
[5] *The Works of Josephus: Complete and Unabridged*, 127.
[6] Motyer, pp 140-141.

and "comes under the same judgment as fallen human nature" (*TDNT*).[7] *Hēdonē* is the same Greek word where our English term "hedonism" originates. J. Ronald Blue describes it as "the playboy philosophy that makes pleasure mankind's chief end."[8] This is an obvious sin of the flesh which must be constantly fought against. God will not facilitate any person's hedonistic desires, where people seek pleasure for their fleshly benefit. 4 Maccabees 1:25-26 describes it as thus: "In pleasure [*hēdonē*] there exists even a malevolent tendency, which is the most complex of all the emotions. In the soul it is boastfulness, covetousness, thirst for honor, rivalry, and malice."

James' word in v. 1, "Where do wars come from? Do people among you fight? It all comes from within, doesn't it—from your desires for pleasure which make war in your members" (Kingdom New Testament), actually has some significant parallels in both the Jewish philosopher Philo and Greek philosopher Plato:

"Perhaps it is a piece of folly to make a long speech upon matters which are so manifest, as to which there is no individual and no city that is ignorant, that they are not only every day, but even every hour, as one may say, supplying a visible proof of the truth of my assertion. Is the love of money, or of women, or of glory, or of any one of the other efficient causes of pleasure, the origin of slight and ordinary evils? Is it not owing to this passion that relationships are broken asunder, and change the good will which originates in nature into an irreconcilable enmity? And are not great countries and populous kingdoms made desolate by domestic seditions, through such causes? And are not earth and sea continually filled with novel and terrible calamities by naval battles and military expeditions for the same reason? For, both among the Greeks and barbarians, the wars between one another, and between their own different tribes, which have been so celebrated by tragedians, have all flowed from one source, namely, desire of money, or glory, or pleasure; for it is on such subjects as these that the race of mankind goes mad" (Philo *On the Decalogue* 151-153).[9]

"And the body fills us with passions and desires and fears, and all sorts of fancies and foolishness, so that, as they say, it really and truly makes it impossible for us to think at all. The body and its desires are the only cause of wars and factions and battles" (Plato *Phaedo* 66c).[10]

4:2 James continues in his stark admonitions: "You desire and do not have, so you murder. You covet and cannot obtain, so you fight and quarrel. You do not have, because you do not ask" (ESV). Rendered as either "lust" (NASU) or "desire" (RSV/ESV/TNIV), the verb *epithumeō* is used in the LXX in the Ten Commandments prohibiting covetousness,

[7] G. Stählin, "*hēdonē*," in *TDNT*, 305.
[8] Blue, in *BKCNT*, 829.
[9] *The Works of Philo: Complete and Unabridged*, 531.
[10] Plato: *Plato in Twelve Volumes*, trans. Harold North Fowler (1966). Accessible online at <http://www.perseus.tufts.edu/hopper/text?doc=Perseus%3atext%3a1999.01.0170%3atext%3dPhaedo>.

translating the Hebrew verb *chamad*: "You shall not covet [*chamad*] your neighbor's house; you shall not covet [*chamad*] your neighbor's wife or his male servant or his female servant or his ox or his donkey or anything that belongs to your neighbor" (Exodus 20:17; cf. Deuteronomy 5:21). This is important to be aware of because *chamad*, in the Qal stem (simple action, active voice), means "**desire** and try to acquire, **crave**, covet" (*CHALOT*).[11] *Epithumeō*, in decisive clarification, means, "To have the affections directed toward something, to lust, desire, long after" (*AMG*).[12] We certainly see instances in the Tanach where murder of someone is used for the acquisition of something, notably with David sending Uriah to the front lines so that he could have Bathsheba (2 Samuel 11), or with Ahab acquiring Naboth's field (1 Kings 21:1-16). In Scripture, coveting can often be tantamount to, or at least closely associated with, murder.

James' remarks about murder have certainly been debated by examiners, some being divided over whether or not he speaks about actual physical murder, or he is using it in a more figurative sense. All are agreed that James warns about the thoughts and attitudes that can certainly lead to physical murder. As the Apostle John would say, "Everyone who hates his brother is a murderer; and you know that no murderer has eternal life abiding in him" (1 John 3:15). In early Christian writing, one sees the sentiment expressed, "Be not prone to anger, for anger leadeth the way to murder; neither jealous, nor quarrelsome, nor of hot temper; for out of all these murders are engendered" (*Didache* 3:2).[13]

Some have speculated that James spoke of murder, because there were Jewish Zealots among his audience. If indeed so, this could have led to actual murder being practiced by a number within the assembly. Ralph P. Martin thinks, "it is quite conceivable that (at least) some of the Jewish Christians were former Zealots," and "the taking of another's life is not out of the realm of possibility for the [assembly] members as a response to disagreement."[14] However, he further notes that "While James' community may have not yet experienced and engaged in literal murder on a mass scale, the contingency is a very real one and must be warned against."[15] Martin argues, "To say that all that James means here is 'hate' (Matt 5:21-22; 1 John 3:15) overlooks the fact that the letter of James was most likely written in a period when murder was accepted as a 'religious' way to solve disagreements,"[16] referencing the attitudes of Saul in Acts 9:1.[17]

Luke T. Johnson is one who disagrees with the Zealot movement being a factor here, stating, "Scholars who imagine that James is warning against some ancient zealot activity

---

[11] William L. Holladay, ed., *A Concise Hebrew and Aramaic Lexicon of the Old Testament* (Leiden, the Netherlands: E.J. Brill, 1988), 108.

[12] Zodhiates, *Complete Word Study Dictionary: New Testament*, 627.

[13] BibleWorks 8.0: Ante-Nicene Fathers.

[14] Martin, 144.

[15] Ibid.

[16] Ibid., 146.

[17] "Now Saul, still breathing threats and murder against the disciples of the Lord, went to the high priest" (Acts 9:1).

miss the mark entirely. He is addressing members of the Christian community who gather in the name of Jesus and profess the faith of the glorious Lord Jesus Christ, but whose attitudes and actions are not yet fully in friendship with God."[18] Scot McKnight is a bit more toned down, as he concludes, "Physical or not, even to this day the words of James should embarrass those who are committed to a Lord who taught the way of love, the way of peace, and whose cross brought into graphic reality a new (cross) way of life."[19]

4:3 Having noted how the source of the problems in his audience are pleasures (v. 1), James asserts, "You ask and do not receive, because you ask with wrong motives so that you may spend it on your passions" (TLV). Apparently, there would have been some who would be praying inappropriate things to God, namely that their lustful desires or hedonistic pleasures, of some kind, be met—*and God was certainly not going to answer these prayers!* While Yeshua does say, "For everyone who asks, receives; and he who seeks, finds; and to him who knocks, it will be opened" (Luke 11:10), this does not mean that the Father is going to grant any request of a sinful nature. As was the case with James' audience, the Lord is certainly not going to answer prayers that may be connected to acts of murder. It is those who are just, who will have their prayers answered (Psalm 34:15-17; Proverbs 10:24).

4 You adulteresses, do you not know that friendship with the world is hostility toward God? Therefore whoever wishes to be a friend of the world makes himself an enemy of God.

4:4 Building upon his previous remarks about murder, pleasures, and asking for things, James issues a serious indictment against at least one sector of his audience in severe error: "You adulteresses, do you not know that friendship with the world is hostility toward God? Therefore whoever wishes to be a friend of the world makes himself an enemy of God." James refers to various "adulterous people" (NIV), although as Peter Davids aptly notes, "the feminine vocative [*moichalides*] clearly calls one back to the whole OT tradition of Israel as God's unfaithful wife denounced in the prophetic books."[20] An entire litany of possible passages and statements encountered in the Tanach, could be in view (Isaiah 1:21; 50:1; 54:1-6; 57:3; Jeremiah ch. 3; 13:27; Ezekiel 16:38; 23:45; Hosea chs. 1-3; 4:12; 9:1).

When James, or any of the Biblical authors for that matter, talk about "the world," what are they specifically referring to? When one is a friend of the world, a person does not only demonstrate a favoritism to its people, but also to its ways and attitudes. According to James, "friendship with the world is hatred toward God" (NIV). The Phillips New Testament actually has an excellent paraphrase of v. 4: "You are like unfaithful wives,

[18] Johnson, in *NIB*, 12:212.
[19] McKnight, 322.
[20] Davids, 160.

never realizing that to be the world's lover means becoming the enemy of God! Anyone who chooses to be the world's friend is thereby making himself God's enemy." When an individual makes God his enemy, nothing can help him. It is sometimes worse than a marriage where a husband or wife has been unfaithful for a season, but then there is reconciliation later. When a person decides that he or she wants nothing more to do with the Creator, you as the created can expect nothing less than eternal punishment.

5 Or do you think that the Scripture speaks to no purpose: "He jealously desires the Spirit which He has made to dwell in us"?

4:5 There is some difficulty regarding what v. 5 communicates, "Or do you suppose it is in vain that the scripture says, 'He yearns jealously over the spirit which he has made to dwell in us'?" (RSV). There is specific difficulty regarding how one takes *graphē legei*, as one might assume some kind of direct Tanach quote to follow. The view of an interpreter like Richard Bauckham is, "Probably James quotes an apocryphal work which is no longer extant."[21] A third possibility is that there is no specific Tanach or Old Testament quote in mind, but instead some kind of a general appeal (cf. as would be seen in John 7:37-39), as Martin concurs, "It may well be that the best we can do is to suggest that he is expressing the theme of God's jealousy contained in the OT."[22] Some passages from the Tanach which may be in view, include:

"for you shall not worship any other god, for the LORD, whose name is Jealous, is a jealous God" (Exodus 34:14).

"Thus says the LORD of hosts, 'I am exceedingly jealous for Zion, yes, with great wrath I am jealous for her'" (Zechariah 8:2).

"As the deer pants for the water brooks, so my soul pants for You, O God. My soul thirsts for God, for the living God; when shall I come and appear before God?" (Psalm 42:1-2).

"My soul longed and even yearned for the courts of the LORD; my heart and my flesh sing for joy to the living God" (Psalm 84:2).

The main thrust of what is intended, by "He yearns jealously over the spirit which He made to dwell in us" (TLV), is to communicate a sense of intimacy and close association between a person and the Creator God. Yet, while it is clear that the verb *katoikizō* means,

---

[21] Bauckham, in *ECB*, 1489.
[22] Martin, 149.

"*cause to dwell, establish, settle*" (BDAG),²³ is the *pneuma* which is to dwell in people the Holy Spirit, or is it the human spirit? Among modern versions, one will encounter "Spirit" both capitalized (NKJV, NASU, HCSB) and in lowercase as "spirit" (RSV, NIV, NRSV, ESV, CJB). In some early Christian writing, we see the sentiment expressed, "Love the truth, and let nothing but truth proceed from your mouth, that the spirit which God has placed in your flesh may be found truthful before all men; and the Lord, who dwelleth in you, will be glorified" (Hermas *Mandates* 3:1),²⁴ which could be used to favor the *pneuma* in v. 5 to be the human spirit.²⁵ The Jewish philosopher Philo, though, expressed the thought that Abraham was given the Holy Spirit because of his belief in God (Genesis 15:6):

"For, indeed, his servants at all times steadfastly observed him, as subjects observe a ruler, looking with admiration at the universal greatness of his nature and disposition, which was more perfect than is customary to meet with in a man; for he did not use the same conversation as ordinary men, but, like one inspired, spoke in general in more dignified language. Whenever, therefore, he was possessed by the Holy Spirit he at once changed everything for the better, his eyes and his complexion, and his size and his appearance while standing, and his motions, and his voice; the Holy Spirit, which, being breathed into him from above, took up its lodging in his soul, clothing his body with extraordinary beauty, and investing his words with persuasiveness at the same time that it endowed his hearers with understanding" (*On the Virtues* 217).²⁶

With cases to be made for the *pneuma* here to be either the Holy Spirit or human spirit, Dan G. McCartney actually concludes, "the 'S/spirit he caused to dwell in us' is a reference to the divine S/spirit considered not as the person of the Holy Spirit but as the presence of God in divinely given wisdom and understanding."²⁷

6 **But He gives a greater grace. Therefore it says, "GOD IS OPPOSED TO THE PROUD, BUT GIVES GRACE TO THE HUMBLE"** [Proverbs 3:34, LXX]. 7 **Submit therefore to God. Resist the devil and he will flee from you.** 8 **Draw near to God and He will draw near to you. Cleanse your hands, you sinners; and purify your hearts, you double-minded.**

4:6 God's personal desire is to see His people worship and commune intimately with Him as sons and daughters, serving Him in the world without any malice or hatred toward others. Accomplishing the purposes and aims of God's Kingdom, though, can only be accomplished if His people have the right attitude when they approach Him. James states that "he gives more grace" (ESV), quoting Proverbs 3:34, "Though He scoffs at the scoffers,

²³ BDAG, 534.
²⁴ BibleWorks 8.0: Ante-Nicene Fathers.
²⁵ McKnight, 339.
²⁶ *The Works of Philo: Complete and Unabridged*, 662.
²⁷ McCartney, 214.

yet He gives grace to the afflicted." V. 6 actually includes a quote from the from the Greek Septuagint, which renders the Hebrew verb *litz* in the Qal stem (simple action, active voice), "to **brag, speak boastfully**" (*HALOT*),[28] as *antitassō*, "*to set opposite to, range in battle against*" (*LS*).[29] This is likely reflective of an interpretive tradition which sees scoffing at sinners tantamount to God fighting against them.

V. 7 following, certainly communicates the reality of how Messiah followers are engaged in a spiritual war against the forces of darkness. Vs. 6-8 in total may be said to parallel 1 Peter 5:5-9:

"[A]nd all of you, clothe yourselves with humility toward one another, for GOD IS OPPOSED TO THE PROUD, BUT GIVES GRACE TO THE HUMBLE [Proverbs 3:34, LXX]. Therefore humble yourselves under the mighty hand of God, that He may exalt you at the proper time, casting all your anxiety on Him, because He cares for you. Be of sober *spirit*, be on the alert. Your adversary, the devil, prowls around like a roaring lion, seeking someone to devour. But resist him, firm in *your* faith, knowing that the same experiences of suffering are being accomplished by your brethren who are in the world."

4:7 James' solution, to not falling into the position of being an opponent of God (v. 6a), is that His people must "Therefore, submit to God. Moreover, take a stand against the Adversary" (CJB), and this should not at all have been a new concept for James' audience, as it is repeated numerous times in the Tanach. Our Heavenly Father wants His people to turn to Him. Zechariah 1:3, for instance, specifically says, "Therefore say to them, 'Thus says the LORD of hosts, "Return to Me," declares the LORD of hosts, "that I may return to you," says the LORD of hosts.'" Psalm 24:4-5 also states, "He who has clean hands and a pure heart, who has not lifted up his soul to falsehood and has not sworn deceitfully. He shall receive a blessing from the LORD and righteousness from the God of his salvation." Interestingly enough, some of the same thoughts expressed by James in v. 7, may be said to also be present in the Second Century B.C.E. *Testament of Dan:*

"And now fear the Lord, my children, be on guard against Satan and his spirits. Draw near to God and to the angel who intercedes for you, because he is the mediator between God and men for the peace of Israel. He shall stand in opposition to the kingdom of the enemy. Therefore the enemy is eager to trip up all who call on the Lord, because he knows that on the day in which Israel trusts, the enemy's kingdom will be brought to an end" (6:1-4).[30]

These are some interesting thoughts, most especially because of the fact that James' audience represents those who are supposed to compose a Kingdom realm of Israel in the process of being restored (1:1).

The result of Believers in Yeshua, turning toward God, is that they will be able to resist Satan and his temptations. James says, "Resist the devil and he will flee from you."

---

[28] *HALOT*, 1:529.

[29] *LS*, 81.

[30] Kee, "Testaments of the Twelve Patriarchs," in *The Old Testament Pseudepigrapha*, Vol 1, 810.

The Greek *diabolos* is frequently used in the LXX to render the Hebrew *satan*, which in its noun form means "**Adversary, one who withstands, Satan**" (*TWOT*).[31] Withstanding Satan requires Divine aid from the Lord, as human strength alone can only resist evil temptations for a short time. As Paul will further state in Ephesians 6:10-12,

"Finally, be strong in the Lord and in the strength of His might. Put on the full armor of God, so that you will be able to stand firm against the schemes of the devil. For our struggle is not against flesh and blood, but against the rulers, against the powers, against the world forces of this darkness, against the spiritual *forces* of wickedness in the heavenly places."

4:8 As Believers in Yeshua turn toward God and resist the Adversary (v. 7), James instructs, "Draw near to God and He will draw near to you. Cleanse your hands, you sinners; and purify your hearts, you double-minded." The need for God's people to turn to Him is a heavy theme of the Tanach (2 Chronicles 15:1-4; Zechariah 1:3; Malachi 3:7). The Talmud regularly counsels Torah study to resist temptation, specifically including the admonition, "Whoever recites the Shema on his bed is as if he holds a twoedged sword in his hand [to fight against demons], as it is said, 'Let the high praises of God be in this mouth, and a two-edged sword in their hand' (Psa. 149:6)" (*b.Berachot* 5a).[32]

One of the important qualifications that a man or woman must undertake, in order to *properly draw near* to the Lord, is the necessity of being spiritually cleansed. It is not unlikely that James intended some sort of allusion to priestly cleansing rites as seen in the Torah (i.e., Exodus 30:17-21),[33] while at the same time, the Prophet Isaiah declares, "So when you spread out your hands *in prayer*, I will hide My eyes from you; yes, even though you multiply prayers, I will not listen. Your hands are covered with blood. Wash yourselves, make yourselves clean; remove the evil of your deeds from My sight. Cease to do evil" (Isaiah 1:15-16). When Isaiah specifically says "Your hands are stained with crime" (NJPS), acts worthy only of Divine vengeance have been performed. James has just warned against possible murder that has been committed by members of his audience (v. 2). Whether this is actual murder or only murderous thoughts will remain debated. But what should not be debated is the fact that people should see to it that they have been thoroughly cleansed, and that all of their individual members (v. 1) are used not to commit sin, but instead serve the Lord.

---

[31] J. Barton Payne, "satan," in *TWOT*, 2:875.

[32] *The Babylonian Talmud: A Translation and Commentary.*

[33] "The LORD spoke to Moses, saying, 'You shall also make a laver of bronze, with its base of bronze, for washing; and you shall put it between the tent of meeting and the altar, and you shall put water in it. Aaron and his sons shall wash their hands and their feet from it; when they enter the tent of meeting, they shall wash with water, so that they will not die; or when they approach the altar to minister, by offering up in smoke a fire sacrifice to the LORD. So they shall wash their hands and their feet, so that they will not die; and it shall be a perpetual statute for them, for Aaron and his descendants throughout their generations'" (Exodus 30:17-21).

Those who do not cleanse themselves are considered to be double-minded or *dipsuchos*, having been previously used in 1:8. Douglas J. Moo remarks, "Its repetition here underscores James's accusation that his readers are attempting to be 'friends' with both God and the world at the same time (v. 4): a conflict of basic allegiance that our jealous God will simply not tolerate...To allow 'the world' to entice us away from total, single-minded allegiance to God is to become people who are divided in loyalties, 'double-minded' and spiritually unstable."[34]

Sirach 2:12 in the Apocrypha says, "Woe to faint hearts and nerveless hands and to the sinner who leads a double life" (NEB). Born again Believers cannot walk both the path of good and the path of evil, as they instead have to choose to follow God's path and submit to Him. By Messiah followers being humbled before Him, the Lord will give each of us the ability to resist the temptations of Satan. But we also must be thoroughly cleansed of anything that might cause us to sin. The Apostle Paul writes that Yeshua has cleansed the assembly "by the washing of water with the word" (Ephesians 5:26). And it is surely not just enough to "pray" for cleansing; cleansing must be coupled with Scriptural instruction and admonition, which will transform us to think and act more like God.

For James' audience in the First Century, much of the sin that he was warning against related to murderous behavior, following the ways of the world, and disloyalty toward God. What might we be facing today? As Messianic Believers who are studying the Torah, do we ever fall short of the Torah's ethical and moral standard that should be second nature to us?

9 Be miserable and mourn and weep; let your laughter be turned into mourning and your joy to gloom. 10 Humble yourselves in the presence of the Lord, and He will exalt you.

4:9 Continuing to admonish his audience, James states further requirements of the necessary spiritual solution for them. He says "Be wretched and mourn and weep" (ESV). The verb *talaipōreō* fully means, "**to experience distress, *endure sorrow/distress, be miserable***" (BDAG).[35] James wants them to "Grieve, mourn and wail" (NIV). He does not want them to feel happy or be comforted, but instead says "Let your laughter be turned to mourning and your joy to dejection" (RSV). Many encountering James' letter must understand how bad they have been in light of God's holiness.

It is possible that v. 9 includes some of the themes of *Yom Kippur* or the Day of Atonement, where God's people are to be focused on their sins and shortcomings, be widely unhappy, and repent of their errors from the previous year. At the same time, eschatological themes of judgment upon the unrepentant are in more concentrated view,

---

[34] Moo, 194.
[35] BDAG, 988.

especially as Yeshua said, "Woe to you who are well-fed now, for you shall be hungry. Woe *to you* who laugh now, for you shall mourn and weep" (Luke 6:25). Laughter is widely the mark of a fool (cf. Proverbs 10:23; Ecclesiastes 7:6; Sirach 27:13). The joy being specifically referenced by James here is not like that of Paul, in a passage like Philippians 4:4,[36] but instead, as Moo properly summarizes,

"[T]he joy James warns about is the fleeting and superficial joy that comes when we indulge in sin. True Christian joy can never be ours if we ignore or tolerate sin; it comes only when we have squarely faced the reality of our sin, brought it before the Lord in repentance and humility, and experienced the cleansing work of the Spirit."[37]

Ward makes the observation of how "the Rabbis did **not** often speak of laughter. It comes from enemies and from fools and in the rabbinic view marks the rejection of God's universal control and the affirmation of human autonomy."[38] James says that his audience's "laughter must change to mourning" (HCSB). If James is at all reflecting on ancient Jewish views of laughter—then the laughter to which he refers is notably not humor, nor laughter which comes from genuine joy, but laughter that is birthed in rejection of God's will and primacy in the lives of human beings that mocks Him.

4:10 Those who truly want to succeed and be recognized as favored by God are directed by James, "Humble yourselves in the sight of ADONAI, and He shall lift you up" (TLV). Humility is a constant theme resonant throughout the Tanach (i.e., Micah 6:8), and surely also of the teaching of Yeshua and the Apostles (i.e., Matthew 23:12; Luke 14:11; 18:14; 1 Peter 5:6). Those who are favored by God will find themselves exalted by Him (Psalm 107:41; 113:7).

Those who are humble before the Lord, are those who will consequently be lifted up and honored by Him. In order to be humbled, though, Believers must know that whatever sin they have done is abhorrent in the eyes of God. It is imperative for a person to have godly sorrow for his or her sins, repent of them, and turn to the salvation available in Messiah Yeshua.

How much emphasis do we hear concerning this today among Believers? *How much emphasis do we hear about it in today's Messianic community?* There is a call going forth in much of the Messianic movement today that we must all return to the Torah. I fully endorse this. However, is this a call of turning from one's evil, sinful ways, and being fully reconciled and transformed by God—resulting in obedience? Or, has such a message largely been one to study the Torah which is resulting in being arrogant, obnoxious, and boastful toward non-Messianic Believers? How many who have adopted a lifestyle of Torah observance have truly humbled themselves in the presence of our Heavenly Father? These will be challenges that face us until the Messiah returns.

---

[36] "Rejoice in the Lord always; again I will say, rejoice!" (Philippians 4:4).
[37] Moo, pp 195-196.
[38] Ward, in *NBCR*, 1232.

11 Do not speak against one another, brethren. He who speaks against a brother or judges his brother, speaks against the law and judges the law; but if you judge the law, you are not a doer of the law but a judge *of* it.

4:11 James writes some very spiritually and theologically probing remarks in v. 11. He says, "Do not speak evil against one another, brothers and sisters. The one who speaks against a brother or judges a brother, speaks evil against the *Torah* and judges the *Torah*. But if you judge the *Torah*, you are not a doer of the *Torah*, but a judge" (TLV). The main thrust of this instruction is that Messiah followers are not to speak against one another, as the verb *katalaleō* means, "*to speak against* one, *to criminate, traduce*" (*Thayer*).[39]

Earlier in his letter, James has addressed the need to control the tongue (1:19; 3:2-8). Perhaps in v. 11, the type of ridicule in view is similar to that seen in Numbers 21:5: "The people spoke against God and Moses, 'Why have you brought us up out of Egypt to die in the wilderness? For there is no food and no water, and we loathe this miserable food.'" For certain, the Tanach is full of references against uncontrolled speech or slander against others:

> "You shall not go about as a slanderer among your people, and you are not to act against the life of your neighbor; I am the LORD" (Leviticus 19:16).

> "You sit and speak against your brother; you slander your own mother's son. These things you have done and I kept silence; you thought that I was just like you; I will reprove you and state *the case* in order before your eyes. Now consider this, you who forget God, or I will tear *you* in pieces, and there will be none to deliver" (Psalm 50:20-22).

> "Whoever secretly slanders his neighbor, him I will destroy; no one who has a haughty look and an arrogant heart will I endure" (Psalm 101:5).

> "The words of a whisperer are like dainty morsels, and they go down into the innermost parts of the body. *Like* an earthen vessel overlaid with silver dross are burning lips and a wicked heart. He who hates disguises *it* with his lips, but he lays up deceit in his heart" (Proverbs 26:22-24).

Wisdom 1:11 in the Apocrypha further says, "Beware then of useless murmuring, and keep your tongue from slander; because no secret word is without result, and a lying mouth destroys the soul."

James directs his audience that "The one who speaks against a brother or judges his brother, speaks evil against the law and judges the law" (ESV). How can one be found to

---

[39] *Thayer*, 332.

actually judge God's Torah or Law? McKnight indicates, "Such a person is actually slandering and judging the Torah because he has usurped the role of God in the act of condemnation and has chosen to defy what God has said not to do. In this way, the slandering damner defies God and transfers authority from God's Torah to himself."[40] A person who thinks that he or she stands in obedience to the instructions of God's Torah, yet who speaks harsh condemnation, can actually be regarded as one who stands as a human judge or evaluator of God's perfect Instruction. Motyer further observes,

"Outwardly we speak against a brother and neighbour, actually we speak *evil against the law* (11). First, we break the law as a precept which we were meant to obey. It commands love; we respond with inflammatory talk. Secondly, we set ourselves up as knowing better than the law, we *judge the law*. In effect we say that the law is mistaken in commanding love. It ought rather to have commanded criticism—and if we were lawgivers it would do so. The law no longer expresses the highest values as far as we are concerned."[41]

While many Christians and Messianic readers of v. 11 are inclined to recognize "law" here, as at least pertaining to the significant part of the Mosaic Instruction—its perceived ethical and moral commandments—it cannot go unnoticed that there is some debate as to what James refers to when he uses the term "law." Moo rather generally concludes, "When James speaks of the law here...we are probably justified in thinking that he refers to the OT law insofar as it has been taken up into the 'law of the kingdom' that Jesus laid upon his followers."[42] Most of today's Messianic Believers should have little problem recognizing "law" in James' epistle as certainly involving the Messiah's own interpretation and application of it. Yet, the view of "law" as being something a bit different, or more narrow than the Torah—such as it almost exclusively involving the instruction to love God and others (Leviticus 19:18; Deuteronomy 6:4-5; cf. Matthew 22:40)—can be found. Martin is one who comes quite close to this:

"[T]he law ([*nomos*]) may be the Mosaic law but an earlier reference to the law (2:8) suggests that what James means is the epitome of the teaching of Jesus, which is summed up by the exhortation 'to love one another as yourself' (cf. Gal. 6:2)."[43]

Bo Ivar Reicke, however, is one who disregards the Torah of Moses as having a place in one's view of "law" in v. 11, and exclusively concludes that it involves the gospel message of salvation in Yeshua:

"To malign and judge one's brother is tantamount to maligning and rejecting the law. As above in i 25, ii 8-12, 'the law' here denotes the word, or the gospel. Since the gospel is directed to all people and invites all all into the fellowship of the church without

[40] McKnight, 363.
[41] Motyer, 159.
[42] Moo, 198.
[43] Martin, 163.

distinction, whether the person is Jewish or Greek, clean or unclean, rich or poor, wise or ignorant, rejection and condemnation of a brother is contradiction of the gospel."[44]

The unfortunate predicament for some interpreters of James' letter is not the high value that they place on loving God and people, showing value to those of more lowly status, or wanting to demonstrate good works of service to those in need. The unfortunate predicament for some interpreters of James' letter is that while not necessarily speaking ill of others, they can haphazardly think that the "law" addressed in v. 11 has little to do with the Torah of Moses. Do they, just as the slanderer who thinks that he or she is superior to God's Torah, also think that they are superior to God's Torah? Or are such people who have a rather narrow view of "law" for v. 11 just limited in how they approach James' direction? It would be best advised that contemporary Messianics who have a fuller view of "law" for v. 11 leave any judging for God alone. We need to seek the Lord, and allow Him to give each of us the wisdom and discernment to ask the necessary questions and inquiries when limited views of "law" present themselves, particularly as Messianics do place a high value on Torah practices such as the seventh-day Sabbath/*Shabbat*, appointed times of Leviticus 23, and the kosher dietary laws.

As the Messianic movement grows and expands, there are many sectors of people who are adopting a lifestyle of so-called "Torah observance," and whether they realize it or not are casting aside the Torah's ethical standards as they relate to slander and speaking against others. Certainly, the sin of slander and insult is an evil to always be on guard against, but there is slander of a particular kind that must be avoided. James specifically warns, "Do not speak evil against one another, brothers and sisters" (NRSV). Sadly, various sectors of the Messianic community have not become known for being beacons of genuine truth, insight, and spiritual maturity—but rather have become infamous for the rhetoric they speak against our Christian brothers and sisters. Rather than taking the Torah's admonitions seriously, about how we must not slander others, many presumed "Torah obedient Messianics" **will**—without any second thoughts or feelings of conviction that it is wrong.[45]

These are the kinds of people, as James talks about, who would find themselves to be judges of God's Torah. Those who speak against others often do so to lift themselves up because they have no internal spiritual assurance or confidence that truly comes from a viable relationship with the Lord. *If you put others down and slander them, then in light of James' words here you should be worried.* You need to seek the Lord and ask Him to convict you of what needs to change in your life and how you can find more constructive and spiritually edifying ways of relating to others. You need to pray that you can be a *proper*

---

[44] Reicke, 47.

[45] Concurrent with this is a growing tide of resentment and unpleasantness directed by many Messianic Jewish leaders toward non-Jewish Believers in their midst. Rather than widely welcome them into their congregations and fellowships, they are patronized and spurned, and hence many are turned away into independent Messianic Hebrew/Hebraic Roots home groups.

example to them—not an example that casts aside the morality of God contained in the Torah.

12 There is *only* one Lawgiver and Judge, the One who is able to save and to destroy; but who are you who judge your neighbor?

4:12 Rather than letting any of his audience think that they can judge the Torah, via disregarding some of its instructions on slander (v. 11), James makes some very candid statements about the origin of the Torah. He says, "There is only one judge, the One who gave the Law, to whom belongs absolute power of life and death. How can you then be your neighbor's judge?" (Phillips New Testament). James identifies that only God Himself is the valid Giver of the Torah or Lawgiver. As the Supreme Creator, He is the only One who gets to decree what human beings are to do, as opposed to sinful persons who might decide that "this" or "that" does not apply to them. There is a likely connection between v. 12 and Deuteronomy 32:39: "See now that I, I am He, and there is no god besides Me; it is I who put to death and give life. I have wounded and it is I who heal, and there is no one who can deliver from My hand." A later statement seen in the Mishnah remarks, "Do not serve as a judge by yourself, for there is only One who serves as a judge all alone" (m.*Avot* 4:8).[46]

James employs an important Greek term for "Lawgiver," *nomothetēs*, which has a background in classicism predating the composition of the Apostolic Scriptures. The figure of the lawgiver came to prominence as the Greek city states of the Seventh-Sixth Centuries B.C.E. emerged out of anarchy and began to establish a proper code of conduct for their people. Historian Oswyn Murray describes, "The figure of the lawgiver (*nomothetēs*) is a response to [the] double need to curb the power of the aristocracy and maintain the force of customary law. The lawgiver was chosen from among the class of experts, and could therefore be given absolute power to establish a written code...He was regarded much as the founder of a colony, for he too was a semi-divine hero whose authority validated the institutions of the city."[47] *LS* indicates, that "at Athens, *the Nomothetae* were a committee of the dicasts charged with the revision of the laws."[48]

James' usage of a classical term like *nomothetēs* should be taken as an indication that his audience was both Jewish *and* non-Jewish. There is no disputing the fact that when James admonishes people for failing to follow the Torah on the issue of slander, that it was something that any person could violate. If Jewish members of James' audience were annulling Torah commandments about morality by their actions, then it would reflect badly on them as those who had been born into and reared in an environment where God's

---

[46] Neusner, *Mishnah*, 682.

[47] Oswyn Murray, *Ancient Greece*, second edition (Cambridge, MA: Harvard University Press, 1993), pp 181-182.

[48] *LS*, 535.

Law was known and regularly taught. Yet at the same time, any Greek or Roman members of James' audience, too, needed to be sure to look to Israel's God as the only viable source of direction.

James emphasizes that the Lord, and Him alone, has the right to issue Law to the people, just as a *nomothetēs* in Ancient Greece was the only one with the authority to determine the law for society. This is the same Supreme God who has absolute control over human history and destiny.

> **13 Come now, you who say, "Today or tomorrow we will go to such and such a city, and spend a year there and engage in business and make a profit." 14 Yet you do not know what your life will be like tomorrow. You are *just* a vapor that appears for a little while and then vanishes away. 15 Instead, *you ought* to say, "If the Lord wills, we will live and also do this or that." 16 But as it is, you boast in your arrogance; all such boasting is evil. 17 Therefore, to one who knows *the* right thing to do and does not do it, to him it is sin.**

4:13-15 The instruction of James 4:13-15 is obviously important as it concerns developing a Biblical view of business ethics. James the Just should not be read from the perspective of him being opposed to people making money, but he is definitely one who stood against inappropriate attitudes concerning wealth and the misuse of wealth. There is an arrogant financial planning for one's future—obviously without the blessing or guidance of God—which James undeniably condemns. James 4:13-15 could be said to be a paraphrase of Proverbs 27:1: "Do not boast about tomorrow, for you do not know what a day may bring forth." Witherington directs our attention,

"James is thinking of a person who runs his own business, sets his own agenda and salary and travels to many different places throughout the Roman Empire. Those who could afford it could travel with some speed on land by horse or horsedrawn carriage or in the Mediterranean by boat. Between the 10% of the population that were rich and the 10% that were absolutely poor lay everyone else, including most of the merchant class, though some of them became rich."[49]

4:13 The breadth of James' audience is realized as he switches some of his attention to those who engage in business. He says, "Now look here, you people who say, 'Today, or tomorrow, we will go to such and such a town and spend a year there, and trade, and make some money'" (Kingdom New Testament). With the theme of business and making money in view, it is not at all inappropriate to be reminded of Yeshua's statement, "For what will it profit a man if he gains the whole world and forfeits his soul? Or what will a man give in exchange for his soul?" (Matthew 16:26). Davids is entirely right to assert, "What bothers James is simply the presumption that one could so determine his future and the fact that

---

[49] Witherington, pp 520-521.

these plans move on an entirely worldly plane in which the chief value is financial profit."[50]

V. 13 is likely, mainly focused on traveling Jewish merchants, who would be transient among potential clients in the First Century Mediterranean.[51] Some have taken historical issues with this, as Josephus said that the Jews of this period largely did not desire to go outside the borders of Israel: "As for ourselves...we neither inhabit a maritime country, nor do we delight in merchandise...but the cities we dwell in are remote from the sea" (*Against Apion* 1.60).[52] Aside from this, however, there is internal Biblical evidence that the Apostles did encounter traveling Jewish merchants in their journeys, notably the tent-makers Aquila and Priscilla (Acts 18:2, 18; Romans 16:3). While it is likely that these people were born and raised in the Diaspora, James' words about people engaging in business and profit remain true to all people of all dispositions.

That there were other traveling merchants in the Mediterranean, to whom James' admonition of vs. 13-15 can be applied, is certain—especially as the good news would impact Jews, Greeks, and Romans across the ancient social spectrum. Those whose lives can be consumed by their work or business, need to decisively have their attention refocused on their Creator. Witherington further observes,

"Traveling merchants were plentiful enough during the imperial age, and since the Pax Romana was generally in place they could go to most places throughout the empire and sell their wares...James has precisely these kinds of persons in mind: people with relative high status, business capital and a business plan. The problem is, they did not factor God or mortality into the equation—two not inconsequential factors!"[53]

4:14 The futility of the traveling merchant planning for the next year is noticed by James, as he poignantly states, "Why, you do not even know what will happen tomorrow. What is your life? You are a mist that appears for a little while and then vanishes" (NIV). The limited and transitory nature of human beings, in contrast to an Eternal God, is certainly witnessed. James' statement is definitely rooted within various thoughts expressed in the Tanach:

"As for man, his days are like grass; as a flower of the field, so he flourishes" (Psalm 103:15).

"For who knows what is good for a man during *his* lifetime, *during* the few years of his futile life? He will spend them like a shadow. For who can tell a man what will be after him under the sun?" (Ecclesiastes 6:12).

---

[50] Davids, 172.
[51] Cf. Moo, 202.
[52] *The Works of Josephus: Complete and Unabridged*, 777.
[53] Witherington, pp 518-519.

"When a cloud vanishes, it is gone, so he who goes down to Sheol does not come up" (Job 7:9).

In comparison to God, human beings may simply be regarded as just a passing mist or vapor. A person who puts too much of his trust in his business, finances, or ability to make money—is not only going to find himself committing much of his energy to things that will decisively pass away—but is probably going to be sorely disappointed when things do not take place as planned. Warnings against putting too much faith in one's ability to control the future are common throughout both Jewish and Greco-Roman literature.

The Dead Sea Scrolls and Mishnah acknowledge the primacy of God in one's plan for life and livelihood:

"Surely a man's way is not his own; neither can any person firm his own step. Surely justification is of God; by His power is the way made perfect. All that shall be, He foreknows, all that is, His plans establish; apart from Him is nothing done" (1QS 11.10-11).[54]

"R. Yose says, 'Let your fellow's money be as precious to you as your own. And get yourself ready to learn Torah, for it does not come as an inheritance to you. And may everything you do be for the sake of Heaven'" (m.Avot 2:12).[55]

"Everything is foreseen, and free choice is given. In goodness the world is judged. And all is in accord with the abundance of deed[s]" (m.Avot 3:15).[56]

The moralist Epictetus emphasized the need to consult higher powers in all human activities, stating, "no one sails from a harbor without sacrificing to the gods, and imploring their assistance; nor do men sow without first invoking Demeter. And shall anyone who has undertaken so great a work undertake it safely without the aid of the gods?" (Discourses 3.21.12).[57]

When one today sees what James says, we should not conclude that God does not want us to have any life dreams or aspirations or desire to achieve great things. James spoke against traveling merchants trying to pre-plan their business activities, likely in micro-managed terms, and without even the hint of trying to seek God's will or favor. Proverbs 16:9 states, "The mind of man plans his way, but the LORD directs his steps." Each one of us has various life plans and dreams we would like to see fulfilled, and some of them are perfectly normal of men and women of God who have preceded us, such as having a spouse and children. *Yet none of us are to so pre-plan our lives, at the expense of letting God sovereignly*

---

[54] Wise, Abegg, and Cook, 143.

[55] Neusner, *Neusner*, 677.

[56] Ibid., pp 680-681.

[57] Epictetus: *The Discourses*, ed. Christopher Gill (London: Everyman, 1995), 188.

move. Many of us have planned for things, and then the Lord has interjected Himself and altered things (quite) a bit, **most often for our protection.** While in the short term, many of us have had our plans changed and it has upset us—in the longer term we tend to be the more grateful for it.

4:15 James does not prohibit anyone from planning for the future, including those in business, but he does say, "Your remarks should be prefaced with, 'If it is the Lord's will, we shall still be alive and will do so-and-so'" (Phillips New Testament). Martin notes, "The idea that what takes place in this life is in the hands of divine power is found in pagan...as well as Jewish...and Christian thought."[58] James could be relying on a variety of ancient thoughts, to get the point across that people cannot meticulously manage their futures without the God of Israel having some part to play. In spite of the fact that limited human beings have tried to control their destinies, there is often still enough of a spiritual component within them that tries to implore Divine intervention in all endeavors.

God's awesome majesty and eternality, compared to humans' limited corporeal existence, is what requires people to beseech Him and seek His will in all things. While specifically applied in James' context to people traveling and doing business, the same is true of all things that people do. The Apostle Paul prayed for God's will to be done in his ministry endeavors:

> "[B]ut taking leave of them and saying, 'I will return to you again if God wills,' he set sail from Ephesus" (Acts 18:21).

> "But I will come to you soon, if the Lord wills, and I shall find out, not the words of those who are arrogant but their power" (1 Corinthians 4:19).

Concurrent with this, is Yeshua's parable of the rich man who built new barns. The rich man spent so much of his time focusing on the accumulation of his own wealth, that he forgot about his spiritual well being. When the time came for him to be held spiritually accountable, he was found wanting:

"And He told them a parable, saying, 'The land of a rich man was very productive. And he began reasoning to himself, saying, "What shall I do, since I have no place to store my crops?" Then he said, 'This is what I will do: I will tear down my barns and build larger ones, and there I will store all my grain and my goods. And I will say to my soul, "Soul, you have many goods laid up for many years *to come*; take your ease, eat, drink *and* be merry."' But God said to him, "You fool! This *very* night your soul is required of you; and *now* who will own what you have prepared?" So is the man who stores up treasure for himself, and is not rich toward God'" (Luke 12:16-21).

The issue of people devoting their time and resources to something that causes them to forget God and their spiritual condition is not something new. *James attests to the fact*

[58] Martin, 167.

that it was going on in the First Century. And, it can more easily happen today in our fast-paced, industrialized, highly mobile and technologically advanced Twenty-First Century world. So, how much more so must we heed James' warnings?

Please keep in mind the fact that James the Just is not speaking against people making money. Every person must earn a living, after all. James rebukes those who place their confidence in their ability to make money and who make their business endeavors the prime element in their lives, when in fact each one of us could die in the next minute. James emphasizes the fact that one's limited human existence is absolutely nothing in the face of who God is. People must consider the Lord's will in everything that they do, so that if they operate a business, He might guide them to opportunities that will help advance His Kingdom. Moo makes the valid remark, "we should guard here against another kind of misinterpretation: the idea that James is forbidding [Believers] from all forms of planning for the future...What James rebukes here, as v. 16 [will make] clear, is any kind of planning for the future that stems from human arrogance in our ability to determine the course of future events."[59]

In an interesting twist, some in the Messianic community today, while probably not preoccupied as traveling merchants who forget or marginalize their relationship with God, do get preoccupied with things that focus less on their relationship with Him. There are many today in our faith community, who in their pursuit of the Torah or Torah study—have focused so much on the Torah and in "falling in love with Torah"—that they have minimized Yeshua, who He is, and His atoning work. Like the businessman who is so caught up in selling a product to make a profit, these people are so focused on Torah study, that they easily forget who the Messiah should be in their lives, and they forget other parts of the Bible outside of the Pentateuch. When you see these people, you wonder whether or not they truly know Yeshua as their Personal Savior, otherwise they would have a more balanced faith of Torah study and insight, coupled with a strong relationship with the Father through His Son. *That is the challenge for us spiritually today.* How do we remain pursuing the deep and forgotten truths of the Torah, while doing everything to imitate our Lord and Savior?

4:16 In spite of James' emphasis that the traveling merchants in his audience (v. 13) need to focus on God's will for their lives, he is forced to tell them, "As it is, you boast in your arrogant schemes. All such boasting is evil" (TNIV). Rendered as "arrogance" is the noun *alazoneia*, with a related term for an "arrogant *person*" being *alazōn*, "'one who makes more of himself than reality justifies,' or 'promises more than he can perform,' often used of orators, philosophers, doctors, cooks, and officials" (*TDNT*).[60] This kind of boasting is considered by James to be evil, because those who think they can "make it big" in their

---

[59] Moo, pp 202-203.
[60] G. Delling, "*alazōn, alazoneía,*" in *TDNT*, 36.

traveling mercantile industries, really cannot. Wisdom 5:7-10 in the Apocrypha sums it up well:

"We took our fill of the paths of lawlessness and destruction, and we journeyed through trackless deserts, but the way of the Lord we have not known. What has our arrogance profited us? And what good has our boasted wealth brought us? All those things have vanished like a shadow, and like a rumor that passes by; like a ship that sails through the billowy water, and when it has passed no trace can be found, nor track of its keel in the waves."

Paul A. Cedar makes the interesting remark, on how the arrogant person in view may be compared to "the characteristic of a wandering quack which was not unlike the medicine man of the frontier days in America. This quack offered cures which were not cures; he boasted of things which he was unable to do."[61] Certainly from a spiritual standpoint, there have been many religious figures over the centuries who have claimed to have "the answers," and have offered quick fixes to the ills of society. The Pentecostal and charismatic movements, in particular, have been riddled with these types of individuals, who through their use, or perhaps manipulation of the Holy Spirit, have been able to get people to believe things that may not necessarily be so.[62] Consider all of the various televangelists who claim that people are physically healed of diseases and debilitating ailments at their crusades, when in actuality nothing happens and such claims are proven fraudulent.

If Christianity has had individuals making great spiritual boasts, which ultimately have no substance, we can be rest assured that the Messianic movement today likewise will probably have the same. Do we not have those in the Messianic community who claim to have "cutting-edge teachings," which no one, save themselves, have heard before? Are there not those who claim that, after centuries of (so-called) "gross misunderstanding of Scripture" by the Church, that now they have all the answers? Are there those in our midst who are making the same mistakes as those who made great prideful boasts about what they can do, when in actuality there is no spiritual or practical substance in what they say? We need to heed James' warnings!

4:17 James' statement in v. 17, "Anyone, then, who knows the right thing to do and fails to do it, commits sin" (NRSV), in view of his immediate admonitions to traveling merchants, would necessarily concern their lack of soliciting Divine favor for their activities. If they fail to seek God's assistance and direction for what they do (v. 15), remaining arrogant about it (v. 16), then they are to be regarded as sinners. An important thought seen in the Pseudepigrapha, which may to a degree be the position of James here, states, "See, I have told you everything, so that I might be exonerated with regard to your

---

[61] Cedar, 87.

[62] For a useful, general review, consult Wayne A. Grudem, gen. ed., *Are Miraculous Gifts for Today? Four Views* (Grand Rapids: Zondervan, 1996).

sin" (*Testament of Simeon* 6:1).[63] James, having just issued some important instruction on the right thing to do, to those in error, is not going to be held responsible by God for those who fail to make the appropriate changes.

While James' specific word in v. 17 concerns what he has said about traveling merchants, the remark "if anyone knows the right thing to do, but doesn't do it, it becomes sin for them" (Kingdom New Testament), can be applied across the board to just about any situation where a teacher or leader has had to issue correction to those needing to change their behavior and attitudes. Consistent with this, the Apostle Paul would say in Galatians 6:9-10, "Let us not lose heart in doing good, for in due time we will reap if we do not grow weary. So then, while we have opportunity, let us do good to all people, and especially to those who are of the household of the faith."

There were likely many traveling merchants among the First Century Believers, who upon encountering James' words in vs. 13-16, changed some of their attitudes and orientations in their business dealings. There were likely many others who did not. While those who did not seek the Lord's favor and direction for what they did, would be regarded as sinners—it would be no fault of James. Similarly, into whatever circumstances any of us may have to speak a word of godly admonition or stern correction—if people do not listen to what we have to say, and continue on a path of error, they should be regarded as the Lord's problem. In remembering that human beings are but a mist or vapor (v. 14), He is the Supreme Judge and Lawgiver (v. 12) who makes the final determination. So, in those circumstances where some of us may have to be firm, may we also be a bit tempered and restrained, knowing our human boundaries.

---

[63] Kee, "Testaments of the Twelve Patriarchs," in *The Old Testament Pseudepigrapha*, Vol 1, 787.

JAMES 5
COMMENTARY

1 Come now, you rich, weep and howl for your miseries which are coming upon you. **2** Your riches have rotted and your garments have become moth-eaten. **3** Your gold and your silver have rusted; and their rust will be a witness against you and will consume your flesh like fire. It is in the last days that you have stored up your treasure!

5:1 James issues some direct words of condemnation upon rich people: "Now listen, you rich people, weep and wail because of the misery that is coming upon you" (NIV). Are these rich people actual Believers, who have fallen into sin, or are they non-Believers who have mistreated the Believers? It is thought by various interpreters that since no alternative behavior is mentioned (i.e., 4:13-17) that non-Believers are in view,[1] with those who draw this conclusion thinking that since there is no mention of repentance or change of behavior, that the rich being condemned are widely beyond hope. There are others, though, who are not convinced that weeping and howling cannot include some, albeit remote, chance for repentance.[2] When the description of these rich people is further evaluated, though, it seems most probable that they are non-Believers, and that their punishment is certain. Douglas J. Moo indicates how, "This was a class of people frequently criticized in the OT, Jewish literature, and the wider Greco-Roman world for their greedy acquisition of land and their exploitation of those forced to work on the land for them."[3]

A key verb, *ololuzō*, rendered as "howl" in the NASU (and also RSV/ESV) and "wail" in the NIV (and also NRSV), is employed in v. 1. As is summarized by *TDNT*, *ololuzō* has some major importance in the Septuagint, particularly in terms of judgment issued by God upon sinners:

"*ololýzō* means 'to make a loud, inarticulate cry' in expression of great stress of soul. It is common in sacral contexts, e.g., at sacrifices or divine epiphanies, usually denoting jubilation (along with dancing etc.). In the LXX it denotes the effect of judgment on those smitten by it (Ezek. 21:17; Zech. 11:2). In crying of this type there comes to expression both horror at oneself (Am. 8:3) and dread at the destruction of worldly

---

[1] Burdick, in *EXP*, 12:199.
[2] Cf. Motyer, 164.
[3] Moo, 210.

power. Hos. 7:14 demands the prayer of the heart in place of such cries. Jms. 5:1 is in line with the prophetic use except that now the fulfillment has come with Christ, and the last and total possibility of repentance will have gone."[4]

Moo goes on further and informs us, "*ololuzō* ('wail' [NIV]) is found only in the prophets in the OT and always in the context of judgment (Isa. 10:10; 13:6; 14:31; 15:2-3; 16:7; 23:1, 6, 14; 24:11; 52:5; 65:14; Jer. 2:23; 31:20, 31; Ezek. 21:17; Hos. 7:14; Amos 8:3; Zech. 11:2). This background makes it clear that *the misery that is coming upon* the rich refers not to earthly, temporal suffering, but to the condemnation and punishment that God will mete out to them on the day of judgment."[5] V. 1 may include an Isaiah 13:6 type of rebuke: "Wail[6], for the day of the LORD is near! It will come as destruction from the Almighty." We might also be reminded of the weeping of the merchants seen in Revelation 18:10-24.

While there are certain details regarding the future Day of the Lord, which as of yet are still widely unknown by us—v. 1 invoking a Day of the Lord style of language, only intensifies that the same God who will judge the unrighteous world in the future, will certainly judge the unrighteous rich in the present (v. 4).

5:2 The present condition of what the rich value is not a good one, as James says first in v. 2, "Your wealth has rotted, and moths have eaten your clothes" (NIV), to then be followed by some statements about their gold and silver (v. 3). Some of what James says might be based in Isaiah 51:8, "For the moth will eat them like a garment, and the grub will eat them like wool. But My righteousness will be forever, and My salvation to all generations." Perhaps more important to be considered would be the words of Yeshua in Matthew 6:19, in His Sermon on the Mount: "Do not store up for yourselves treasures on earth, where moth and rust destroy, and where thieves break in and steal." Also to keep in mind are Yeshua's words of the foolish person who has stored up too much (Matthew 25:24-30).[7]

Popular concepts of modern wealth see it primarily portrayed in the form of a large bank account, but much of ancient wealth was composed of agricultural produce and expensive clothing.[8] Ralph P. Martin describes, "The hoarding of wealth—as understood in the ancient Mediterranean Levant world in terms of the items of grain, garments, and

---

[4] H.W. Heidland, "*ololýzō*," in *TDNT*, 682.

[5] Moo, 211.

[6] Heb. verb *yalal*; Grk. LXX verb *ololuzō*.

[7] "And the one also who had received the one talent came up and said, 'Master, I knew you to be a hard man, reaping where you did not sow and gathering where you scattered no *seed*. And I was afraid, and went away and hid your talent in the ground. See, you have what is yours.' But his master answered and said to him, 'You wicked, lazy slave, you knew that I reap where I did not sow and gather where I scattered no *seed*. Then you ought to have put my money in the bank, and on my arrival I would have received my *money* back with interest. Therefore take away the talent from him, and give it to the one who has the ten talents.' For to everyone who has, *more* shall be given, and he will have an abundance; but from the one who does not have, even what he does have shall be taken away. Throw out the worthless slave into the outer darkness; in that place there will be weeping and gnashing of teeth" (Matthew 25:24-30).

[8] 2 Kings 5:5, 22; 1 Maccabees 11:24.

gold—has brought its own inevitable nemesis. Food has gone bad; clothes have become riddled with moth-holes; and the much vaunted treasure of gold has been tarnished and has lost its sheen."[9] In terms of their usage, Peter Davids observes how "The garments which are food for moths and the money which is tarnishing are not being used by their owner, and yet they could have been used by the poor."[10]

In vs. 2-3a, Greek readers encounter three perfect tense verbs, which describe what has taken place to the unrighteous rich: *ho ploutos humōn* **sesēpen** *kai ta himatia humōn sētobrōta* **gegonen,** *ho chrusos humōn kai ho arguros* **katiōtai.**[11] The three perfect tense verbs are *sesēpen* or "rotted," *gegonen* or "become [moth-eaten]," and *katiōtai* or "rusted." In the estimation of Moo, "the normal meaning of the perfect tense in Greek—to state a condition—makes perfect sense here. Although the rich people do not, or cannot, see it, their great wealth has already lost its luster. It stands already under the doom of the things of this world that will fade away and can provide no foundation for the life to come."[12]

5:3 James' further condemnation of the rich, as he has just mentioned their moth-eaten garments, now involves the deterioration of their gold and silver: "Your gold and silver have rusted, and their rust will be evidence against you and will eat your flesh like fire. You have laid up treasure for the last days" (RSV). While ancient wealth was centered around physical items like food and clothing much more than it is today, gold and precious metals were mainly where wealth was based. James says that the gold and silver of the rich have suffered "corrosion" (NIV, ESV). Martin concludes, "The rusting of the gold testifies to the social injustice the rich have committed. Instead of using their wealth to aid the poor in time of need, the rich agriculturists have amassed their possessions to see them destroyed."[13] While gold and silver as precious metals are often considered to have long-lasting value, their value is limited. The faith and trust that the rich have placed in such things, will ultimately be a part of their undoing.

Perhaps the closest parallel we see in the Tanach to wealth deteriorating is in Ezekiel 7:19: "They will fling their silver into the streets and their gold will become an abhorrent thing; their silver and their gold will not be able to deliver them in the day of the wrath of the LORD [*b'yom evrat ADONAI*]. They cannot satisfy their appetite nor can they fill their stomachs, for their iniquity has become an occasion of stumbling." James' reference to "the last days" (*en eschatais hēmerais*)[14] may be taken via a theme of realized eschatology,[15] as

---

[9] Martin, 173.

[10] Davids, 176.

[11] "the wealth of you has rotten and the clothes of you have become~moth-eaten, the gold of you and the silver has been corroded" (Robert K. Brown and Philip W. Comfort, trans., *The New Greek-English Interlinear New Testament* [Carol Stream, IL: Tyndale House, 1990], 804).

[12] Moo, 213.

[13] Martin, 174.

[14] The CJB includes "This is the *acharit-hayamim*" for its rendering of v. 3.

[15] McKnight, 389.

future judgment upon the corporate wicked by God has already manifested itself in the individuals being condemned.

While the wicked rich are condemned by James the Just (vs. 1-6), the attention of readers, both ancient and modern, should be more focused upon those who were being oppressed. Donald W. Burdick states, after all, "The tragic fact is that the rich had hoarded so much food and clothing that it was going to waste. Their crime was uncontrolled greed that resulted in oppression of the poor (v.4)."[16] Sirach 29:9-11 in the Apocrypha gives instruction on the proper way to use one's wealth and resources:

"Help a poor man for the commandment's sake, and because of his need do not send him away empty. Lose your silver for the sake of a brother or a friend, and do not let it rust under a stone and be lost. Lay up your treasure according to the commandments of the Most High, and it will profit you more than gold."

> **4 Behold, the pay of the laborers who mowed your fields, *and* which has been withheld by you, cries out *against you*; and the outcry of those who did the harvesting has reached the ears of the Lord of Sabaoth. 5 You have lived luxuriously on the earth and led a life of wanton pleasure; you have fattened your hearts in a day of slaughter. 6 You have condemned and put to death the righteous *man*; he does not resist you.**

5:4 In James' continuing rebuke of the rich, his words come quite close to that of a prophet from the Tanach: "Behold, the wages of the workers who mowed your fields—which you kept back by fraud—are crying out against you. And the cries of the harvesters have reached the ears of the Lord of Hosts" (TLV). James is doubtlessly appealing to various instructions in the Torah, which require that a hired hand be paid at the close of the work day:

"You shall not oppress your neighbor, nor rob *him*. The wages of a hired man are not to remain with you all night until morning" (Leviticus 19:13).

"You shall not oppress a hired servant *who is* poor and needy, whether *he is* one of your countrymen or one of your aliens who is in your land in your towns. You shall give him his wages on his day before the sun sets, for he is poor and sets his heart on it; so that he will not cry against you to the LORD and it become sin in you" (Deuteronomy 24:14-15).

Luke T. Johnson actually makes the assertion, "James appears to be making an allusion to the scriptural context of the law of love in Leviticus,"[17] as though withholding wages from

---

[16] Burdick, in *EXP*, 12:199.
[17] Johnson, in *NIB*, 12:217.

a hired laborer is a manifestation of love-lessness. More significant, to be certain, would be various statements expressed elsewhere in the Tanach, Apocrypha, and Pseudepigrapha, on how important it was in ancient times to see that a hired laborer received his proper wages:

"Woe to him who builds his house without righteousness and his upper rooms without justice, who uses his neighbor's services without pay and does not give him his wages" (Jeremiah 22:13).

"'Then I will draw near to you for judgment; and I will be a swift witness against the sorcerers and against the adulterers and against those who swear falsely, and against those who oppress the wage earner in his wages, the widow and the orphan, and those who turn aside the alien and do not fear Me,' says the LORD of hosts" (Malachi 3:5).

"Do not hold over till the next day the wages of any man who works for you, but pay him at once; and if you serve God you will receive payment. Watch yourself, my son, in everything you do, and be disciplined in all your conduct" (Tobit 4:14).

"To take away a neighbor's living is to murder him; to deprive an employee of his wages is to shed blood" (Sirach 34:22).

"At evening, as he was about to leave for home, he would be compelled to take wages from me as I would say, 'I know you are a workingman counting on and *looking for your wages*. You must accept.' Nor did I allow the wage earner's pay to remain at home with me in my house" (*Testament of Job* 12:2-4).[18]

"Give the laborer his pay, do not afflict the poor" (*Pseudo-Phocylides* 19).[19]

Workers not being paid for their labor is something that has occurred all throughout human history. This can especially be true of those who perform agricultural work, and are relatively poor. Richard Bauckham summarizes the place of the worker in view for v. 4:

"[T]he day laborer was a significant category of the poor. He neither owned land or rented land, but was employed a day at a time on the estates of others and paid his wages at the end of each day's work. Of all peasant workers, he was in the most vulnerable position. His employment could be terminated at a few hours' notice. He might often be unemployed. His wages were too small to make savings possible. He and his family lived from hand to mouth, and withholding his wages even until next morning was a serious matter. An employer who did so could be accused of murder without hyperbole."[20]

Dan G. McCartney further observes, "It is endemic to human behavior everywhere for the rich to oppress the poor, and the Greco-Roman world was no exception, and James's

---

[18] R.P. Splittler, "Testament of Job," in *The Old Testament Pseudepigrapha*, Vol 1, 844.

[19] P.W. Van der Horst, "Psuedo-Phocylides," in *The Old Testament Pseudepigrapha*, Vol 2, 574.

[20] Bauckham, in *ECB*, 1490.

condemnation applies to every manifestation of greed and the abuse of power, not just the withholding of wages."[21]

It is not just enough for James to inform his audience, particularly those who were being oppressed by the rich, that the Supreme God was going to come down and vindicate them. James specifically says, as the CJB has rendered it, "the outcries of those who harvested have reached the ears of ADONAI-Tzva'ot." The Greek source text uses *Kuriou sabaōth*, which is the LXX form of ADONAI *Tzavaot*, "the LORD of hosts" or "HASHEM, Master of Legions" (ATS). This is a very important designation for God, as it has both military and kingly attributes. *TWOT* remarks, "Although the title has military overtones, it points directly to Yahweh's rulership over the entire universe. He continually rules, but at times he directly intervenes to secure his own victory and insure the direction of history for the salvation of his people."[22]

While there are many potential places within the Tanach where "the Lord of hosts" is used as a title for God, Isaiah 5:9 is widely believed to be what is specifically in the mind of James: "In my ears the LORD of hosts *has sworn*, 'Surely, many houses shall become desolate, *even* great and fine ones, without occupants."[23] J.A. Motyer, noting the reference to Isaiah ch. 5, comments,

"It may be that the unexpected description of God as *the Lord of hosts* is intended to do more than achieve this cross-reference to Isaiah 5 and thereby to bring an even deeper reassurance and comfort to the Lord's beleaguered people...The message through Isaiah all those years ago proved to be a word from the Lord. He did step in to judge the oppressor— and he will still do so today...No power, however great or solid to the earthly eye, is beyond his capacity; no need, however pressing, is beyond his means, or outside his attention."[24]

James has said that the wages which have been withheld cry out; James has said that the laborers themselves cry out; Proverbs 21:13 says, "He who shuts his ear to the cry of the poor will also cry himself and not be answered." Indeed, the Lord of Hosts will make Himself known to the wicked rich, whose possessions can do nothing to save them, and who will not be helped when they finally are in need of God when it is too late.

5:5 James continues his words of condemnation against the oppressive rich: "You have lived on the earth in luxury and in self-indulgence. You have fattened your hearts in a day of slaughter" (ESV). Rendered as "led a life of wanton pleasure" (NASU), the verb *spatalaō* means "**to indulge oneself beyond the bounds of propriety, live luxuriously/voluptuously**" (BDAG).[25] The implication is that the rich are getting richer

---

[21] McCartney, 234.

[22] John E. Hartley, "tzavaot," in *TWOT*, 2:751.

[23] Cf. Erwin Nestle and Kurt Aland, eds., *Novum Testamentum Graece, Nestle-Aland 27th Edition* (New York: American Bible Society, 1993), 596; Kurt Aland, et. al., *The Greek New Testament, Fourth Revised Edition* (Stuttgart: Deutche Bibelgesellschaft/United Bible Societies, 1998), 782.

[24] Motyer, 167.

[25] *BDAG*, 936.

while the poor are getting poorer. The rich landowners here have likely not only withheld wages from their workers (v. 4), but they have also used their wealth to extort, rather than deter the plight of those in need.

James' words evoke significant prophetic themes of the Tanach, as Davids indicates how the terminology "day of slaughter" (*hēmera sphagēs*), "is part of a long tradition of the day of God's judgment as a day of the slaughter of his enemies."[26] The theme of slaughter, as God judges His enemies, is encountered numerous times (Isaiah 34:5-8; Jeremiah 46:10; 50:26-27; Ezekiel 39:17; Lamentations 2:21-22; cf. Revelation 19:17-21). Moo takes this admonition in the direction of realized eschatology, concluding, "The 'last days' have already begun; the judgment *could* break in at any time—yet the rich, instead of acting to avoid that judgment, are, by their selfish indulgence, incurring greater guilt. They are like cattle being fattened for the kill."[27] Bauckham, however, takes the theme of "day of slaughter" as being associated with Ezekiel 39:17-20,[28] and asserts, "The rich who have gorged themselves at the expense of the poor are depicted as food for birds and animals at the gruesome eschatological feast of judgment."[29]

Regardless of the specificities—as final judgment upon sinners is a role reserved entirely to God, in His timing—these rich have not at all heeded the warnings of Scripture, and they will ignore James' own words as well.

5:6 James' final rebuke of the ungodly rich is, "You have condemned and murdered the righteous one, who does not resist you" (NRSV). Translated as "resist," the verb *antitassō* was used previously in 4:6 to describe how "GOD IS OPPOSED [*antitassō*] TO THE PROUD..." Martin makes the important point, "The poor do not resist because they *cannot*. They are helpless. If they cannot even hold their own when it comes to securing the wages due to them, then it should come as no surprise that they are victims to the point of having their blood shed."[30]

There has actually been some discussion among examiners regarding the identity of *ton dikaion* or "the righteous."[31] In light of the surrounding cotext, it would seem most natural to take "the righteous" to be the poor person who has had his wages unjustly withheld from him, and who may be regarded as murdered by not receiving any money for

---

[26] Davids, 178.

[27] Moo, 218.

[28] "As for you, son of man, thus says the Lord GOD, 'Speak to every kind of bird and to every beast of the field, "Assemble and come, gather from every side to My sacrifice which I am going to sacrifice for you, as a great sacrifice on the mountains of Israel, that you may eat flesh and drink blood. You will eat the flesh of mighty men and drink the blood of the princes of the earth, as *though they were* rams, lambs, goats and bulls, all of them fatlings of Bashan. So you will eat fat until you are glutted, and drink blood until you are drunk, from My sacrifice which I have sacrificed for you. You will be glutted at My table with horses and charioteers, with mighty men and all the men of war,"' declares the Lord GOD" (Ezekiel 39:17-20).

[29] Bauckham, in *ECB*, 1490.

[30] Martin, 181.

[31] The REB actually has "the innocent one."

living. Yet, there are some, like N.T. Wright, who take *ton dikaion* as actually being Yeshua the Messiah. He thinks, "The final condemnation of 'the rich' is not that they are oppressive, living in luxury and denying the workers their wages. The worst thing they have done is that *they have condemned the Righteous One and killed him.* They are responsible for the death of Jesus."[32] He goes on to associate the condemned rich as actually being the Sadducees and chief priests.[33]

While there is no doubting that the trial and death of Yeshua were conducted unjustly and with corrupt motives, it is too much of a stretch for us to conclude that "the righteous" in view in v. 5, is specifically Yeshua the Messiah. Davids details, "there is no tradition that the rich in particular either killed Jesus or James, although the author would surely include Jesus under this general category of righteous sufferer."[34] One can (metaphorically) conclude that just as the wealthy wicked often embody the worst of humanity, that they may be regarded as having killed the Righteous One Himself, Yeshua, who in turn is representative of the company of all the righteous as King Messiah. Beyond this, we should not push the content of v. 5.

Rather than suggesting that the condemned wealthy are Sadducees or chief priests, Scot McKnight instead interjects, "The best explanation….is that James writes to messianic communities that are embedded in Jewish communities, with boundary lines that are simply not clear. Some in the crosshairs of James, so we think the evidence suggests, are violent. It also appears that they are leaders at some level, for they have enough influence to shape who sits in the synagogue and can dominate the courtroom. I lean toward the view that these violent people are not messianists, though that is far from clear."[35] His suggestion, that the condemned wealthy are some kind of local Jews of influence, not being Believers, is to be far preferred than them being Sadducees and chief priests. Yet, while there is some interesting speculation as to who the condemned wealthy specifically are— there is nothing in the text that *requires* them, or at least all of them, to be a part of the Jewish Synagogue. James' admonition is general enough, that while it would seem likely that those condemned are a part of the Jewish community—that they could just as well be wealthy Greeks or Romans who were greedy and corrupt, and would have shown contempt for Biblical admonitions when issued to them.

---

[32] Wright, 33.
[33] Ibid., 34.
[34] Davids, 180; cf. Martin, pp 181-182.
[35] McKnight, 397.

7 Therefore be patient, brethren, until the coming of the Lord. The farmer waits for the precious produce of the soil, being patient about it, until it gets the early and late rains. 8 You too be patient; strengthen your hearts, for the coming of the Lord is near.

5:7 James' words from v. 7 until the end of his epistle, shift toward addressing people within the community of Messiah followers. Having just issued condemning admonitions to the wealthy unrighteous (vs. 1-6), he now says to the Believers, "be patient, brothers and sisters, until the coming of the Lord" (a, TLV), *heōs tēs parousias tou Kuriou*. While this is general enough to be issued to any group of Messiah followers, it is especially important for any group which has been marginalized, abused, or persecuted. Those who are oppressed must be patient until the coming of the Lord, as God will vindicate them in the prophesied eschatological judgment.

James actually tells his audience to be more than just "patient," as some versions have "long-suffering" (LITV). The verb *makrothumeō* has a variety of connotations, notably "**to remain tranquil while waiting, *have patience, wait*,**" and "**to bear up under provocation without complaint, *be patient, forbearing***" (BDAG).[36] *TDNT* notes, "Divine forbearance imposes a demand for human forbearance too."[37] The imagery connected with the Lord's "coming" or *parousia* is one where He not only returns to Planet Earth, but where He defeats His enemies. This is something that only He can perform, and human beings cannot. People have to be longsuffering, as opposed to being impatient and wanting to take justice into their own hands. People should turn to God and to His justice, the same way as the Ancient Israelites turned to Him in Egypt (Exodus 2:23-24).

Continuing in v. 7, James specifies the kind of patience or longsuffering that his audience needs to have: "See how the farmer waits for the precious fruit of the earth, being patient for it until it receives the early and late rain" (b, TLV). This is a probable reflection on the author's geographical location somewhere within First Century Israel, as its "autumn rains came in October and November, and winter rains (roughly three-quarters of the year's rainfall) in December and January. But residents of Syria-Palestine eagerly anticipated the late rains of March and April, which were necessary to ready their late spring and early summer crops" (*IVPBBC*).[38] An important theme of the Tanach is that God demonstrates His faithfulness to Israel through the rains, by which the crops grow and are thus harvested:

> "It shall come about, if you listen obediently to my commandments which I am commanding you today, to love the LORD your God and to serve Him with all your heart and all your soul, that He will give the rain for your land in its season, the early and late rain, that you may gather in your grain and your new wine and your oil" (Deuteronomy 11:13-14).

---

[36] *BDAG*, 612.
[37] J. Horst, "patience, forbearance," in *TDNT*, 550.
[38] Keener, pp 701-702.

"But this people has a stubborn and rebellious heart; they have turned aside and departed. They do not say in their heart, 'Let us now fear the LORD our God, who gives rain in its season, both the autumn rain and the spring rain, who keeps for us the appointed weeks of the harvest.' Your iniquities have turned these away, and your sins have withheld good from you" (Jeremiah 5:23-25).

"So let us know, let us press on to know the LORD. His going forth is as certain as the dawn; and He will come to us like the rain, like the spring rain watering the earth" (Hosea 6:3).

While God is faithful in sending the rains, which will help crops grow and provide food for the people, notice how the Lord requires obedience to send the rain. He requires His people "to love the LORD your God and to serve him with all your heart and with all your soul" (Deuteronomy 11:13, NIV). This means a full obedience of not just outward commandments, but also of a proper heart attitude. For James to tell his audience that they need patience or longsuffering, and connecting that with the required patience of a farmer, he alludes to all of the important qualities that must be present in a Believer. The steadfastness of a farmer is necessary if one hopes to be a useful servant in the Kingdom of God (2 Timothy 2:6).

5:8 James' statement in v. 8, "You also be patient. Establish your hearts, for the coming of the Lord is at hand" (RSV), is certainly not without some controversy. While his admonition to be patient and to "take courage" (NLT) is fairly straightforward, his remark "the coming of the Lord is near" can be confusing. It is very true that in the First Century many of the Believers expected the return of Yeshua in their lifetimes, but is this what is being communicated by James in this passage? Pre-tribulationists who believe in the any-moment return of the Lord can use this reference as a support for their position. Likewise, various other end-time views, such as preterism, which conclude that the bulk of the prophecies of the Last Days occurred in the First Century, may also claim support from v. 8.

James says *hē parousia tou Kuriou ēngiken*, "the coming of the Lord has drawn near" (LITV). The verb *engizō*, rendered as either "at hand" or "near," means "*approach, come or draw near*" (CGEDNT).[39] Specifically in view is how *ēngiken* appears in the perfect active indicative tense, which may be taken to describe something which has occurred in the past, but has continuing results in the future. It is not as though James has said that the Lord *generally* is near (i.e., Psalm 34:17-18; 145:18-19; Philippians 4:4-6), as meaning that He is present and will answer the urgent cries of His people; James has said that the coming or arrival of the Lord is *specifically* near. In the view of Ben Witherington III, "James believes

---

[39] *CGEDNT*, 50.

the Lord is spatially near the righteous in his audience, and he also believes that Christ could return at any time and so could be also temporally near."[40]

How are readers to appropriately approach James' assertion, "for the coming of the Lord is near"? Preterists who think that the destruction of Jerusalem in 70 C.E. involved the "coming" of the Lord think that they have the answer, and they conclude that a majority of end-time events have already occurred in past history.[41] This is certainly one way to approach what James has claimed, but one which is often marked by a great deal of supersessionism or replacement theology, as such First Century events can be stigmatized by interpreting them as God being finished with Israel's Kingdom and the Jewish people.

Pre-millennialists, who consider Yeshua's Olivet Discourse teaching of Matthew 24 to be largely futuristic, might be prone to view James' assertion "for the coming of the Lord is near" in view of how the Last Days technically began with the Messiah's First Coming and will consummate at His Second Coming (cf. Hebrews 1:1-2; 1 John 2:18). Moo is one who is particularly insistent that the presumed "nearness" of the *parousia* of the Lord, be viewed salvation-historically, directing readers,

"Many scholars are convinced that Jesus himself predicted he would return within the lifetime of the disciples, and that the earliest Christians shared this expectation of an immediate *parousia*. Gradually, however, as time went by and the *parousia* did not occur, Christians began to 'postpone' the *parousia* to an indefinite time in the future. James, of course, would seem to share the earlier perspective. But this scenario raises an insistent issue for those, like me, who credit the NT with complete truthfulness: Jesus, Paul, Peter, James, and others [would be apparently] wrong about the timing of the *parousia*."[42]

Moo, as a relatively conservative Christian interpreter, is right to insist on the Apostolic Scriptures or New Testament being reliable on the issue of the Second Coming, and that the Believers did not just keep "postponing" it. Rather than v. 8 implying some kind of any-moment return of the Lord, or a return of the Lord which should have occurred in the First Century and obviously did not, he takes the "nearness" of the *parousia* "as the next event in the salvation-historical timetable...from the time of the early [First Century] church to our own day, [as being] 'near,' or 'imminent.'"[43] This would mean that time needs to be especially viewed from the perspective of an Eternal God who sits outside of time, and not the perspective of limited mortals who often fail to consider time decade-to-decade, much less century-to-century or millennium-to-millennium.

The coming or *parousia* of the Lord should be a motivating factor for all Believers to do the right thing, and to check themselves daily. Consider the fact that the return of the Lord is so awesome, that Paul will write, "the Lord will slay" the antimessiah "with the breath of

---

[40] Witherington, 537.
[41] McKnight, pp 406, 412-413.
[42] Moo, pp 223-224.
[43] Moo, 224.

His mouth and bring [him] to an end by the appearance of His coming" (2 Thessalonians 2:8). Evil will be rooted out of this world by Yeshua's Divine power at His return.

Elsewhere in the Apostolic Scriptures, especially in 2 Thessalonians ch. 2, it is specified how there must be various events which precede the return of the Lord. Today in the Twenty-First Century, many of us believe that we are much closer to the Lord's return than the early Believers actually were in the First Century. *We need to have the faith and the patience that at His Second Coming things that we have been wronged in the world will be made right.* At the same time, we have to be careful with our approach to "at hand" or "nearing." There are some in the Messianic, or Christian, community today, who while correctly believing in the Messiah's post-tribulational return (Matthew 24:29-31; 1 Corinthians 15:51-52; Revelation 11:15), are not patient and actually want the horrors of the end-times to come upon Planet Earth. They want the final judgment of humanity to take place, and they have little or no concern for the salvation of others. Those who would wish a harsh judgment are not going to receive the rewards they think they are going to receive in His Kingdom. If you might be one of those people, consider what the Prophet Amos says:

"Woe to you who desire the day of the LORD! Why would you have the day of the LORD? It is darkness, and not light; as if a man fled from a lion, and a bear met him; or went into the house and leaned with his hand against the wall, and a serpent bit him. Is not the day of the LORD darkness, and not light, and gloom with no brightness in it?" (Amos 5:18-20).[44]

> **9 Do not complain, brethren, against one another, so that you yourselves may not be judged; behold, the Judge is standing right at the door. 10 As an example, brethren, of suffering and patience, take the prophets who spoke in the name of the Lord. 11 We count those blessed who endured. You have heard of the endurance of Job and have seen the outcome of the Lord's dealings, that the Lord is full of compassion and *is* merciful.**

5:9 As James begins to close his letter, he issues a final plea for proper speech and communication. He admonishes his audience, "Don't grumble against one another, brothers and sisters, or you will be judged. The Judge is standing at the door!" (TNIV). James' word might be said to have a slight connection to Leviticus 19:18a, "You shall not take vengeance, nor bear any grudge against the sons of your people." There may certainly also be connections to be made from the Ancient Israelites' Exodus from Egypt and trek through the wilderness, of how they often grumbled and complained toward God (Exodus 16:7-8; Numbers 14:36; 16:11). The inevitable result, of complaining about or toward other people, is that (harsh) judgment will be passed. When judgment toward other people—especially

---

[44] For a further review of the end-times, consult the author's publications *When Will the Messiah Return?* and *The Dangers of Pre-Tribulationism.* Also to be considered would be his commentary *1&2 Thessalonians for the Practical Messianic.*

those inside the community of faith—is issued, one can often find himself or herself usurping the position of God as Judge (cf. 4:12).

James emphasizes the eschatological judgment by the Judge, God Himself, in saying, "the Judge is standing right at the door." From the eternal perspective of our Creator, when He will directly intervene in human history via the Second Coming of the Messiah and the judgment of His enemies, is quite soon. Biblically speaking, "the Last Days" have been occurring ever since the First Century (Acts 2:17; Hebrews 1:1-2). When we look at things from God's perspective, the Last Days are not a small period of just a few years,[45] but the final few millennia prior to the restoration of His Kingdom on Earth. But the Judge standing at the door, need not only be an omen of Divine retribution. Yeshua says in Revelation 3:20, "Behold, I stand at the door and knock; if anyone hears My voice and opens the door, I will come in to him and will dine with him, and he with Me." The Messiah, waiting at the door, wants to come into our lives and transform us from within. While all too frequently, God portrayed as Judge is present to issue punishment to sinners—this same Judge is there to offer forgiveness to those who are truly repentant, and who are willing to change their ways.

5:10 With the Judge standing at the door (v. 9), James directs his audience, "As an example of suffering mistreatment and being patient, brothers, take the prophets who spoke in the name of ADONAI" (CJB). While it is most appropriate for readers to consider these figures to mainly include the Hebrew Prophets of the Tanach, many of whom died horrific deaths, Davids indicates, "the author is referring to well-known stories of the worthies of the OT and Hasmonean periods that his readers had probably heard from childhood."[46] The example of the Maccabean martyrs, in particular, was one of intense suffering prior to death (i.e., 2 Maccabees 6:26-28).[47] The endurance required of Messiah followers, similar to the Prophets of the Tanach, is something that Yeshua Himself mentions in His Sermon on the Mount:

"Blessed are you when *people* insult you and persecute you, and falsely say all kinds of evil against you because of Me. Rejoice and be glad, for your reward in heaven is great; for in the same way they persecuted the prophets who were before you" (Matthew 5:11-12).

In terms of the timing of James' composition, the death of Stephen had likely already taken place (Acts 7). The suffering that the poor among James' audience would have to endure, would sadly intensify as hostilities toward the First Century Believers became more pronounced and targeted. Whatever difficulties they were to endure, they were to count themselves among the company of the significant figures of faith who had preceded them (cf. Hebrews 11:32-38).

---

[45] Against: McKnight, 416 who takes v. 9 as speaking of the destruction of Jerusalem to the Romans in 70 C.E.

[46] Davids, 186.

[47] Consult the relevant sections of the *Messianic Winter Holiday Helper* by Messianic Apologetics.

5:11 Having just mentioned the patience of the Prophets, James now mentions the steadfastness or endurance (*hupomonē*) of Job: "we consider those blessed who remained steadfast. You have heard of the steadfastness of Job, and you have seen the purpose of the Lord, how the Lord is compassionate and merciful" (ESV). Do note, though, that James does not say that Job had "patience" (Job 3; 12:1-3; 16:1-4; 21:4); Job only had "endurance" (Job 1:20-22; 2:9-10; 13:15). It is commonly thought among expositors that James relies upon some ancient concepts of Job as one who was "fully engaged in endurance" (*Testament of Job* 1:5; cf. 4:6).[48]

How are readers to approach the clause *to telos Kuriou*? Is this "the end *intended by* the Lord" (NKJV), or more the "outcome" (NASU) or "purpose" (RSV/ESV)? *Telos* is the key term here, which can mean "*the fulfilment or completion of anything...i.e. its consummation, issue, result, end*" (LS).[49] Even "goal" could be a possible rendering for *telos* in v. 11. Mainly, these different renderings vary as an interpreter considers the manner in which the compassion and mercy of God are displayed. For many throughout Biblical history, suffering and hardship endured, are the means by which God can demonstrate Himself to be God.

12 But above all, my brethren, do not swear, either by heaven or by earth or with any other oath; but your yes is to be yes, and your no, no, so that you may not fall under judgment.

5:12 Just as with Yeshua's words in Matthew 5:33-37,[50] so is there some discussion and controversy over what James says regarding oath taking in v. 12: "But above all, my brothers and sisters, do not swear—either by heaven, or by the earth, or by any other oath. But let your 'yes' be 'yes,' and your 'no,' be 'no'—so that you may not fall under judgment" (TLV). One of the main Torah instructions regarding swearing an oath is Leviticus 19:12, "You shall not swear falsely by My name, so as to profane the name of your God; I am the LORD," which does not at all prohibit oath-taking, but does assume that any oaths taken will be fulfilled (cf. Numbers 30:3; Deuteronomy 32:22; Ecclesiastes 5:4). So in view of what James says in v. 12, one does have to wonder if what he directs is a situational-driven application prohibiting all oaths and vows, and/or if frivolous remarks that appeal to some kind of Divine authority are in view. Among ancient sects of Judaism, the Essenes were a community that did not take oaths (Josephus *Wars of the Jews* 2.135).

---

[48] Splittler, in *The Old Testament Pseudepigrapha*, Vol 1, 839.

[49] *LS*, 799.

[50] "Again, you have heard that the ancients were told, 'YOU SHALL NOT MAKE FALSE VOWS, BUT SHALL FULFILL YOUR VOWS TO THE LORD' [Leviticus 19:12; Numbers 30:3; Deuteronomy 32:22]. But I say to you, make no oath at all, either by heaven, for it is the throne of God, or by the earth, for it is the footstool of His feet, or by Jerusalem, for it is THE CITY OF THE GREAT KING [Psalm 48:2]. Nor shall you make an oath by your head, for you cannot make one hair white or black. But let your statement be, 'Yes, yes' or 'No, no'; anything beyond these is of evil" (Matthew 5:33-37).

James' (and also Yeshua's) words on not making vows or swearing at all, and instead simply saying "yes" to something or "no" to something, could very well be historical reflections of how flippantly invoking God in a commitment became. A similar warning is encountered in Sirach 23:9, 11, composed in the preceding century:

"Do not accustom your mouth to oaths, and do not habitually utter the name of the Holy One...A man who swears many oaths will be filled with iniquity, and the scourge will not leave his house; if he offends, his sin remains on him, and if he disregards it, he sins doubly; if he has sworn needlessly, he will not be justified, for his house will be filled with calamities."

The Jewish philosopher Philo also describes,

"The next commandment is, 'not to take the name of God in vain.'...Now the principle on which this order or arrangement proceeds is very plain to those who are gifted with acute mental vision; for the name is always subsequent in order to the subject of which it is the name; being like the shadow which follows the body. Having, therefore, previously spoken of the existence of God, and also of the honour to be paid to the everlasting God; he then, following the natural order of connection proceeds to command what is becoming in respect of his name; for the errors of men with respect to this point are manifold and various, and assume many different characters" (*Decalogue* 82-83).[51]

We should not dismiss some of these ancient thoughts, for as Moo describes, "concern about the devaluation of oaths through their indiscriminate use and a growing tendency to 'weasel out' of oaths by swearing by less sacred things...led to warnings against using them too often."[52] Once again, there is no Torah or Tanach prohibition on making vows, but it is witnessed how people can swear things to God that they have no intention of fulfilling or completing. Johnson draws the conclusion that "James forbids oaths, because he desires a community of solidarity based in mutual trust. Such trust is possible only where speech is simple and unadorned with false religiosity."[53] His observation is hardly invalid, because in a community where the implanted word (1:21) is able to manifest itself via acts of kindness and mercy one to another (1:27; 2:14-17), and in edifying speech (3:13), making oaths or vows should not be necessary. Commitments need only be designated by a person's simple "yes" or "no," because there will be a demonstrated track record of actions to show whether someone will be consistent in what is to be done. McCartney observes in this regard,

"The use of oaths...is contrary to faith; it marks unbelief. Faith always means yes when it says yes; that is, people of faith have no need of oaths, either to give their words weight or to prompt a solution to suffering; they wait patiently and prayerfully for the Lord and always keep their promises, cognizant that God always keeps his."[54]

---

[51] *The Works of Philo: Complete and Unabridged*, 525.
[52] Moo, pp 232-233.
[53] Johnson, in *NIB*, 12:222.
[54] McCartney, 247.

It cannot be overlooked, however, that interpreters have widely taken both James' and Yeshua's words about oath-taking as not being a blanket prohibition, but instead have viewed them as being limited to casual oaths and not serious oaths. Psalm 110:4 would be an example of such a serious oath: "The Lᴏʀᴅ has sworn and will not change His mind, 'You are a priest forever according to the order of Melchizedek.'" Also to be weighed in, is how a figure like the Apostle Paul took oaths on rather serious matters (i.e., Romans 1:9; 2 Corinthians 1:23; Galatians 1:20). Burdick concludes that "casual use of oaths in informal conversation—not formal oaths in places as courts of law" are what are spoken against.[55] Davids also recognizes, "James...prohibits not official oaths, such as in courts...but the use of oaths in everyday discourse to prove integrity. The community member ought not to use oaths, for his yes or no should be totally honest, making oaths unnecessary; truthfulness is the issue."[56] Indeed, the bulk of oaths and vows people make are not on serious matters, but on frivolous things spoken in casual conversation which are quickly dismissed and forgotten.

13 Is anyone among you suffering? *Then* he must pray. Is anyone cheerful? He is to sing praises. 14 Is anyone among you sick? *Then* he must call for the elders of the [assembly] and they are to pray over him, anointing him with oil in the name of the Lord; 15 and the prayer offered in faith will restore the one who is sick, and the Lord will raise him up, and if he has committed sins, they will be forgiven him. 16 Therefore, confess your sins to one another, and pray for one another so that you may be healed. The effective prayer of a righteous man can accomplish much.

5:13 James asks his audience, "Is any one of you in trouble? He should pray. Is anyone happy? Let him sing songs of praise" (NIV). While in vs. 14-16 following, much of what James discusses takes on a theme of being healed from sickness or disease, the statement, "Does anyone suffer ill among you?" (LITV), need not only apply to physical illness. The verb *kakopatheō* can mean, "*to suffer ill, to be in ill plight, be in distress*" (LS).[57] YLT actually has "Doth any one suffer evil among you?" The Message might be said to go even a step even further, paraphrasing v. 13 with, "Are you hurting? Pray. Do you feel great? Sing." While there are specific directions given by James on what to do with sick people in the assembly, not everyone in trouble is going to be physically ill. Anyone who suffers through persecution, a retention of wages earned, or some kind of intense emotional situation, surely also classifies as a man or woman who needs to pray to the Lord for His intervention. When an answer is found and resolution is enacted, praise to God should surely follow.

[55] Burdick, in *EXP*, 12:203; cf. Davids, 189; Motyer, 183.
[56] Davids, 190.
[57] *LS*, 393.

5:14 Vs. 14-16 largely carry a motif of how sick people in the local assembly are to be handled, although there are surely applications of James' original instruction that can be made beyond sick people. James first states, "Is anyone among you sick? Let him call for the elders of Messiah's community, and let them pray over him, anointing him with oil in the name of the Lord" (TLV).

Those who perform the function described by James are *tous presbuterous tēs ekklēsias*, "the elders of the assembly" (LITV). An elder or *presbuteros* holds an important position of leadership within the local community of faith (i.e., Acts 11:30; 14:23; 20:17; 1 Timothy 5:17-19; 1 Peter 5:1; 2 John 1), and is not just an older person with some greater degree of experience. The general position of an elder (and also deacon) for the First Century Messianic community was widely inherited from the leadership structure of the ancient Jewish Synagogue. While in much of the modern charismatic Christian movement, the function of an elder can be somewhat skewed with just about anyone who feels "led by the Spirit" operating in the specific duties described in vs. 14-16—it cannot go unnoticed that what James describes, when further considered, involves much more than fellow Believers praying for those in need, extending a hand of prayer to someone, or even offering some level of forgiveness Believer-to-Believer. The elders' service is likely one of having to go to a bedridden individual, offering intensive prayer to the Lord for healing and physical restoration, and also consultation with the infirmed person on his or her spiritual status before the Lord. Much of the elders' service is likely also to be conducted on a confidential basis.

There is actually some interesting discussion that can take place among examiners, per James' statement about anointing with oil (*aleipsantes [auton] elaiō*), and whether what is intended is to be: medicinal, pastoral, sacramental, or symbolic.[58] None of us should dismiss that anointing with oil has an important symbolic, religious function, as seen throughout Holy Scripture, particularly to consecrate either people or objects to the Lord's service, such as priests or the Tabernacle (i.e., Exodus 29:7; 40:9). An elder anointing someone who was ill would be an important gesture of acknowledging the man or woman as a member of God's own. Beyond the spiritual significance of anointing someone with oil, is how olive oil was an important medicine of ancient times (Isaiah 1:6; Luke 10:33-34). Is it possible that James' reference to "oil" could be synonym for "medicine"? In Mark 6:13, oil is used in a dual sense, for both physical and spiritual healing: "And they were casting out many demons and were anointing with oil many sick people and healing them." *ISBE* summarizes a few of the ancient applications of oil as a medicine:

"Olive oil has certain curative qualities and is still used in modern medicine. Celsus mentioned its use for fevers, and Josephus (*Ant.*xvii.6.5 [172]) said that Herod was given an oil bath in an attempt to cure him of his deadly disease. Isaiah wrote of it as softening

---

[58] Cf. Moo, 238-240.

wounds (1:6). The Good Samaritan mixed it with wine and poured the resultant antiseptic fluid into the wounds of the stricken traveler."[59]

If James' reference to anointing a sick person with oil is to be taken beyond its spiritual or symbolic function, then it would also involve the role of the elder in seeing that those who are stricken with disease receive appropriate medical treatment. Given the importance of olive oil for ancient medicine, it should not be a stretch, or at all inappropriate, to apply James' anointing with oil reference to mean a combination of consecrating someone to God for healing, along with some sort of medical action. As an elder anoints one who is infirm, so can the elder be present to consult with a doctor on how someone can be restored to full health. History certainly bears out the fact that whether it be those who bear the title of elder, or more generally pastor or rabbi, that such spiritual leaders have often had to play an important role counseling those who are sick, as well as conferring with the various medical practitioners.

5:15 James further specifies in v. 15, "the prayer of faith will save the one who is sick, and the Lord will raise him up. And if he has committed sins, he will be forgiven" (ESV). This can be a bit confusing, if some of the important details are not evaluated.

James labels the person in view with the participle *ton kamnonta*, "the distressed one" (YLT) or "the sick one." Is it at all significant that the verb *kamnō*, while meaning "generally, to suffer, be distressed or afflicted" (LS),[60] is used in a place like Wisdom 4:16 in the Apocrypha, to describe one who has died? "The righteous man who had died [*kamnō*] will condemn the ungodly who are living, and youth that is quickly perfected will condemn the prolonged old age of the unrighteous man." Is the sick person of v. 15 to be taken as one who is just badly ill, or is the sick person one who is on the verge of dying? It would seem likely, that while prayer for healing from disease is important for all manner of ailments—from a two-day sore throat or a bug, all the way to a terminal illness or cancer or a heart condition—that the most serious of afflictions are what James has in mind. It might also be detectable that the kind of prayer in view, a prayer of faith (*hē euchē tēs pisteōs*), is the kind that involves the trust in God to, if necessary, not only raise the sick out of their beds, but also resurrect people from the dead.

These are factors to be considered, given the presence of how the prayer of faith is to actually "save" (RSV/NRSV/ESV/HCSB) the sick person, with the verb *sōzō* sometimes translated with "restore" (NASU) or "make the sick person well" (NIV). Here, it needs to be kept in mind that the saving in view is not being offered eternal salvation via the gospel message, but instead a being restored to physical, and quite possibly also, spiritual pristineness. The verb *sōzō* is certainly used in the Gospels to describe physical healing.[61] Yet, given the presence of the conditional statement by James, "and if he has committed sins, they will be forgiven him," that some people are (deathly) ill as a consequence of sin in

---

[59] J.A. Balchin, "Oil," in *ISBE*, 3:586.
[60] *LS*, 398.
[61] Matthew 9:21-22; Mark 3:4; 5:23, 28, 34; 6:56; 10:52; Luke 7:50; 8:48, 50; 17:19; 18:42; John 11:12.

their lives, is not something to be ignored. However, while many people come to saving faith while suffering or enduring through a debilitating disease or ailment, for those who have been truly redeemed by Yeshua, the presence of disease or ailment caused by sin may be unresolved pre-salvation issues, or a temporary season of faithlessness.

5:16 James' direction, while surely involving the interactions between the elder and sick person (vs. 14-15), is something that can be more widely applied to those within the faith community: "confess your sins to one another and pray for one another, that you may be healed. The prayer of a righteous person has great power as it is working" (ESV). No reader of v. 16 denies the significance of *ischuei deēsis*; "effective prayer" (NASU) or "urgent request" (HCSB). However, as can be demonstrated throughout religious history, the admonition of people to confess their sins to each other, has been applied in some extremely useful, and some not so useful ways. The verb *exomologeō* means both "**to make an admission of wrong-doing/sin, confess, admit**" and "**to declare openly in acknowledgment, profess, acknowledge**" (*BDAG*).[62] The confession of sins is to occur *allēlois* or "to one another," which is a bit different than just personally confessing sins to God (cf. Psalm 38:15-18).

A commentator like McCartney, in considering the circumstances described in James' letter, takes the perspective that "James is probably thinking about those sins that involve the whole body, such as the 'wars' mentioned in 4:1. If an individual has sinned against the whole body, then confession to the whole body by way of its elders is appropriate, and sins that disrupt the harmony and peace of the community must be dealt with within the community, not by posting them in public, not even by putting them on display before everyone in the church, but by way of the elders who represent the body as a whole."[63] His conclusions should certainly be considered by Messianic congregational or fellowship leaders today, who want to see people restored and cleared of any errors committed, but who also may want to contain any potential damage to the assembly as a whole.

At the same time, it cannot at all go overlooked how James 5:16 has played an important role in supporting the traditional Roman Catholic practice of Extreme Unction,[64] whereby individual Christians are thought to have a responsibility to regularly confess their sins to a priest, who will then offer them forgiveness on the part of God. It is not surprising to see that the Reformer John Calvin offered a different approach to James 5:16:

"[James] puts mutual prayer together with mutual confession, and he means that the advantage of confession is to find assistance from the prayers of our brethren in the sight of God. Such as appreciate our real needs are prompted to intercede on our behalf, while those who have no knowledge of our troubles are less forward in bringing help. I am amazed at

---

[62] *BDAG*, 351.
[63] McCartney, 258.
[64] Cf. Motyer, 191.

the folly of the papists—or is it wickedness?—who attempt to extract their whispering confessional from this proof."[65]

John Wesley would later observe, "[James] does not say, to the elders: this may, or may not, be done; for it is nowhere commanded. We may confess them to any who can pray in faith: he will then know how to pray for us, and be more stirred up so to do."[66]

The obvious intention of James is to convey a sense of mutual support and accountability of Believers one to another. In many cases, elders or other leaders are involved, but in others it may be some other kind of close confidant. The practice, of confessing one's faults or errors to those we can trust, is not only therapeutic, but it is to facilitate a spiritual environment where people can look out for others, and warn others of potential temptations. All of us need to be able to help one another spiritually, and we need close friends who are Believers in whom we can confide with our personal problems and struggles. This is especially true of a Messianic movement that is still relatively small, spiritually and theologically maturing, and whose challenges will persist until the Messiah returns.

17 Elijah was a man with a nature like ours, and he prayed earnestly that it would not rain, and it did not rain on the earth for three years and six months. 18 Then he prayed again, and the sky poured rain and the earth produced its fruit.

5:17-18 James describes the nature and intensity of prayer that Messiah followers should possess, noting the Prophet Elijah as a point of comparison. He says, "Eliyahu was only a human being like us; yet he prayed fervently that it might not rain, and no rain fell on the Land for three years and six months" (CJB). Elijah's tenacity to pray for rain in Israel is described within 1 Kings chs. 17-18:

"Now Elijah the Tishbite, who was of the settlers of Gilead, said to Ahab, 'As the LORD, the God of Israel lives, before whom I stand, surely there shall be neither dew nor rain these years, except by my word'...Now Elijah said to Ahab, 'Go up, eat and drink; for there is the sound of the roar of a *heavy* shower.' So Ahab went up to eat and drink. But Elijah went up to the top of Carmel; and he crouched down on the earth and put his face between his knees. He said to his servant, 'Go up now, look toward the sea.' So he went up and looked and said, 'There is nothing.' And he said, 'Go back' seven times. It came about at the seventh *time*, that he said, 'Behold, a cloud as small as a man's hand is coming up from the sea.' And he said, 'Go up, say to Ahab, "Prepare *your chariot* and go down, so that the *heavy* shower does not stop you."' In a little while the sky grew black with clouds and wind, and there was a heavy shower. And Ahab rode and went to Jezreel. Then the hand of the LORD was on Elijah, and he girded up his loins and outran Ahab to Jezreel" (1 Kings 17:1; 18:41-46).

---

[65] Calvin, 316.
[66] Wesley, *Explanatory Notes Upon the New Testament*, 870.

There is no specific reference in the Tanach to Elijah praying for up to three-and-a-half years, and so it may have been popularly understood in the Jewish community of the First Century C.E. that the time elapsed between 1 Kings chs. 17-18 is about three-and-a-half years.[67] It would be attested later in the Mishnah, for certain, that "He who answered Elijah at Mount Carmel will answer you and hear the sound of your cry this day. Blessed are you, O Lord, who hears a cry" (m.Ta'anit 2:4).[68] Elijah, among other important figures of the Tanach, is one whose example is to provide encouragement to the people of God, when they cry out to Him for help. Some additional thoughts of interest, regarding the Prophet Elijah, are encountered in the Talmud:

> "And Elijah, the Tishbite, who was one [o]f the inhabitants of Gilead, said to Ahab, 'As the Lord God of Israel lives, before whom I stand, there shall not be dew or rain these years, but according to my word' (1Ki. 17:1). *He sought mercy, and the key of rain was given to him. He got up and went his way.* And the word of the Lord came to him, saying, 'Go away and turn eastward and hide yourself by the brook Cherith, that is before Jordan...And the ravens brought him bread and flesh in the morning' (1Ki. 17:2, 6). *Where did they get [validly slaughtered meat]? Said R. Judah said Rab, 'They got it from the butchery of Ahab.'* 'And it came to pass, after a while, that the brook dried up, because there had been no rain in the land' (1Ki. 17:7). *When [God] saw that there was suffering in the world, it is written,* 'And the work of the Lord came to him saying, Arise, go to Zarephath' (1Ki. 17:8-9). And it is written, 'And it came to pass after these things that the son of the woman, mistress of the house, fell sick' (1Ki. 17:17). *[Elijah] prayed for mercy that the keys of the resurrection of the dead might be given to him. They said to him, 'Three keys are not handed over to a messenger: those of birth, rain, and the resurrection of the dead. For will people say, "Two already are in the hand of the disciple [he already had the one for rain] and one in the hand of the master?" Bring the one and take the other.'* For it is written, 'Go, appear to Ahab, and I will send rain upon the earth' (1Ki. 18:1)" (b.Sanhedrin 113a).[69]

For ancient times, not experiencing rain, for a period of three-and-a-half years, is something that would have caused a great amount of pain and hardship for people, obviously necessitating a figure like Elijah praying as intensely and devotedly as he did. Certainly in history since, there have been similar circumstances, requiring multiple years of prayer, intercession, and regular communication to God. *Perseverance in petitioning the Lord is a necessity for spiritual maturity and vitality.* Famines still come and go, there are still wars and battles waging on the Earth, and the economy seems to never improve. People inside the community of faith do not seem to always get along, friends have strained relationships with other friends, and too many marriages are places of contention and not

---

[67] Cf. Witherington, 547.
[68] Neusner, *Mishnah*, 309.
[69] *The Babylonian Talmud: A Translation and Commentary.*

love. The need to pray and seek God, the way Elijah did, had not gone away for those within James' First Century audience—and it has certainly not gone away for Twenty-First Century Believers, either.

> **19 My brethren, if any among you strays from the truth and one turns him back,**
> **20 let him know that he who turns a sinner from the error of his way will save his soul from death and will cover a multitude of sins.**

5:19 James ends his epistle with an urgent summons to action, first stating, "My brothers and sisters, if any among you strays from the truth and someone turns him back..." (TLV). The verb *planaō* can mean "*to lead astray, mislead, deceive*" (*LS*).[70] It is rendered as "wanders" in the RSV/NRSV/ESV, although the KJV actually has "err from the truth." One can detect a definite echo in v. 19, from a Tanach passage like Ezekiel 33:11: "Say to them, 'As I live!' declares the Lord GOD, 'I take no pleasure in the death of the wicked, but rather that the wicked turn from his way and live. Turn back, turn back from your evil ways! Why then will you die, O house of Israel?'"

For certain, when encountering James' word, "My dear family, if someone in your company has wandered from the truth, and someone turns him back..." (Kingdom New Testament), it can be debated whether or not the one who has wandered, or strayed, is actually a Believer **or** a non-Believer in the assembly of Believers. Is the person wandering to the brink of being hopelessly lost, going to lose his or her salvation, **or** is the person wandering already an unregenerate soul on the fringe in a community of Believers, and is about to leave the sphere influence of where he or she can actually be saved? Without getting into too much unnecessary debate (particularly over the Calvinist-Arminian disagreement over eternal security), with not enough details provided in James' statement, it might be best for a reader to assume that an unrepentant sinner is in view. No one can disagree that those people within a local assembly or fellowship of Messiah followers, who have been truly redeemed from their sins and born again, have a responsibility to see that others within that same group also come to saving faith. Men and women within the assembly have to take charge of seeing that the will of God is being accomplished among them, and that sinners can come to repentance.

One of the major ways, how those who are truly redeemed can have the impetus instilled in them to see other people come to saving faith, is to see that they themselves are discipled in God's Word and hence growing in sanctification. Motyer, observing more modern-day occurrences, makes the important comment, "Sunday school attendance has plummeted from that which we remember in the late 1940s and early 1950s. Its descending graph has been matched by the rising graph of juvenile delinquency, just as the churchs' abandonment of biblical truth has been matched by the increasingly open licentiousness

---

[70] *LS*, 643.

and lasciviousness of adolescent and adult life-styles."[71] And obviously, since Motyer wrote this in 1985, things have gotten much, much worse for much of Western evangelicalism.

How do we see James' statement of v. 19 adequately applied within the contemporary, and still-developing, Messianic movement? There is no easy answer, and there are many case-by-case examples to be considered, given the fact that no two Messianic congregations are alike. Too many Messianic Jewish congregations do not serve the spiritual needs of their non-Jewish constituents, and do not even offer membership to them, and might not be too concerned with the type of issue presented by James 5:19 for even the Jews in their midst. Likewise, too many of the independent Hebrew/Hebraic Roots fellowships out there (which may call themselves "Messianic"), to their discredit, might be so preoccupied with Torah study, that by widely ignoring the New Testament, James 5:19 would not even factor into their Bible reading or contemplation.

What we do know for certain is that congregations, assemblies, and fellowships of people are made up of individuals. Individual Believers, who make up the whole, need to be fervent in their prayers, in regular communication with God (vs. 16-17), and as they commune with the Lord they need to ask Him for wisdom, discernment, and guidance as to when they can speak a word of admonition to those straying. Individual Messianic Believers also need to be well rounded in their Bible studies and personal reading of Holy Scripture, even if the congregation or fellowship they associate with might not be.

5:20 James' thought from v. 19 finishes, as his epistle comes to a quick close: "let him know that the one who turns a sinner from the error of his way shall save a soul from death and cover a multitude of sins" (TLV). This statement could likely be based on Proverbs 10:12, "Hatred stirs up strife, but love covers all transgressions." The Prophet Ezekiel also says, "However, if you have warned the righteous man that the righteous should not sin and he does not sin, he shall surely live because he took warning; and you have delivered yourself" (Ezekiel 3:21). Also important to be considered are the thoughts expressed in 2 *Clement* 15:1, seemingly based on James 5:19-20:

"Now I do not think I have given you any light counsel concerning self-control, which if any one do he will not repent of it, but will save both himself and me who counseled him. For it is no light reward to turn again a wandering and perishing soul that it may be saved."[72]

Those, who are truly redeemed and are spiritually mature, have a significant job to perform in making sure that the influences of sin are not present within the local faith community. They have a responsibility of being aware of those who bring in sinful behavior, and to see them turn toward the truth. The reward is surely great for those who are able to do this! For especially, "How blessed is he whose transgression is forgiven, whose

---

[71] Motyer, 210.
[72] BibleWorks 8.0: Ante-Nicene Fathers.

sin is covered!" (Psalm 32:1). Even more so, eternal rewards are accrued by those who play a role in seeing that sinners are brought to redemption.

Readers of the Epistle of James often notice how with v. 20, the letter just ends. Was this done on purpose? Or is the Epistle of James a collection of sayings, later formatted into a letter for easy reference? McKnight offers a number of options, as he states, "the letter ends abruptly, and we can only guess why. My intuition is that it is less an official letter and more a letter-shaped collection of the teaching of James...One can suggest that James ends on this note because he wants his readers to repent and be restored, which makes sense for the last few verses, but it is a stretch to think that 5:19-20 represents the purpose of James."[73]

The Epistle of James is a bit broad in the content it addresses, which mainly concerns the ethics and morality of ancient Messiah followers, the need to be urgently loving God and neighbor (2:8), making sure that the implanted word is present within them (1:21), and that their speech is tempered (1:26; 3:2-11), among other things. While McKnight would seemingly disagree, *what if* the over-arching purpose of the Epistle of James is indeed to see mature people emerge, who are making sure that the main job of seeing people turn from their sins and to a path of holiness? Those who are striving to see others rescued from a path of eternal punishment, and changed by the power of the good news of salvation in Yeshua, should not have either the time or the inclination to participate in any of the sinful activities and behaviors James has admonished his audience about. And without question, if the Epistle of James closes with an evangelistic bent to see others rescued from sins, then questions pertaining to the Torah of liberty (1:25), and the necessary good works of Believers (2:10-26), are quite important—**as God's people are to demonstrate the trust they have placed in Him via tangible actions of grace and mercy toward others.**

---

[73] McKnight, pp 460-461.

EPILOGUE

Implementing James' words, for either his original First Century recipients, down to Christians in the Reformation and post-Reformation, and now to today's Messianic people—has not always been something easy. Any reader of the Epistle of James, whether the letter is simply surveyed for its high points, or whether the letter is probed in more detail, per the study we have just completed—**is going to be challenged.** While we can only deduce some of the specific ancient circumstances in view for James' ancient audience, generally speaking, the human corruption, immorality, oppression, and foul communication encountered in his admonitions, have not changed that much over the centuries. James presents us as modern readers—and most especially people who make up a still-maturing and still-developing Messianic movement—with many areas of our spirituality which require improvement.

Perhaps because of a manifold of human limitations, many of the statements and challenges that James presents will be corporately impossible to fulfill as a Messianic faith community—although they will be individually implementable for Messianic Believers. Some of the important points that each of you who have gone through this study need to remember, as you now have been able to investigate James a bit more in detail, include:

- **"[A] man is justified by works and not by faith alone"** (James 2:24): The statement presented here will be a continual theological challenge for many Messianic readers. Is this an observation that people can be redeemed from their sins by human action? Or, is this an indication of being "the friend of God" (James 2:23), meaning reckoned as a member of God's own? Given wider theological debates over places in Galatians and Romans where "justification" might involve membership in God's people and not forgiveness from sins, keeping this in mind also for places in James will be highly important for Messianic soteriology.

- **"Let not many *of you* become teachers, my brethren, knowing that as such we will incur a stricter judgment"** (James 3:1): The questions asked by this statement, both for the qualifications not present among various First Century teachers and leaders—and for what it means for modern-day teachers and leaders in the contemporary Messianic movement, are quite immense. Some of the initial issues to be considered, pertain to whether the personal ethics and morality of the teachers today's Messianic people submit themselves to, are concurrent with what James communicates in his letter. Beyond this, making sure that teachers are relatively qualified, to speak on theological and spiritual matters of substance, has likely been an area where corners have been cut. Given the fact that we are nearing the return of the Lord, this is also likely to be an area which will get more complicated, requiring individuals to have significant wisdom and discernment.

- **"Therefore, putting aside all filthiness and *all* that remains of wickedness, in humility receive the word implanted, which is able to save your souls"** (James 1:21): If "the word planted in you" (NIV) may be regarded as the New Covenant promise to supernaturally transcribe the instructions of God's Torah onto the heart and mind (Jeremiah 31:31-34; Ezekiel 36:25-27), then how is this imperative to decisively change the attitudes and behaviors of individual Messianic Believers today? How much in our current, overall Messianic spiritual culture needs to change—to make sure that a Supernatural Compulsion model of keeping the Torah is emphasized, as opposed to the more common legalistic alternatives?

- **"My brethren, if any among you strays from the truth and one turns him back, let him know that he who turns a sinner from the error of his way will save his soul from death and will cover a multitude of sins"** (James 5:19-20): How many readers of James overlook the decisive fact that the letter's author is concerned for the straying and the lost? Could it be that when James' message is heeded by people of faith, that it will actually enable them to have a greater concern for the salvation and redemption of sinners?

There should be little doubt in our minds that the standard of perfection or maturity presented by James is something that each of us needs to be pursuing. Let me be clear: much of James' message is hard for us to often bear. Today's Messianic community on the whole, unfortunately, falls short of what James presents—particularly in its manner of communication (1:26; 3:2-12; 4:11). It does not matter which sector of the Messianic world one encounters; it can be easily detected that there is factionalism, rejection toward others, and gross unfairness toward others manifested. There are unbalanced levels of human emotion interjected into theological and spiritual topics, which need to be examined by people with level and cool heads. It is hard to say if various denominations and organizations among us will be able to moderate themselves. This is why individual Messianic Believers need to be sure that they are maturing spiritually, that they stay encouraged, and that they are accomplishing some of the main tasks as presented in Biblical texts like the Epistle of James.

How easy or difficult will it be for any of us to simply, **"Draw near to God and He will draw near to you. Cleanse your hands, you sinners; and purify your hearts, you double-minded. Be miserable and mourn and weep; let your laughter be turned into** mourning and your joy to gloom. **Humble yourselves in the presence of the Lord, and He will exalt you**" (4:8-10)? Only those people who have been humbled before their Creator, cleansed of their sins and spiritually regenerated, and are pursuing a mature faith—can be able to sort through the different theological issues of a text like James. They will be able to balance the inward and outward works or deeds that they need to be accomplishing. They will have love toward one another, and will be able to control their speech. Corporately, they will facilitate an environment where favoritism is not shown (2:2-3), and where selfish ambition will have no place (3:16). Yet, as many generations of those who have encountered the Epistle of James can probably attest, *talking* about these things is much easer than actually *doing* them. May each of us be committed to doing them, with the Lord's help!

THE MESSAGE OF JAMES

a summary for Messianic teaching and preaching

Much of today's Messianic movement places a high value on the Epistle of James and its message for Believers.[1] In a Christian world that has lost much of its moral compass, an emphasis on practical holiness, and a realization that good works are required of God's people—James offers an antidote to counter much contemporary complacency. To the brother of Yeshua, faith in God is not just about some kind of mental ascent or speaking written creeds; it is about performing the actions which are reflective of one's deeply held convictions. This letter is very easy to read, as it is full of important sayings and admonitions about upstanding living in the Lord. James has, at times, been compared to some of the Wisdom literature of the Tanach or Apocrypha, a Rabbinic composition such as Mishnah tractate Pirkei Avot, and most especially the Sermon on the Mount. The Epistle of James contains important instructions for a developing and still-maturing Messianic movement, and how it is to focus its attitudes and attention on the mission of the Messiah.

James considers the audience of his letter to be of the assembly of Israel (1:1), and offers them encouragement in the midst of the trials that they have been facing (1:2), asserting "that the testing of your faith develops perseverance. Perseverance must finish its work so that you may be mature and complete, not lacking anything" (1:3). Among conservative interpreters, it is sometimes thought that James' epistle was composed around the time following the martyrdom of Stephen (Acts 7), and that the pressure that these Believers were likely experiencing was a result of the persecution which followed (Acts 8:1), having largely fled out of Judea. James recognizes that such trials and tribulations have an important role in the formation of one's personal character, and that wisdom is available from God to those who ask sincerely, so that they can be stable and secure people (1:5-8).

An important feature of James' message is how he does not waste any time in telling the rich to be careful with their wealth, as those who are truly wealthy are humble people of God (1:9-11). Most frequently, this involves those who endure trial (1:12). Yet, God does not tempt people to sin—which is different than experiencing hard times—as sin begins in the human heart and then manifests in deathly behavior (1:13-15). Much sin can be associated with the acquisition of wealth, and James is clear on how the gifts that God's people truly need are given to them by the Creator (1:16-18).

[1] Unless otherwise noted, Biblical quotations in this article are from the New International Version (NIV).

One of the most important words that appears in James' letter, **which every reader must heed,** is seen very early. The Lord's brother expresses a direct concern in saying, "My dear brothers, take note of this: Everyone should be quick to listen, slow to speak and slow to become angry, for man's anger does not bring about the righteous life that God requires" (1:19-20). There are many possible applications of this, but one of the major ones involves how the people of God should approach **conflict resolution.** If there is a possible conflict or fight brewing between Believers, within a community of Believers, James instructs his audience to be very careful and not get too emotionally involved. *Human anger will not accomplish that much.* People who can listen to what others are saying, carefully thinking through what information they see presented, are more likely to use the God-given wisdom He has granted them and make reasonable decisions. This is contrasted to those who act rashly and do not pause to ask whether or not how they act will accomplish something, or be a waste of their time and energy.

James urged his ancient audience not to deceive themselves, and not fail to heed the Word of God, as it is to reveal any flaws in their character (1:22-25). It is insufficient for any born again Believer to simply read the Scriptures, and then do nothing. Not only does the Bible implore God's people to guard what they say and what they do with their mouths and tongues (1:26), but we need to each take an active interest in the downtrodden in society, getting out of our comfort zones and helping those in need. James' almost timeless remedy is, "Religion that our God and Father accepts as pure and faultless is this: to look after orphans and widows in their distress and to keep oneself from being polluted by the world" (1:27).

How we can demonstrate upstanding spirituality can be determined by how we treat those in the local assembly we may attend. James was most serious about how the rich were not to be favored at the expense of the poor (2:1-4). He expresses how, "Has not God chosen those who are poor in the eyes of the world to be rich in faith and to inherit the kingdom he promised to those who love him?" (2:5). Most frequently, it is poor people who have to entreat their Creator every day for their basic needs to be met, unlike the rich who often do not think about such matters. In the case of James' audience, he reminds them, "Is it not the rich who are exploiting you?...Are they not the ones who are slandering the noble name of him to whom you belong?" (2:6, 7). The rich to whom his readers would pay attention were likely some kind of wealthy business owners or merchants, who required the regular services of poor people in order for them to maintain their lifestyle. Rather than showing them a degree of kindness and generosity, they instead took advantage of them. Certainly in the Twenty-First Century, the tendency to exploit the poor and weak has not changed that much.

The main imperative of Holy Scripture is to "Love your neighbor as yourself" (2:8; Leviticus 19:18), labeled by James to be "the royal law." However, James is also clear that those who show favoritism to those in the assembly are considered by God to be violating His Torah (2:9), to the point where if one "stumbles at just one point [he] is guilty of breaking all of it" (2:10). His analogy is that those who do not commit adultery, but do commit murder, are guilty of disregarding all of the Torah of God (2:11). James' direction is to "Speak and act as those who are going to be judged by the law that gives freedom," precisely "because judgment without mercy will be shown to anyone who has not been merciful. Mercy triumphs over judgment!" (2:12-13).

Too frequently in our Messianic faith community, James 2:10-11 is used as a sharp rebuke of many of our Christian brothers and sisters who often disregard things like *Shabbat*, the appointed times, or kosher—but are most eager to accomplish things like taking care of widows, orphans, and the homeless. Their Messianic accusers, contrary to this, will often not even venture out beyond the "safe confines" of their assemblies or fellowships. If Torah observant Messianic Believers would take James' letter a bit more seriously and really consider the need to be full of the Father's grace and mercy to all, then perhaps we might make a more sizeable impact when others ask us about the importance and relevance of the Law of Moses. Can we be a little more tempered in our approach to Torah validity?

I do not believe that James the Just would have had any problems with anyone diligently keeping the Sabbath or appointed times, given his own reputation as steadfastly obedient to the Torah (Eusebius *Ecclesiastical History* 2.23.4-5). **James expects God's people to obey Him,** asking, "What good is it, my brothers, if a man claims to have faith but has no deeds? Can such faith save him?" (2:14). If one is diligently following the example of the Lord, then it is to be followed by the right actions. James would not stand against anyone wanting to rest on the Sabbath or eat appropriately, but he is most concerned with *the actions of service* to others. If a person needs food and clothing, and all you do is bless someone by words and really do nothing about it (2:15-16), then as he directly says, "faith by itself, if it is not accompanied by action, is dead...Show me your faith without deeds, and I will show you my faith by what I do" (2:17, 18). This is something that Abraham of old did when he presented his son Isaac to be sacrificed at God's request (2:19-24), or Rahab when she helped the Israelites spies in Jericho (2:25).

James spends some time discussing the heavy responsibilities which have been placed upon those who serve the Body of Messiah as teachers, issuing the stern warning, "Not many of you should presume to be teachers, my brothers, because you know that we who teach will be judged more strictly" (3:1). Teachers are human the same as any other person, and they will err even if relatively spiritually mature (3:2). The specific area of maturity that James focuses on is that of speaking with the tongue (3:3-12). While a proper usage of the tongue, a small organ of the body with which "we praise our Lord and Father, and with it we curse men" (3:9), should concern all Believers—**teachers are most especially in view here.** If those who instruct God's people in the Scriptures do not focus their attention on how to demonstrate greater holiness and love, then teachers might instead set them on a course toward eternal punishment (3:5-6). James' poignant observation is, "For every species of beast and bird, of reptile and sea creature, can be tamed and has been tamed by the human species, but no one can tame the tongue—a restless evil, full of deadly poison" (3:7-8, NRSV).

Wise and understanding persons, according to James, are to "show it by [their] good life, by deeds done in the humility that comes from wisdom" (3:13). At the same time, he delivers extreme caution against harboring bitterness and selfish ambition in the heart (3:14), specifying, "Such 'wisdom' does not come down from heaven but is earthly, unspiritual, of the devil. For where you have envy and selfish ambition, there you find disorder and every evil practice" (3:15-16). While there is such a thing as demonic "wisdom," something which seems to have some semblance of insight and intelligence—even though it brings nothing but devastation in its path—"the wisdom that comes from heaven is first of all pure; then peace-loving, considerate, submissive, full of mercy and good fruit, impartial and sincere" (3:17). When one is full of godly wisdom, then "Peacemakers who sow in peace raise a harvest of righteousness" (3:18). True wisdom from the Holy One is able to enact true *shalom*,[2] where peace between the Creator and man, one's fellow human beings, and nature as a whole, can be realized. Any of us, who truly desire the wisdom of the Lord present in our hearts, should desire to help see such tranquility be enacted.

For various reasons, James had to express how many in his audience were not adhering to a basic Biblical code of conduct. Perhaps issued for some rhetorical effect, he asks them, "What causes fights and quarrels among you? Don't they come from your desires that battle within you? You want something but don't get it. You kill and covet, but you cannot have what you want. You quarrel and fight. You do not have, because you do not ask God" (4:1-2). Much of what they wanted caused them, at the very least, to entertain a most ungodly approach to living. While it is doubtful that people within James' audience were directly responsible for murdering, their lack of care for the starving poor could be associated with "killing." James rebukes any person who asks God for the fulfillment of their own personal pleasures, as He will not grant such a request (4:3). He further rebukes Believers who choose to become friends of the fallen world and its baseness, and as a result make themselves out to be enemies of the Lord (4:4-6).

Not all hope is lost! James urges, "Submit yourselves, then, to God. Resist the devil, and he will flee from you. Come near to God and he will come near to you. Wash your hands, you sinners, and purify your hearts, you double-minded. Grieve, mourn and wail. Change your laughter to mourning and your joy to gloom. Humble yourselves before the Lord, and he will lift you up" (4:7-10). James admonishes that those who have been sinners need to change their behavior, including any attitudes where others appropriate the position of judging one's neighbor (4:11), when the Lord alone is the "only Lawgiver and Judge" (4:12). Human beings are to be compared to a small mist, one that "appears for a little while and then vanishes" (4:14). They are to appeal to the will of God in all of life's experiences, especially those of business (4:13-16).

---

[2] Grk. *eirēnē*; cf. G. Lloyd Carr, "shālôm," in *TWOT*, 2:931.

James again discusses the plight of many rich people, who are to "weep and wail because of the misery that is coming" (5:1). He says, "Your wealth has rotted, and moths have eaten your clothes. Your gold and silver are corroded. Their corrosion will testify against you and eat your flesh like fire. You have hoarded wealth..." (5:2-3). All of the things that they looked to for satisfaction and reliability will waste away. And the reason is most severe: "The wages you failed to pay the workmen who mowed your fields are crying out against you. The cries of the harvesters have reached the ears of the Lord Almighty. You have lived on earth in luxury and self-indulgence. You have fattened yourselves in the day of slaughter. You have condemned and murdered innocent men, who were not opposing you" (5:4-6). Such rich people could have used their means as a way to help others, giving the needy employment and steady jobs, and distributing their agricultural goods to the hungry—or at least selling them at an affordable price. Instead, those who got rich on the backs of the poor, gouging them from wages due, will get what is coming to them.

Believers who are suffering at the hands of greedy bosses are to simply be patient, because at the Lord's coming the evil world will have to answer to the Supreme King (5:7); they are to not "grumble against each other...or you will be judged" (5:9). Instead, those suffering are to consider examples like those of Job or the Hebrew Prophets (5:10-11). Just like Yeshua admonished (Matthew 5:34-37), so does James say, "Above all, my brothers, do not swear—not by heaven or by earth or by anything else. Let your 'Yes' be yes, and your 'No,' no, or you will be condemned" (5:12). The need to speak honestly is paramount for God's holy people.

James' epistle ends with a description of what is to happen when one of the Believers is sick. The elders of a congregation are to lay their hands on the infirm, and anoint him with oil (5:14). Prayer is to heal the illness, and sins are to be forgiven as public confession is important for the well being of the assembly (5:15-16). It may be that "oil" is not necessarily a reference to just a symbolic act, but rather "oil" used as an ancient medicine—hence prayer *and* a doctor's care together can help heal a sick person. But prayer is the most important: "The prayer of a righteous man is powerful and effective" (5:16b). The need to pray, especially like figures such as Elijah (5:17-18), is most critical not only in terms of seeing sick people healed, but also in turning a sinner back to a path of righteousness (5:19-20).

It is not difficult to see why a new appreciation needs to come forth in the worldwide Body of Messiah for the Epistle of James: James challenges Believers to have the right attitudes *and* actions becoming of those who claim Yeshua (Jesus) as Lord. James does not affirm any kind of salvation-by-works doctrine, but he does affirm that without works one's faith is quantitatively dead (cf. Ephesians 2:8-10). In too much of today's Christianity, there is an overemphasis on a faith in God that is not necessarily followed by the deeds which reflect the internal transformation that the gospel is to enact within Believers. Conversely in much of today's Messianic movement, there can sometimes be an unhealthy emphasis on various outward works, that we forget to guard our tongues, our thoughts, and perform acts of helps to the destitute. A fair re-appreciation of *all* of what James exhorts needs to be enacted in the hearts and minds of *all* who desire to walk the path of the Messiah. If we can do this, we will be much closer to not only accomplishing the mission of God, but seeing the Kingdom of God made manifest on the Earth!

EPISTLE OF JAMES

adapted from the 1901 American Standard Version,
incorporating the conclusions made and defended in this commentary

1

Salutation
[1] James, a servant of God and of the Lord Yeshua the Messiah, to the twelve tribes in the Diaspora: Greetings.

Faith and Wisdom
[2] Consider it all joy, my brothers and sisters, when you fall into[a] various trials,

[3] knowing that the testing of your faith produces endurance[b].

[4] And let endurance have *its* perfect work[c], that you may be perfect and complete, lacking in nothing.

[5] But if any of you lacks wisdom, let him ask of God, who gives to all generously and without reproaching, and it will be given to him.

[6] But let him ask in faith, without any doubting, for the one who doubts is like the surf of the sea, driven by the wind and tossed.

[7] For that person must not suppose that he will receive anything from the Lord,

[8] being a double-minded man[d], unstable in all his ways.

Poverty and Riches
[9] But let the brother[e] of humble circumstances glory in his high position;

[10] and the rich in his humiliation, because like the flower of the grass he will pass away.

---

[a] Grk. verb *peripiptō*; "**to encounter at hazard, *fall in with, fall into***" (*BDAG*, 804).

[b] Grk. *katergazetai hupomonēn*; "produces steadfastness" (RSV); "develops perseverance" (NIV).

[c] Grk. *ergon teleion*; sometimes rendered as "perfect result" (NASU); better rendered as something like "complete work" (CJB/HCSB).

[d] Grk. *anēr dispuchos*.

[e] Grk. *ho adelphos*; "believer" (NRSV).

[11] For the sun rises with a scorching wind, and withers the grass; and its flower falls off and the beauty of its appearance perishes; so also will the rich fade away in his pursuits.

Trial and Temptation

[12] Blessed is the man[a] who endures trial; for when he has been approved, he will receive the crown of life, which *the Lord* has promised to those who love Him.

[13] Let no one say when he is tempted, "I am being tempted by God"; for God cannot be tempted by evil, and He Himself tempts no one.

[14] But each one is tempted, when he is drawn away by his own lust, and enticed.

[15] Then the lust, when it has conceived, gives birth to sin; and the sin, when it is fully grown, brings forth death.

[16] Do not be deceived, my beloved brothers and sisters.

[17] Every good gift and every perfect gift is from above, coming down from the Father of lights, with whom there is no variation or shifting shadow[b].

[18] Of His own will He brought us forth by the word of truth, so that we would be a kind of firstfruits of His creatures.

Hearing and Doing the Word

[19] *This* you know, my beloved brothers and sisters. But let everyone be quick to hear, slow to speak, slow to wrath;

[20] for the wrath of man[c] does not work the righteousness of God[d].

[21] Therefore, putting away all filthiness and rank growth of wickedness, receive with meekness the implanted word, which is able to save your souls.

[22] But be doers of the word, and not hearers only, deluding yourselves.

[23] For if anyone is a hearer of the word and not a doer, he is like a man[e] who observes his natural face in a mirror;

[24] for he observes himself and goes away, and immediately forgets what he was like.

[25] But one who looks into the perfect Torah, the *Torah* of liberty, and abides by it, being no hearer who forgets but a doer who works[f], this one will be blessed in his doing.

[26] If anyone thinks himself to be religious, not bridling his tongue but deceiving his heart, this person's religion is worthless.

[27] Pure and undefiled religion before our God and Father is this: to visit orphans and widows in their affliction[g], *and* to keep oneself unstained from the world.

---

[a] Grk. *Makarios anēr.*

[b] Grk. *tropēs aposkiasma*; "shadow of turning" (KJV/NKJV); "shadow due to change" (RSV/NRSV/ESV).

[c] Grk. *orgē andros.*

[d] Grk. *dikaiosunēn Theou ouk ergazetai*; "does not achieve the righteousness of God" (NASU); "does not produce the righteousness of God" (ESV).

[e] Grk. *eoiken andri.*

[f] Grk. *poiētēs ergou*; "effectual doer" (NASU); "doer that/who acts" (RSV/ESV).

[g] Grk. *thilipsis*; or "distress" (NASU); possibly even "tribulation."

2

Warning against Partiality

¹ My brothers and sisters, do not hold the faith of our Lord Yeshua the Messiah, *the Lord* of glory, with *an attitude of* personal favoritism.

² For if a man comes into your synagogue with a gold ring, in fine clothing, and a poor man comes also in dirty clothing,

³ and you pay special attention to the one who is wearing the fine clothing, and say, "You sit here in a good place," and you say to the poor one, "You stand over there, or sit down under my footstool,"

⁴ have you not made distinctions among yourselves, and become judges with evil thoughts?

⁵ Listen, my beloved brothers and sisters: did not God choose those who are poor in the world *to be* rich in faith and heirs of the Kingdom which He promised to those who love Him?

⁶ But you have dishonored the poor one. Is it not the rich who oppress you, and personally drag you before the courts?

⁷ Do they not blaspheme the honorable name by which you were called?

⁸ If, however, you fulfill the royal Torah[a], according to the Scripture, "YOU SHALL LOVE YOUR NEIGHBOR AS YOURSELF" [Leviticus 19:18], you do well.

⁹ But if you show partiality, you are committing sin, being convicted by the Torah as transgressors.

¹⁰ For whoever keeps the whole Torah and yet stumbles in one *point*, he has become guilty of all.

¹¹ For He who said, "DO NOT COMMIT ADULTERY" [Exodus 20:14; Deuteronomy 5:18], also said, "DO NOT COMMIT MURDER" [Exodus 20:13; Deuteronomy 5:17]. Now if you do not commit adultery, but you do commit murder, you have become a transgressor of the Torah.

¹² So speak and so act as those who are to be judged by a Torah of liberty[b].

¹³ For judgment *is* without mercy to one who has shown no mercy; mercy triumphs over judgment[c].

Faith and Works

¹⁴ What does it profit, my brothers and sisters, if someone says he has faith, but has no works? Can that faith save him?

---

[a] Grk. *nomon teleite basilikon*; "the goal of Kingdom *Torah*" (CJB); "the royal law" (TLV).

[b] Grk. *dia nomous eleutherias*; correctly rendered as "by *the* law of liberty" (NASU, NRSV) or "by the law that gives freedom" (NIV); incorrectly rendered as "under the law of liberty" (RSV/ESV).

[c] Grk. *katakauchatai eleos kriseōs*; "mercy glorieth against judgment" (ASV).

¹⁵ If a brother or sister is naked and in lack of daily food,

¹⁶ and one of you says to them, "Go in peace, be warmed and filled," and yet you do not give the things needed for the body, what does it profit?

¹⁷ Even so faith, if it has no works, is dead by itself.

¹⁸ But someone will say, "You have faith, and I have works; show me your faith apart from your works, and I by my works will show you my faith."

¹⁹ You believe that God is one; you do well. The demons also believe, and shudder.

²⁰ But do you want to know, you foolish fellow[a], that faith apart from works is barren[b]?

²¹ Was not Abraham our father justified by works, when he offered up Isaac his son upon the altar?

²² You see that faith was working with his works[c], and by works faith was perfected;

²³ and the Scripture was fulfilled which says, "AND ABRAHAM BELIEVED GOD, AND IT WAS RECKONED TO HIM AS RIGHTEOUSNESS" [Genesis 15:6], and he was called the friend of God.

²⁴ You see that a person is vindicated[d] by works and not by faith alone.

²⁵ And in the same way was not also Rahab the harlot justified by works when she received the messengers and sent them out another way?

²⁶ For as the body apart from the spirit is dead, so faith apart from works is dead.

3

The Tongue

¹ Let not many *of you* become teachers, my brothers and sisters, knowing that we will receive a stricter judgment.

² For we all stumble in many *ways*. If anyone does not stumble in what he says[e], he is a perfect man[f], able to bridle the whole body also.

³ Now if we put bits into the mouths of horses so that they may obey us, we guide their whole body as well.

⁴ Behold, the ships also, though they are so great and are driven by strong winds, are guided by a very small rudder, wherever the inclination of the pilot directs.

---

[a] Grk. *ō anthrōpe kene*; "you shallow man" (RSV); "O vain man" (ASV).

[b] Grk. *hē pistis chōris tōn ergōn argē estin*; "faith without works is dead" (KJV); "faith without works is useless" (NASU).

[c] Grk. *hē pistis sunergei tois ergois autou*; "faith was active along with his works" (RSV/NRSV/ESV); "his faith and his actions were working together" (NIV).

[d] Grk. verb *dikaioō*; more traditionally rendered as "justified."

[e] Grk. *en logō*; lit. "in word" (ASV).

[f] Grk. *teleios anēr*; "mature man" (HCSB).

⁵ So also the tongue is a small member, and *yet* it boasts of great things. Behold, how great a forest is set ablaze by such a small fire!

⁶ And the tongue is a fire. The world of unrighteousness among our members is the tongue, which defiles the whole body, and sets on fire the cycle of nature[a], and is set on fire by Gehenna.

⁷ For every species of beasts and birds, of reptiles and creatures of the sea[b], is tamed, and has been tamed by the human species[c].

⁸ But no human being can tame the tongue; *it is* a restless evil, full of deadly poison.

⁹ With it we bless the Lord and Father; and with it we curse people, who are made in the likeness of God;

¹⁰ from the same mouth come *both* blessing and cursing. My brothers and sisters, these things ought not to be so.

¹¹ Does a spring pour forth from the same opening *both* fresh and bitter *water*?

¹² Can a fig tree, my brothers and sisters, yield olives, or a grapevine figs? Neither *can* salt water yield fresh.

The Wisdom from Above

¹³ Who is wise and understanding among you? Let him show by his good behavior[d] his works in meekness of wisdom.

¹⁴ But if you have bitter jealousy and selfish ambition in your heart, do not boast and *so* lie against the truth.

¹⁵ This wisdom is not such as comes down from above, but is Earthly, sensual, demonic.

¹⁶ For where jealousy and selfish ambition are, there is confusion[e] and every vile deed.

¹⁷ But the wisdom from above is first pure, then peaceable, gentle, reasonable, full of mercy and good fruits, unwavering, without hypocrisy.

¹⁸ And the fruit of righteousness is sown in peace for those who make peace.

Friendship with the World

¹ Where do conflicts and where do fightings among you *come* from? *Are they* not from here: from your pleasures that wage war in your members?

---

[a] Grk. *ton trochon tēs geneseōs*; "wheel of nature" (ASV); often extrapolated as "the course of *our* life" (NASU).

[b] Grk. *pasa gar phusis thēriōn te kai peteinōn, herpetōn te kai enaliōn damazetai*.

[c] Grk. *tē phusei tē anthrōpinē*; "the human species" (NRSV).

[d] Grk. *anastrophē*; **"conduct expressed according to certain principles *way of life, conduct, behavior*"** (BDAG, 73).

[e] Grk. *akatastasia*; "instability, a state of disorder, disturbance, confusion" (*Thayer*, 21).

[2] You lust and you do not have; *so* you murder. And you envy[a] and cannot obtain; *so* you have conflict and war. You do not have, because you do not ask.

[3] You ask and do not receive, because you ask wrongly, so that you may spend *it* on your pleasures.

[4] You adulteresses, do you not know that the friendship with the world is enmity with God? Therefore whoever wishes to be a friend of the world makes himself an enemy of God.

[5] Or do you think that the Scripture speaks in vain: "He yearns jealously over the Spirit which He caused to dwell in us"?

[6] But He gives more grace. Therefore *it* says, "GOD OPPOSES THE PROUD, BUT GIVES GRACE TO THE HUMBLE" [Proverbs 3:34, LXX].

[7] Submit therefore to God. But resist the Devil, and he will flee from you.

[8] Draw near to God and He will draw near to you. Cleanse your hands, you sinners; and purify your hearts, you double-minded.

[9] Be miserable and mourn and weep; let your laughter be turned into mourning, and your joy to gloom.

[10] Humble yourselves in the sight of the Lord, and He will exalt you.

Judging a Brother or Sister

[11] Do not speak evil against one against another, brothers and sisters. He who speaks evil against a brother or sister, or judges his brother or sister, speaks evil against the Torah, and judges the Torah; but if you judge the Torah, you are not a doer of the Torah, but a judge *of it*.

[12] *Only* one is the Giver of the Torah[b] and Judge, He who is able to save and to destroy. But who are you that you judge your neighbor?

Warning against Boasting

[13] Come now, you who say, "Today or tomorrow we will go into this or that city, and spend a year there and trade and make a profit";

[14] whereas you do not know about tomorrow. What is your life? For you are a vapor that appears for a little while and then vanishes.

[15] Instead *you ought* to say, "If the Lord wills, we will live and do this or that."

[16] But as it is, you boast in your arrogance; all such boasting is evil.

[17] Therefore, to one who knows *the* right thing to do, and does not do it, to him it is sin.

---

[a] Grk. verb *zēloō*; or "are zealous" (YLT).

[b] Grk. *nomothetēs*; a Messianic version like the TLV has the more standard, "lawgiver"; the rendering here follows the CJB.

5

Warning to the Rich

[1] Come now, you rich, weep and howl for your miseries which are coming upon you.

[2] Your riches have rotted and your garments are moth-eaten.

[3] Your gold and your silver have rusted; and their rust will be a testimony against you and will eat your flesh like fire. You have laid up treasure for the last days.

[4] Behold, the wages of the laborers who mowed your fields, which you kept back by fraud, cries out *against you*; and the cries of the harvesters have reached[a] the ears of the Lord of Sabaoth[b].

[5] You have lived luxuriously on the Earth and in self-indulgence[c]; you have fattened your hearts in a day of slaughter.

[6] You have condemned, you have murdered the righteous *one*; he does not resist you.

Patience and Prayer

[7] Be patient, therefore, brothers and sisters, until the coming of the Lord. Behold, the farmer waits for the precious fruit of the land[d], being patient about it, until it receives the early and late rain.

[8] You also be patient; establish your hearts, for the coming of the Lord is at hand.

[9] Do not grumble, brothers and sisters, against one another, that you may not be judged; behold, the Judge is standing at the doors.

[10] As an example of suffering and patience, brothers and sisters, take the prophets who spoke in the name of the Lord.

[11] Behold, we call those blessed who endured. You have heard of the patience of Job, and you have seen the purpose of the Lord, how the Lord is full of compassion and *is* merciful.

[12] But above all, my brothers and sisters, do not swear, either by the Heaven or by Earth or by any other oath; but let your yes be yes and your no be no; so that you may not fall under judgment[e].

[13] Is anyone among you suffering? Let him pray. Is anyone cheerful? Let him sing praise.

---

[a] Grk. verb *eiserchomai*; more lit. "entered into the" (ASV).

[b] Grk. *Kuriou sabaōth*; Heb. equiv. *Adonai Tzavaot* (Delitzsch); Messianic versions vary on what to include, having a standard English "Lord of Hosts" (TLV); "Commander of all forces" (The Messianic Writings); or "*Adonai-Tzva'ot*" (CJB). The inclusion of the Tetragrammaton (YHWH/YHVH) in various modern Hebrew versions, is most perplexing, considering the fact that Second Temple Judaism would not readily pronounce the Divine Name of God.

[c] Grk. *etruphēsate epi tēs gēs kai espatalēsate*; "you lived in indulgence upon the earth and lived luxuriously, you nourished the hearts of you [as] in a day of slaughter" (Brown and Comfort, 804).

[d] Grk. *ton timion karpon tēs gēs*; "the precious produce of the soil" (NASU).

[e] Grk. *hupo krisin*; "under condemnation" (RSV/NRSV/ESV).

[14] Is anyone among you sick? Let him call for the elders of the assembly, and let them pray over him, anointing him with oil in the name of the Lord;

[15] and the prayer of faith will save the one who is sick, and the Lord will raise him up; and if he has committed sins, he will be forgiven.

[16] Therefore confess your sins to one another, and pray one for another, that you may be healed. The effective petition[a] of a righteous person can accomplish much.

[17] Elijah was a human being with a nature like ours, and he prayed fervently that it might not rain; and it did not rain on the Earth for three years and six months.

[18] And he prayed again, and the sky gave rain, and the ground brought forth its fruit.

[19] My brothers and sisters, if any among you wanders from the truth and one turns him back,

[20] let him know that he who turns a sinner from the error of his way will save a soul from death and will cover a multitude of sins.

---

[a] Grk. *ischuei deēsis*; "effective prayer" (NASU); "urgent request" (HCSB); "power [the] petition" (Brown and Comfort, 806).

ABOUT THE AUTHOR

John Kimball McKee is an integral part of Outreach Israel Ministries, and serves as the editor of Messianic Apologetics. He is a graduate of the University of Oklahoma (Class of 2003) with a B.A. in political science, and holds an M.A. in Biblical Studies from Asbury Theological Seminary (Class of 2009). He is a 2009 recipient of the Zondervan Biblical Languages Award for Greek. John has held memberships in the Evangelical Theological Society, the Evangelical Philosophical Society, and Christians for Biblical Equality, and is a longtime supporter of the perspectives and views of the Creationist ministry of Reasons to Believe. In 2019, John was licensed as a Messianic Teacher with the International Alliance of Messianic Congregations and Synagogues (IAMCS), and was officially ordained as a Messianic Teacher in 2022.

Since the 1990s, John's ministry has capitalized on the Internet's ability to reach people all over this planet. He has spoken with challenging and probing articles to a wide Messianic audience, and those evangelical Believers who are interested in Messianic things. Given his generational family background in evangelical ministry, as well as in academics and the military, John carries a strong burden to assist in the development and maturation of our emerging Messianic theology and spirituality. John has had the profound opportunity since 1997 to engage many in dialogue, so that they will consider the questions he postulates, as his only agenda is to be as Scripturally sound as possible. John believes in demonstrating a great deal of honor and respect to both his evangelical Protestant, Wesleyan and Reformed family background, as well as to the Jewish Synagogue, and together allowing the strengths and virtues of our Judeo-Protestant heritage to be employed for the Lord's plan for the Messianic movement in the long term future.

J.K. McKee is the son of the late K. Kimball McKee (1951-1992) and Margaret Jeffries McKee Huey (1953-), and stepson of William Mark Huey (1951-), who married his mother in 1994, and who is the executive director of Outreach Israel Ministries. Mark Huey is the Director of Partner Relations for the Joseph Project, a ministry of the Messianic Jewish Alliance of America (MJAA).

John has a very strong appreciation for those who have preceded him. His father, Kimball McKee, was a licensed lay minister in the Kentucky Conference of the United Methodist Church, and was a very strong evangelical Believer, most appreciable of the Jewish Roots of the faith. Among his many ministry pursuits, Kim brought the Passover *seder* to Christ United Methodist Church in Florence, KY, was a Sunday school teacher, and was extremely active in the Walk to Emmaus, leading the first men's walk in Madras, India in 1991. John is the grandson of the late Prof. William W. Jeffries (1914-1989; CDR USN WWII), who served as a professor at the United States Naval Academy in Annapolis, MD from 1942-1989, notably as the museum director and founder of what is now the William W. Jeffries Memorial Archives in the Nimitz Library. John is the great-grandson of Bishop Marvin A. Franklin (1894-1972), who served as a minister and bishop of the Methodist Church, throughout his ministry serving churches in Georgia, Florida, Alabama, and Mississippi. Bishop Franklin was President of the Council of Bishops from 1959-1960. John is also the first cousin twice removed of the late Charles L. Allen (1913-2005), formerly the senior pastor of Grace Methodist Church of Atlanta, GA and First Methodist Church of Houston, TX, and author of numerous books, notably including *God's Psychiatry*. John can also count among his ancestors, Lt. Colonel, By Brevet, Dr. James Cooper McKee (1830-1897), a Union veteran of the U.S. Civil War and significant contributor to the medical science of his generation.

J.K. McKee is a native of the Northern Kentucky/Greater Cincinnati, OH area. He has also lived in Dallas, TX, Norman, OK, Kissimmee-St. Cloud, FL, and Roatán, Honduras, Central America. He presently resides in McKinney, TX, just north of Dallas.

BIBLIOGRAPHY

Articles

Balchin, J.A. "Oil," in *ISBE*.

Barabas, Steven. "James, Letter of," in *NIDB*, pp 494-495.

Barnett, A.E. "James, Letter of," in *IDB*, 2:794-799.

Beardsless, W.A. "James," in *IDB*, 2:790-794.

Büchsel, F. "*epithymía, epithyméō*," in *TDNT*.

Bultmann, R. "to believe, trust," in *TDNT*.

Carr, G. Lloyd. "shālôm," in *TWOT*.

Delling, G. "*alazōn, alazoneía*," in *TDNT*.

_____. "*téleios*," in *TDNT*.

Douglas, J.D. "James," in *NIDB*.

Gaster, T.H. "Gehenna," in *IDB*.

Gillman, Florence Morgan. "James, Brother of Jesus," in *ABD*, 3:620-621.

Hagner, Donald A. "James," in *ABD*, 3:616-618.

Harris, R.L. "James," in *ISBE*, 2:958-959.

Hartley, John E. "*tzevaot*," in *TWOT*.

_____. "*tzlm*," in *TWOT*.

Heidland, H.W. "*ololýzō*," in *TDNT*.

Horst J. "patience, forbearance," in *TDNT*

Kaiser, Walter C. "b^{e}lîya'al," in *TWOT*.

Kittel, G. "glory," in *TDNT*.

Laws, Sophie. "James, Epistle of," in *ABD*, 3:621-628.

McCartney, Dan G. Review of *The Letter of James* in <u>Journal of the Evangelical Theological Society</u> Vol. 54 No. 4 (2011).

Oswalt, John N. "*kaveid*," in *TWOT*.

Payne, J. Barton. "*satan*," in *TWOT*.

Pratt, D.M. "Catholic Epistles," in *ISBE*.

Schmidt, K.L. "*basilikós*," in *TDNT*

_____. "*diasporá*," in *TDNT*.

Scott, Jack B. "*aman*," in *TWOT*.

Stählin, G. "anger, wrath," in *TDNT*.

_____. "*hēdonē*," in *TDNT*.

Stigers, Harold G. "*tzadeq*," in *TWOT*.

Van Voorst, Robert E. "James," in *EDB*, pp 669-670.

Wall, R.W. "James, Letter of," in *Dictionary of the Later New Testament & Its Developments*, pp 545-561.

Ward, R.B. "James, Letter of," in *IDBSup*, pp 469-470.

Webb, Robert L. "Epistles, Catholic," in *ABD*.

Wessel, W.W. "James, Epistle of," in *ISBE*, 2:959-966.

Wilckens, U. "wisdom," in *TDNT*.

Würthwein, E. "*katanoéō*," in *TDNT*.

Yetzer Ha-Ra," in *The New Jewish Encyclopedia*.

Bible Versions & Study Bibles

Abegg, Jr., Martin, Peter Flint, and Eugene Ulrich, trans. *The Dead Sea Scrolls Bible* (New York: HarperCollins, 1999).

American Standard Version (New York: Thomas Nelson & Sons, 1901).

Barker, Kenneth L., ed., et. al. *NIV Study Bible* (Grand Rapids: Zondervan, 2002).

Berlin, Adele, and Marc Zvi Brettler, eds. *The Jewish Study Bible* (Oxford: Oxford University Press, 2004).

Bratcher, Robert G., ed. *Good News Bible: The Bible in Today's English Version* (New York: American Bible Society, 1976).

Esposito, Paul W. *The Apostles' Bible, An English Septuagint Version* (http://www.apostlesbible.com/).

Garrett, Duane A., ed., et. al. *NIV Archaeological Study Bible* (Grand Rapids: Zondervan, 2005).

Green, Jay P., trans. *The Interlinear Bible* (Lafayette, IN: Sovereign Grace Publishers, 1986).

Green, Joel B., ed. *The Wesley Study Bible* (Nashville: Abingdon, 2009).

God's Game Plan: The Athlete's Bible 2007, HCSB (Nashville: Serendipity House Publishers, 2007).

Grudem, Wayne, ed. *ESV Study Bible* (Wheaton, IL: Crossway, 2008).

Harrelson, Walter J., ed., et. al. *New Interpreter's Study Bible*, NRSV (Nashville: Abingdon, 2003).

Harris, W. Hall, ed. *The Holy Bible: The Net Bible*, New English Translation (Dallas: Biblical Studies Press, 2001).

Holman Christian Standard Bible (Nashville: Broadman & Holman, 2004).

Holy Bible, King James Version (edited 1789).

Holy Bible, New International Version (Grand Rapids: Zondervan, 1978).

LaHaye, Tim, ed. *Tim LaHaye Prophecy Study Bible*, KJV (Chattanooga: AMG Publishers, 2000).

Lattimore, Richmond, trans. *The New Testament* (New York: North Point Press, 1996).

May, Herbert G., and Bruce M. Metzger, eds. *The New Oxford Annotated Bible With the Apocrypha*, RSV (New York: Oxford University Press, 1977).

Meeks, Wayne A., ed., et. al. *The HarperCollins Study Bible*, NRSV (New York: HarperCollins, 1993).

Messianic Jewish Shared Heritage Bible, JPS/TLV (Shippensburg, PA: Destiny Image, 2012).

Newman, Barclay M., ed. *Holy Bible: Contemporary English Version* (New York: American Bible Society, 1995).

New American Standard Bible (La Habra, CA: Foundation Press Publications, 1971).

New American Standard, Updated Edition (Anaheim, CA: Foundation Publications, 1995).

New English Bible (Oxford and Cambridge: Oxford and Cambridge University Presses, 1970).

New King James Version (Nashville: Thomas Nelson, 1982).

New Revised Standard Version (National Council of Churches of Christ, 1989).

Packer, J.I., ed. *The Holy Bible, English Standard Version* (Wheaton, IL: Crossway Bibles, 2001).

Peterson, Eugene H. *The Message: The Bible in Contemporary Language* (Colorado Springs: NavPress, 2002).

Phillips, J.B., trans. *The New Testament in Modern English* (New York: Touchstone, 1972).

Pietersma, Albert, and Benjamin G. Wright, eds. *A New English Translation of the Septuagint* (Oxford and New York: Oxford University Press, 2007).

Ryrie, Charles C., ed. *The Ryrie Study Bible*, NASB (Chicago: Moody Press, 1978).

Scherman, Nosson, and Meir Zlotowitz, eds. *ArtScroll Tanach* (Brooklyn: Mesorah Publications, 1996).

Siewert, Frances E., ed. *The Amplified Bible* (Grand Rapids: Zondervan, 1965).

Suggs, M. Jack, and Katharine Doob Sakenfeld, and James R. Mueller, et. al. *The Oxford Study Bible*, REB (New York: Oxford University Press, 1992).

Stern, David H., trans. *Jewish New Testament* (Clarksville, MD: Jewish New Testament Publications, 1995).

_____, trans. *Complete Jewish Bible* (Clarksville, MD: Jewish New Testament Publications, 1998).

Tanakh: The Holy Scriptures (Philadelphia: Jewish Publication Society, 1999).

The Holy Bible, Revised Standard Version (Nashville: Cokesbury, 1952).

The Jerusalem Bible (Jerusalem: Koren Publishers, 2000).

Today's New International Version (Grand Rapids: Zondervan, 2005).

Tree of Life Messianic Family Bible—New Covenant (Shippensburg, PA: Destiny Image, 2011).

Williams, Charles B., trans. *The New Testament: A Private Translation in the Language of the People* (Chicago: Moody Publishers, 1937).

Wright, N.T. *The Kingdom New Testament: A Contemporary Translation* (New York: HarperCollins, 2011).

Young, Robert, trans. *Young's Literal Translation.*

Zodhiates, Spiros, ed. *Hebrew-Greek Key Study Bible*, NASB (Chattanooga: AMG Publishers, 1994).

Books

Berkowitz, Ariel and D'vorah. *Torah Rediscovered* (Lakewood, CO: First Fruits of Zion, 1996).

_____. *Take Hold* (Littleton, CO: First Fruits of Zion, 1999).

Bruce, F.F. *New Testament History* (New York: Doubleday, 1969).

Carson, D.A., and Douglas J. Moo. *An Introduction to the New Testament*, second edition (Grand Rapids: Zondervan, 2005).

Cohen, Mitchell, and Nicole Fermon, eds. *Princeton Readings in Political Thought* (Princeton, NJ: Princeton University Press, 1996).

Cohn-Sherbok, Dan, ed. *Voices of Messianic Judaism* (Baltimore: Lederer Books, 2001).

Dillard, Raymond B., and Tremper Longman III. *An Introduction to the Old Testament* (Grand Rapids: Zondervan, 1994).

Fee, Gordon D., and Douglas Stuart. *How to Read the Bible for All Its Worth* (Grand Rapids: Zondervan, 2003).

Friedman, David. *They Loved the Torah* (Baltimore: Lederer Books, 2001).

_____, with D.B. Friedman. *James the Just Presents Applications of Torah* (Clarksville, MD: Lederer, 2012).

Fructenbaum, Arnold G. *Ariel's Bible Commentary: The Messianic Jewish Epistles* (Tustin, CA: Ariel Ministries, 2005).

Gundry, Robert H. *A Survey of the New Testament*, third edition (Grand Rapids: Zondervan, 1994).

Guthrie, Donald. *New Testament Introduction* (Downers Grove, IL: InterVarsity, 1990).

Harrison, R.K. *Introduction to the Old Testament* (Grand Rapids: Eerdmans, 1969).

Hegg, Tim. *Interpreting the Bible* (Tacoma, WA: TorahResource, 2000).

_____. *The Letter Writer: Paul's Background and Torah Perspective* (Littleton, CO: First Fruits of Zion, 2002).

_____. *It is Often Said: Comments and Comparisons of Traditional Christian Theology and Hebraic Thought*, 2 vols. (Littleton, CO: First Fruits of Zion, 2003).

Juster, Dan, and Keith Intrater. *Israel, the Church and the Last Days* (Shippensburg, PA: Destiny Image, 1990).

Juster, Daniel C. *Jewish Roots* (Shippensburg, PA: Destiny Image, 1995).

Kaiser, Walter C. *Toward Old Testament Ethics* (Grand Rapids: Zondervan, 1983).

_____. *The Old Testament Documents: Are They Reliable & Relevant?* (Downers Grove, IL: InterVarsity, 2001).

_____. *The Promise-Plan of God: A Biblical Theology of the Old and New Testaments* (Grand Rapids: Zondervan, 2008).

_____, Peter H. Davids, F.F. Bruce, and Manfred T. Brauch. *Hard Sayings of the Bible* (Downers Grove, IL: InterVarsity, 1996).

Kaiser, Walter C., and Moisés Silva. *An Introduction to Biblical Hermeneutics* (Grand Rapids: Zondervan, 1994).

McGrath, Alister E. *Christian Theology: An Introduction* (Oxford: Blackwell Publishing, 2001).

McKee, J.K. *Torah In the Balance, Volume I* (Kissimmee, FL: TNN Press, 2003).

_____. *The New Testament Validates Torah* (Kissimmee, FL: TNN Press, 2004).

_____. *James for the Practical Messianic* (Kissimmee, FL: TNN Press, 2005).

_____. *Hebrews for the Practical Messianic* (Kissimmee, FL: TNN Press, 2006).

_____. *A Survey of the Apostolic Scriptures for the Practical Messianic* (Kissimmee, FL: TNN Press, 2006).

_____. *Philippians for the Practical Messianic* (Kissimmee, FL: TNN Press, 2007).

_____. *Galatians for the Practical Messianic*, second edition (Kissimmee, FL: TNN Press, 2007).

_____. *Ephesians for the Practical Messianic* (Kissimmee, FL: TNN Press, 2008).

_____. *A Survey of the Tanach for the Practical Messianic* (Kissimmee, FL: TNN Press, 2008).

_____. *Colossians and Philemon for the Practical Messianic* (Kissimmee, FL: TNN Press, 2010).

_____. *Acts 15 for the Practical Messianic* (Kissimmee, FL: TNN Press, 2010).

_____. *The Pastoral Epistles for the Practical Messianic* (Kissimmee, FL: TNN Press, 2012).

_____. *1&2 Thessalonians for the Practical Messianic* (Kissimmee, FL: TNN Press, 2012).

Patzia, Arthur G. *The Making of the New Testament: Origin, Collection, Text & Canon* (Downers Grove, IL: InterVarsity, 1995).

Ross, Hugh. *The Genesis Question: Scientific Advances and the Accuracy of Genesis*, second expanded edition (Colorado Springs: NavPress, 2001).

_____. *A Matter of Days: Resolving a Creation Controversy* (Colorado Springs: NavPress, 2004).

_____. *Why the Universe Is the Way It Is* (Grand Rapids: Baker Books, 2008).

Strickland, Wayne G., ed. *Five Views on Law and Gospel* (Grand Rapids: Zondervan, 1996).

Thompson, David L. *Bible Study That Works* (Nappanee, IN: Evangel Publishing House, 1994).

Wesley, John. *A Plain Account of Christian Perfection* (Kansas City: Beacon Hill Press, 1966).

Wilson, Marvin R. *Our Father Abraham* (Grand Rapids: Eerdmans, 1989).

Wright, Christopher J.H. *The Mission of God: Unlocking the Bible's Grand Narrative* (Downers Grove, IL: InterVarsity, 2006).

Christian Reference Sources

Alexander, T. Desmond, and David W. Baker, eds. *Dictionary of the Old Testament Pentateuch* (Downers Grove, IL: InterVarsity, 2003).

Arnold, Bill T., and H.G.M. Williamson, eds. *Dictionary of the Old Testament Historical Books* (Downers Grove, IL: InterVarsity, 2005).

Bercot, David W., ed. *A Dictionary of Early Christian Beliefs* (Peabody, MA: Hendrickson, 1998).

Boda, Mark J., and J. Gordon McConville, eds. *Dictionary of the Old Testament Prophets* (Downers Grove, IL: InterVarsity, 2012).

Bromiley, Geoffrey, ed. *International Standard Bible Encyclopedia*, 4 vols. (Grand Rapids: Eerdmans, 1988).

Buttrick, George, ed. et. al. *The Interpreter's Dictionary of the Bible*, 4 vols. (Nashville: Abingdon, 1962).

Cairns, Alan. *Dictionary of Theological Terms* (Greenville, SC: Ambassador Emerald International, 2002).

Crim, Keith, ed. *Interpreter's Dictionary of the Bible: Supplementary Volume* (Nashville: Abingdon, 1976).

Evans, Craig A., and Stanley E. Porter, eds. *Dictionary of New Testament Background* (Downers Grove, IL: InterVarsity, 2000).

Freedman, David Noel, ed. *Anchor Bible Dictionary*, 6 vols. (New York: Doubleday, 1992).

_____, ed. *Eerdmans Dictionary of the Bible* (Grand Rapids: Eerdmans, 2000).

Geisler, Norman L., ed. *Baker Encyclopedia of Christian Apologetics* (Grand Rapids: Baker, 1999).

Green, Joel B., Scot McKnight, and I. Howard Marshall, eds. *Dictionary of Jesus and the Gospels* (Downers Grove, IL: InterVarsity, 1992).

Grenz, Stanley J., David Guretzki, and Cherith Fee Nordling. *Pocket Dictionary of Theological Terms* (Downers Grove, IL: InterVarsity, 1999).

Harrison, Everett F., ed. *Baker's Dictionary of Theology* (Grand Rapids: Baker Book House, 1960).

Hawthorne, Gerald F., Ralph P. Martin, and Daniel G. Reid, eds. *Dictionary of Paul and His Letters* (Downers Grove, IL: InterVarsity, 1993).

Longman III, Tremper, and Peter Enns, eds. *Dictionary of the Old Testament Wisdom, Poetry & Writings* (Downers Grove, IL: InterVarsity, 2008).

Martin, Ralph P., and Peter H. Davids, eds. *Dictionary of the Later New Testament & its Developments* (Downers Grove, IL: InterVarsity, 1997).

McKim, Donald S. *Westminster Dictionary of Theological Terms* (Louisville: Westminster John Knox, 1996).

McLay, R. Timothy. *The Use of the Septuagint in New Testament Research* (Grand Rapids: Eerdmans, 2003).

Patzia, Arthur G., and Anthony J. Petrotta. *Pocket Dictionary of Biblical Studies* (Downers Grove, IL: InterVarsity, 2002).

Roberts, Alexander, and James Donaldson, eds. *The Apostolic Fathers*, American Edition.

Schaff, Philip. *History of the Christian Church*, 8 vols. (Grand Rapids: Eerdmans, 1995).

Tenney, Merrill C., ed. *The New International Dictionary of the Bible* (Grand Rapids: Zondervan, 1987).

The Book of Common Prayer (New York: Oxford University Press, 1990).

Commentaries

Bauckham, Richard. "James," in James D.G. Dunn and John W. Rogerson, eds. *Eerdmans Commentary on the Bible* (Grand Rapids: Eerdmans, 2003), pp 1483-1492.

Blue, J. Ronald. "James," in John F. Walvoord and Roy B. Zuck, eds. *The Bible Knowledge Commentary: New Testament* (Wheaton, IL: Victor Books, 1983), pp 815-836.

Burdick, Donald W. "James," in Frank E. Gaebelein, ed. et. al. *Expositor's Bible Commentary* (Grand Rapids: Zondervan, 1981), 12:161-205.

Calvin, John. *Calvin's New Testament Commentaries: A Harmony of the Gospels Matthew, Mark & Luke and James & Jude*, trans. A.W. Morrison (Grand Rapids: Eerdmans, 1972).

Cedar, Paul A. *The Preacher's Commentary: James, 1&2 Peter, Jude*, Vol 34 (Nashville: Thomas Nelson, 1984).

Davids, Peter. *New International Greek Testament Commentary: The Epistle of James* (Grand Rapids: Eerdmans, 1982).

Hamilton, Victor P. *New International Commentary on the Old Testament: The Book of Genesis, Chapters 1-17* (Grand Rapids: Eerdmans, 1990).

Johnson, Luke T. "The Letter of James," in Leander E. Keck, ed., et. al. *New Interpreter's Bible* (Nashville: Abingdon, 1998), 12:177-225.

Keener, Craig S. *The IVP Bible Background Commentary: New Testament* (Downers Grove, IL: InterVarsity, 1993).

Keil, C., and F. Delitzsch, eds. *Commentary on the Old Testament*, 10 vols.

Martin, Ralph P. *Word Biblical Commentary: James*, Vol. 48 (Nashville: Thomas Nelson, 1988).

McCartney, Dan G. *Baker Exegetical Commentary on the New Testament: James* (Grand Rapids: Baker Academic, 2009).

McKnight, Scot. *New International Commentary on the New Testament: The Letter of James* (Grand Rapids: Eerdmans, 2011).

Moo, Douglas J. *Pillar New Testament Commentary: The Letter of James* (Grand Rapids: Eerdmans, 2000).

Motyer, J.A. *The Message of James* (Downers Grove, IL: InterVarsity, 1985).

Reicke, Bo Ivar. *The Anchor Bible: The Epistles of James, Peter, and Jude* (Garden City, NY: Doubleday, 1964).

Sarna, Nahum M. *JPS Torah Commentary: Genesis* (Philadelphia: Jewish Publication Society, 1989).

Scheef, Jr., Richard L. "The Letter of James," in Charles M. Laymon, ed. *The Interpreter's One-Volume Commentary on the Bible* (Nashville: Abingdon, 1971), pp 916-923.

Stern, David H. *Jewish New Testament Commentary* (Clarksville, MD: Jewish New Testament Publications, 1995).

Tigay, Jeffrey H. *JPS Torah Commentary: Deuteronomy* (Philadelphia: Jewish Publication Society, 1996).

Walton, John H., and Victor H. Matthews and Mark W. Chavalas. *The IVP Bible Background Commentary: Old Testament* (Downers Grove, IL: InterVarsity, 2000).

Walvoord, John F., and Roy B. Zuck, eds. *The Bible Knowledge Commentary: Old Testament* (Wheaton, IL: Victor Books, 1985).

Ward, Ronald A. "James," in D. Guthrie and J.A. Motyer, eds. *The New Bible Commentary Revised* (Grand Rapids: Eerdmans, 1970), pp 1222-1235.

Wesley, John. *Explanatory Notes Upon the New Testament*, reprint (Peterborough, UK: Epworth Press, 2000).

Witherington III, Ben. *Letters and Homilies for Jewish Christians: A Socio-Rhetorical Commentary on Hebrews, James and Jude* (Downers Grove, IL: IVP Academic, 2007).

Wright, Christopher. *New International Biblical Commentary: Deuteronomy* (Peabody, MA: Hendrickson, 1996).

Wright, N.T. *The Early Christian Letters for Everyone: James, Peter, John, and Judah* (Louisville: Westminster John Knox, 2011).

Greek Language Resources

Aland, Kurt, et. al. *The Greek New Testament, Fourth Revised Edition* (Stuttgart: Deutche Bibelgesellschaft/United Bible Societies, 1998).

Black, David Alan. *Learn to Read New Testament Greek* (Nashville: Broadman and Holman, 1994).

_____. *It's Still Greek to Me* (Grand Rapids: Baker Books, 1998).

Brenton, Sir Lancelot C. L., ed & trans. *The Septuagint With Apocrypha* (Peabody, MA: Hendrickson, 1999).

Bromiley, Geoffrey W., ed. *Theological Dictionary of the New Testament*, abridged (Grand Rapids: Eerdmans, 1985).

Brown, Robert K., and Philip W. Comfort, trans. *The New Greek-English Interlinear New Testament* (Carol Stream, IL: Tyndale House, 1990).

Croy, N. Clayton. *A Primer of Biblical Greek* (Grand Rapids: Eerdmans, 1999).

Danker, Frederick William, ed., et. al. *A Greek-English Lexicon of the New Testament and Other Early Christian Literature*, third edition (Chicago: University of Chicago Press, 2000).

Liddell, H.G., and R. Scott. *An Intermediate Greek-English Lexicon* (Oxford: Clarendon Press, 1994).

Metzger, Bruce M. *A Textual Commentary on the Greek New Testament* (London and New York: United Bible Societies, 1975).

Mounce, William D. *Basics of Biblical Greek Grammar* (Grand Rapids: Zondervan, 2009).

Nestle, Erwin, and Kurt Aland, eds. *Novum Testamentum Graece, Nestle-Aland 27th Edition* (New York: American Bible Society, 1993).

Nestle-Aland Greek-English New Testament, NE27-RSV (Stuttgart: United Bible Societies/Deutche Bibelgesellschaft, 2001).

Newman, Jr., Barclay M. *A Concise Greek-English Dictionary of the New Testament* (Stuttgart: United Bible Societies/Deutche Bibelgesellschaft, 1971).

Rahlfs, Alfred, ed. *Septuaginta* (Stuttgart: Deutsche Bibelgesellschaft, 1979).

Rogers, Cleon L., Jr., and Cleon L. Rogers III. *The New Linguistic and Exegetical Key to the Greek New Testament* (Grand Rapids: Zondervan, 1998).

Thayer, Joseph H. *Thayer's Greek-English Lexicon of the New Testament* (Peabody, MA: Hendrickson, 2003).

Vine, W.E. *Vine's Expository Dictionary of New Testament Words* (Nashville: Thomas Nelson, 1968).

Wallace, Daniel B. *Greek Grammar Beyond the Basics* (Grand Rapids: Zondervan, 1996).

Zodhiates, Spiros, ed. *Complete Word Study Dictionary: New Testament* (Chattanooga: AMG Publishers, 1993).

Hebrew Language Resources

Arnold, Bill T., and John H. Choi. *A Guide to Biblical Hebrew Syntax* (New York: Cambridge University Press, 2003).

Baker, Warren, and Eugene Carpenter, eds. *Complete Word Study Dictionary: Old Testament* (Chattanooga: AMG Publishers, 2003).

Brown, Francis, S.R. Driver, and Charles A. Briggs. *Hebrew and English Lexicon of the Old Testament* (Oxford: Clarendon Press, 1979).

Davidson, Benjamin. *The Analytical Hebrew and Chaldee Lexicon* (Grand Rapids: Zondervan, 1970).

Dotan, Aron, ed. *Biblia Hebraica Leningradensia* (Peabody, MA: Hendrickson, 2001).

Elliger, Karl, and Wilhelm Rudolph, et. al., eds. *Biblica Hebraica Stuttgartensia* (Stuttgart: Deutche Bibelgesellschaft, 1977).

Gabe, Eric S., ed. *New Testament in Hebrew and English* (Hitchin, UK: Society for Distributing the Hebrew Scriptures, 2000).

Harris, R. Laird, Gleason L. Archer, Jr., and Bruce K. Waltke, eds. *Theological Wordbook of the Old Testament* (Chicago: Moody Press, 1980).

Holladay, William L., ed. *A Concise Hebrew and Aramaic Lexicon of the Old Testament* (Leiden, the Netherlands: E.J. Brill, 1988).

Jastrow, Marcus. *Dictionary of the Targumim, Talmud Bavli, Talmud Yerushalmi, and Midrashic Literature* (New York: Judaica Treasury, 2004).

Kelley, Page H., Daniel S. Mynatt, and Timothy G. Crawford, eds. *The Masorah of Biblia Hebraica Stuttgartensia* (Grand Rapids: Eerdmans, 1998).

Koehler, Ludwig, and Walter Baumgartner, eds. *The Hebrew & Aramaic Lexicon of the Old Testament*, 2 vols. (Leiden, the Netherlands: Brill, 2001).

Kohlenberger III, John R., trans. *The Interlinear NIV Hebrew-English Old Testament* (Grand Rapids: Zondervan, 1987).

Pratico, Gary D., and Miles V. Van Pelt. *Basics of Biblical Hebrew Grammar* (Grand Rapids: Zondervan, 2007).

Seow, C.L. *A Grammar for Biblical Hebrew*, revised edition (Nashville: Abingdon, 1995).

Tov, Emanuel. *Textual Criticism of the Hebrew Bible* (Minneapolis: Fortress Press, 1992).

Torah Nevi'im Ketuvim v'ha'Brit haChadashah (Jerusalem: Bible Society in Israel, 1991).

Unger, Merrill F., and William White. *Nelson's Expository Dictionary of the Old Testament* (Nashville: Thomas Nelson, 1980).

Historical Sources & Ancient Literature

Epictetus: *The Discourses*, ed. Christopher Gill (London: Everyman, 1995).

Eusebius of Caesarea: *Ecclesiastical History*, trans. C.F. Cruse (Peabody, MA: Hendrickson, 1998).

González, Justo L. *The Story of Christianity*, Vol. 1 (San Francisco: Harper Collins, 1984).

Harrington, Joel F., ed. *A Cloud of Witnesses: Readings in the History of Western Christianity* (Boston: Houghton Mifflin, 2001).

Irvin, Dale T., and Scott W. Sunquist. *History of the World Christian Movement*, Vol. 1 (Maryknoll, NY: Orbis Books, 2001).

Josephus, Flavius: *The Works of Josephus: Complete and Unabridged*, trans. William Whiston (Peabody, MA: Hendrickson, 1987).

Judeaus, Philo: *The Works of Philo: Complete and Unabridged*, trans. C.D. Yonge (Peabody, MA: Hendrickson, 1993).

Murray, Oswyn. *Ancient Greece*, second edition (Cambridge, MA: Harvard University Press, 1993).

Plato: *Timaeus and Critias*, trans. Desmond Lee (London: Penguin Books, 1977).

Shanks, Hershel, ed. *Ancient Israel: From Abraham to the Roman Destruction of the Temple* (Washington, D.C.: Biblical Archaeology Society, 1999).

Virgil: *The Aeneid*, trans. David West (London: Penguin Classics, 1990).

Jewish Reference Sources

Bridger, David, ed. et. al. *The New Jewish Encyclopedia* (West Orange, NJ: Behrman House, 1976).

Cohen, Abraham. *Everyman's Talmud: The Major Teachings of the Rabbinic Sages* (New York: Schoken, 1995).

Eisenberg, Ronald L. *The JPS Guide to Jewish Traditions* (Philadelphia: Jewish Publication Society, 2004).

Encyclopaedia Judaica. MS Windows 9x. Brooklyn: Judaica Multimedia (Israel) Ltd, 1997.

Frank, Daniel H., Oliver Leaman, and Charles H. Manekin, eds. *The Jewish Philosophy Reader* (London and New York: Routledge, 2000).

Harlow, Jules, ed. *Siddur Sim Shalom for Shabbat and Festivals* (New York: Rabbinical Assembly, 2007).

Hertz, J.H., ed. *Pentateuch & Haftorahs* (London: Soncino, 1960).

_____, ed. *The Authorised Daily Prayer Book*, revised (New York: Bloch Publishing Company, 1960).

Kolatch, Alfred J. *The Jewish Book of Why* (Middle Village, NY: Jonathan David Publishers, 1981).

_____. *The Second Jewish Book of Why* (Middle Village, NY: Jonathan David Publishers, 1985).

Levine, Amy-Jill, and Marc Zvi Brettler, eds. *The Jewish Annotated New Testament*, NRSV (Oxford: Oxford University Press, 2011).

Lieber, David L. *Etz Hayim: Torah and Commentary* (New York: Rabbinical Assembly, 2001).

Neusner, Jacob, trans. *The Mishnah: A New Translation* (New Haven and London: Yale University Press, 1988).

_____, ed. *The Tosefta: Translated from the Hebrew With a New Introduction*, 2 vols. (Peabody, MA: Hendrickson, 2002).

_____, and William Scott Green, eds. *Dictionary of Judaism in the Biblical Period* (Peabody, MA: Hendrickson, 2002).

Scherman, Nosson, ed., et. al. *The ArtScroll Chumash, Stone Edition*, 5th ed. (Brooklyn: Mesorah Publications, 2000).

Miscellaneous Texts & Lexicons

Charlesworth, James H., ed. *The Old Testament Pseudepigrapha*, Vol 1 (New York: Doubleday, 1983).

_____. *The Old Testament Pseudepigrapha*, Vol 2 (New York: Doubleday, 1985).

Gruber, Daniel, trans. *The Messianic Writings* (Hanover, NH: Elijah Publishing, 2011).

Robinson, James M., ed. *The Nag Hammadi Library* (San Francisco: HarperCollins, 1990).

Vermes, Geza, trans. *The Complete Dead Sea Scrolls in English* (London: Penguin Books, 1997).

Webster's New World Dictionary and Thesaurus, second edition (Cleveland: Wiley Publishing, Inc, 2002).

Wise, Michael, Martin Abegg, Jr., and Edward Cook, trans. *The Dead Sea Scrolls: A New Translation* (San Francisco: HarperCollins, 1996).

Young, Robert. *Young's Analytical Concordance to the Bible* (Grand Rapids: Eerdmans, 1977).

Online Resources

Christian Classics Ethereal Library. <http://www.ccel.org/>.

Plato: *Plato in Twelve Volumes*, trans. Harold North Fowler (1966). Accessible online at <http://www.perseus.tufts.edu/hopper/text?doc=Perseus%3atext%3a1999.01.0170%3atext%3d Phaedo>.

Plutarch: *Moralia: On Talkativeness*, Loeb Classical Library edition (1939). Accessible online at: <http://penelope.uchicago.edu/Thayer/E/Roman/Texts/Plutarch/Moralia/De_garrulitate*.htm l>.

Software Programs

BibleWorks 5.0. MS Windows 9x. Norfolk: BibleWorks, LLC, 2002. CD-ROM.

BibleWorks 7.0. MS Windows XP. Norfolk: BibleWorks, LLC, 2006. CD-ROM.

BibleWorks 8.0. MS Windows Vista/7 Release. Norfolk: BibleWorks, LLC, 2009-2010. DVD-ROM.

E-Sword 9.9.1. MS Windows Vista/7. Franklin, TN: Equipping Ministries Foundation, 2011.

The Babylonian Talmud: A Translation and Commentary. MS Windows XP. Peabody, MA: Hendrickson, 2005. CD-ROM.

Printed in Great Britain
by Amazon

29431128R00137